Faulkner and History
FAULKNER AND YOKNAPATAWPHA
2014

Faulkner and History

FAULKNER AND YOKNAPATAWPHA, 2014

EDITED BY
JAY WATSON
AND
JAMES G. THOMAS, JR.

UNIVERSITY PRESS OF MISSISSIPPI
JACKSON

www.upress.state.ms.us

The University Press of Mississippi is a member of
the Association of American University Presses.

Copyright © 2017 by University Press of Mississippi
All rights reserved
Manufactured in the United States of America

First printing 2017
∞
Library of Congress Cataloging-in-Publication Data

Names: Faulkner and Yoknapatawpha Conference (41st : 2014 : University of
Mississippi) | Watson, Jay, editor. | Thomas, James G., Jr., editor.
Title: Faulkner and history / edited by Jay Watson, James G. Thomas.
Description: Jackson : University Press of Mississippi, 2017. | Series:
Faulkner and Yoknapatawpha series | Includes bibliographical references
and index.
Identifiers: LCCN 2016025868 (print) | LCCN 2016031609 (ebook) | ISBN
9781496809971 (hardback) | ISBN 9781496809988 (epub single) | ISBN
9781496809995 (epub institutional) | ISBN 9781496810007 (pdf single) |
ISBN 9781496810014 (pdf institutional)
Subjects: LCSH: Faulkner, William, 1897–1962—Criticism and
interpretation—Congresses. | Faulkner, William,
1897–1962—Knowledge—History—Congresses. | History in
literature—Congresses. | BISAC: LITERARY CRITICISM / American / General.
| LITERARY COLLECTIONS / American / General.
Classification: LCC PS3511.A86 Z783173 2014 (print) | LCC PS3511.A86 (ebook)
| DDC 813/.52—dc23
LC record available at https://lccn.loc.gov/2016025868

British Library Cataloging-in-Publication Data available

In Memoriam

Elizabeth Nichols Shiver
June 28, 1932–October 26, 2014

Dorothy Lee Tatum
May 3, 1924–August 20, 2015

Billy Ross Brown Jr.
August 5, 1934–September 12, 2015

Contents

Introduction

William Faulkner was, and remains, a historian's writer. C. Vann Woodward, dean of his generation of southern historians, kept a portrait of Faulkner in his academic study at Yale; according to Candace Waid, who studied and taught at Yale in the 1980s and 1990s, the portrait was "the only visible image in the room."[1] Leon Litwack routinely assigned *The Unvanquished* as the opening text in his southern history class at the University of California, Berkeley, and Joel Williamson, the distinguished scholar of southern history and US race relations, taught Faulkner often at the University of North Carolina.[2] In Faulkner's hometown of Oxford, my colleague David Sansing, author of scholarly histories of the state and of the University of Mississippi, assigned *Intruder in the Dust* in his Mississippi history course and was known to recommend another Faulkner novel as well. "I told my students, 'If you don't have a Mississippi history textbook, buy *Absalom, Absalom!* That's the finest Mississippi history there is!'"[3] An equally accomplished roster of professional historians, including Woodward, Williamson, Richard H. King, Daniel Singal, Morton Sosna, Grace Elizabeth Hale, Ted Ownby, Don H. Doyle, James C. Cobb, Charles Reagan Wilson, Barbara Jeanne Fields, and Matthew Guterl, has drawn on Faulkner in their published work: as a fellow historian, a shaper of narrative reflections on the meaning of the past; as a historiographer, a theorist, and a dramatist of the fraught epistemological enterprise of doing history; and as a historical figure himself, especially after his midcentury, post-Nobel emergence as a sometimes reluctant, sometimes not-reluctant-enough public intellectual.

Or we could turn to the student of Faulkner who served as the nation's historian in chief. When, as a presidential candidate in 2008, Barack Obama felt the need to talk about history at a key moment in his campaign, he turned for wisdom to a perhaps surprising source. "A More Perfect Union," Obama's closely scrutinized, justly celebrated speech on race, traced "many of the disparities that exist in the African-American community today" to "inequalities passed on from . . . the brutal legacy of slavery and Jim Crow."[4] To underscore the importance of understanding the work of such legacies in the present, Obama cited William Faulkner,

who in the candidate's words "once wrote, 'The past isn't dead and buried. In fact, it isn't even past.'"[5] Cutting the president a little slack on
the accuracy of his quotation allows us to recognize its aptness. Indeed,
had Obama delved further into the Mississippian's body of work—as I
suspect he actually has[6]—he could have referenced any number of vivid
accounts and scenes of the human damage wrought by racial oppression
in the United States, the human courage that rose to meet that systematic injustice, and the historical persistence of both the damage and
the courage across generations and even centuries. Perhaps just such
an awareness lay behind Obama's decision to channel Faulkner's voice,
lending the quoted words, from *Requiem for a Nun*, additional authority,
nuance, and resonance. At any rate, here was William Faulkner in 2008:
dead nearly half a century, but not even past.

Faulkner once told an interviewer, "There is no such thing as *was*—
only *is*."[7] On the face of it, this would not seem to be the remark of a
writer with a particularly strong interest in history. Why, then, have so
many historians enlisted Faulkner as a source, inspiration, and fellow
practitioner of the craft? Part of the answer may lie in the novelist's
awareness, as profound as that of any writer before or since, that the past
as the stuff of history does not exist in amber, locked away in moments
irrevocably gone and thus to the present either immaterial or all-deter-
mining. Rather, the past exists and exerts its force now and only now,
in the minds and lives, the aspirations and anxieties, of people striving
to honor it, to resist or undo it, to transcend it, or simply to understand
it—to probe it for insight into where and how they live now—or "why
. . . they live at all," as Shreve McCannon might say.[8] Faulkner knows,
even when his characters don't, that this is what history *is*. Its meaning, as Michel-Rolph Trouillot explains, "is also in its purpose."[9] This is
precisely why, and how, it is used and abused: for the present moment,
or as Friedrich Nietzsche put it, "for life."[10] The intensity and haunting
power that history assumes for Faulkner's twentieth-century southerners in particular should not misdirect us from the fact that this past that
seems to assault them exists only in, and is accessible only through, their
memories and the oral and material culture that surrounds them—in the
now of their awareness and their lifeworld. As such, writes philosopher
of history R. G. Collingwood, "All history is contemporary history," perhaps nowhere more than in the fictional world of William Faulkner.[11]

In his important study of what he calls "the process of historical production" (24), Trouillot offers a useful distinction between "two sides of
historicity" (4). "In vernacular use, history means both the facts of the
matter and a narrative of those facts, both 'what happened' and 'that
which is said to have happened.' The first meaning places the emphasis on

the sociohistorical process, the second on our knowledge of that process or a story about that process" (2). If the first meaning (or "historicity 1") stresses "what history is," the second (or "historicity 2") reflects "how history works" (25; see also 28). Turning to literature, "what happened" is the domain of the historical novelist like Walter Scott, who hurls his protagonists into the turbulence of historical events and clashing historical forces while reserving a kind of historical omniscience, an uncontested possession of the underlying direction and meaning of those events, for his third-person narrators.[12] What is said to have happened, however, is the province of a different, more historiographically oriented fiction, in which historical facts are themselves contested, debated, and revised and the historical consciousness grows contingent and problematic in its own right (Rollyson, 106).

Faulkner's greatest achievements as a historically oriented writer of fiction lay in the domain of historicity 2. He may have been a historian's novelist, in other words, but he was not primarily a historical novelist in the conventional sense of the term. Though he often dealt with the sweeping historical events that are the stock in trade of the historical novelist (the Civil War and the Great War, for instance, serving him much as the Napoleonic Wars once served Tolstoy or the Jacobite rising served Scott), he seems, notes Michael Millgate, to have opted away from the genre, as though "the recording and attempted re-creation of specific periods . . . did not greatly interest him."[13] As Carl E. Rollyson Jr., author of the most thorough study of the subject to date, observes, Bayard Sartoris of *The Unvanquished* is probably the closest Faulkner came to creating the kind of protagonist that populates the historical novel proper: a representative figure who embodies the values of a society undergoing historical conflict and transformation, who serves as a human arena for the contending forces of his era while exhibiting only limited understanding of those forces, yet who "earns our trust by appreciating the humanity on both sides" of the struggle (40; see also 98). With Bayard serving as the novel's first-person narrator, however, *The Unvanquished* lacks the omniscient narrating presence common to most historical fiction, a figure "who can confidently summarize the meaning" of Bayard's reminiscences and reflections in their totality (106). According to Rollyson, the nearest thing to that sort of figure is to be found in the prologues of *Requiem for a Nun*: "nowhere else" in Faulkner "does the narrator function more like . . . an authority, a superbly informed historian" presiding over the text's "historical world" (245–46). What is missing from the prologues, however, is precisely the sort of unwitting world-historical protagonist, the Edward Waverly or Bayard Sartoris figure around and upon whom the forces of that history converge. Nor are the continuities between the prologues and the dramatic scenes sufficiently integrated for the latter to supply such a figure, leaving the text adrift to some degree between the natural, social, and personal histories it attempts to navigate. Ultimately, concludes Rollyson, Faulkner is neither, strictly speaking, a historian "primarily concerned with authenticating facts about the past" nor a historical novelist per se, since he "never exclusively concentrates on the manners of a past period of time" (257).

Instead, in his most accomplished historical narratives, *Absalom, Absalom!* and *Go Down, Moses*, Faulkner perfected a technique that brilliantly dramatized and interrogated Trouillot's process of historical production itself. As Rollyson echoes many other critics in noting, at issue in these novels is not what actually happened so much as "what the characters *think* really happened" (20), and Millgate agrees that their focus lies less "on accuracy of historical representation" than "on the act of historical interpretation itself" (5), as performed explicitly by character-historians and character-narrators whose stories about the past reflect their own contemporary preoccupations and answer their contemporary needs. For figures like Quentin Compson, Shreve McCannon, Mr. Compson, Rosa Coldfield, Isaac McCaslin, Cass Edmonds, and Buck and Buddy McCaslin (who joust over the meaning of slave histories in the McCaslin plantation ledgers), the endeavor to make narrative sense of the past is all too susceptible to the projections and transferential effects that according to Dominick LaCapra inevitably shadow historical production.[14] Their tales and musings also, in a peculiarly Faulknerian twist, abound in telltale omissions and reverberant silences. As Trouillot observes, "any historical narrative is a particular bundle of silences" (27) because "any single event enters history with some of its constituent parts missing" (49). Few novelists working in English—perhaps only Conrad and Morrison—have registered this truth as consistently, and insistently, as Faulkner.

Because "the personality of the historian (narrator)" explicitly "enters into the process of turning the historical event into an historical narrative" (Rollyson, 114), these great novels achieve a dynamic quality in their representations of the past, along with a sophistication, complexity, and mystery, that the conventional historical novel rarely if ever approaches.[15] This, I take it, was precisely Faulkner's point when he wrote to his publisher in 1934 that resurrecting Quentin Compson as the central consciousness of *Absalom, Absalom!* was a way "to keep the hoop skirts and plug hats out" of his first extended novelistic foray into the antebellum era, "to get more out of the story itself than a historical novel would."[16] The effects of this strategy go beyond the characters to leave a powerful impression on the reader: rather than spoon-feeding historical information to his readers, Faulkner forces them to participate in the process of historical inquiry and judgment:

> Since the "authorities" on the past cannot wholly be trusted, and since the novels themselves refuse to yield up a definitive or conclusive "formula" that would neatly link up the conflicting testimony, it is imperative that we assemble our own evidence, become our own historians, and interact, personally and individually, with the experience of the past. (Rollyson, 268)

If this technique anticipates the mode of "historiographic metafiction" that Linda Hutcheon has famously associated with literary postmodernism, that in turn may help explain why Brian McHale could declare *Absalom, Absalom!* (or more precisely, Quentin and Shreve's great breakthrough in chapter 8) to be a harbinger of—a kind of tipping point for—the emergence of postmodern narrative and its "ontological dominant."[17] Yet the historical imagination at work in and behind Faulkner's fiction is irreducible to mere language games. Indeed, it carries an agonizing intensity, a life-and-death urgency, particularly for Quentin, Rosa, and Ike. The fact that history is first and foremost "a hermeneutical discipline" for Faulkner (Rollyson, 217) only raises its stakes higher, for characters and author alike.

Faulkner's stories, novels, essays, letters, interviews, and public statements are also, of course, fascinating historical artifacts and symptoms in their own right. Not only do they theorize history as a human endeavor, a personal or cultural form of meaning-making, they also offer a revealing historical window onto the era of their composition, publication, and reception through their close engagement with the cultural forces—intellectual, popular, material—that shaped the life and times of the author and his audience. And they do so not only by documenting their time and place in overt ways but also, as the scholarship of John T. Matthews and Richard Godden has abundantly and ingeniously demonstrated, by secreting or "sedimenting" historical conflicts and contradictions, from the macro level of aesthetic form to the micro level of the individual word or even the phoneme, vibrating with polysemantic possibility.[18] For these critics, as for Karl Marx, Faulknerian language is preeminently practical consciousness, saturated with economic, social, and (thus) historical content. For these reasons, Faulkner's texts have paid especially rich dividends for new historicist scholars and for other historically informed critics, from Lawrence H. Schwartz to Pascale Casanova and David M. Earle, who have shed important light on Faulkner as a historical phenomenon in his own right, a figure whose literary reputation then and now can be seen as the complex, evolving product of forces at work within the publishing industry, the institutions of literary criticism and higher learning, the mass media, American popular culture, and the cultural geopolitics of the Cold War.[19]

This volume seeks to advance an already lively dialogue into new territory by bringing together an interdisciplinary group of historians and literary scholars—some eminent in their field, others in the process of emerging there—to explore the many facets of Faulkner's relationship to history. We begin with a trio of essays that seeks to define, expand, and complicate the model of temporality that governs most historically oriented discussions of Faulkner's work. As an alternative to a post-Enlightenment sense of history predicated on "the violence of rupture" or "a fatalistic sense of closure," Wai Chee Dimock proposes a network-based model of historical connectivity that trades in forms of "low-bar" affiliation across local worlds with seemingly little in common. "Faulkner Networked: Indigenous, Regional, Trans-Pacific" locates a structure of feeling, "locally felt yet globally shareable," that links Faulkner's viewpoint to that of the readers he encountered on his post-war travels to Japan and that of twenty-first-century Native American writers like Gerald Vizenor and Jim Barnes. This affective network, "a sense of being somehow on the wrong side of history" that characterizes populations who "have fought for something and fought in vain," surfaces in the give and take, "happening as much by chance as by design," between Faulkner and his interlocutors at the Nagano seminars in 1955. Moreover, the novelist's remarks at Nagano on the origins of the word "Yoknapatawpha," a name that evokes another "defeated but honored people" whose dispossession prefigures those of postbellum US southerners and the postwar Japanese, form an illuminating "weak network" with Vizenor's 2003 novel *Hiroshima Bugi* and Barnes's 2001 poem, "The Only Photograph of Quentin at Harvard," texts in which Native histories that go "unactualized" in Faulkner are brought forward into a different future. Approaching history as network, Dimock argues, repositions Faulkner as "an intensely local author with a sustained global outreach."

"The animal," Nietzsche claimed, "lives *unhistorically*."[20] Colin Dayan's "Salvific Animality, or Another Look at Faulkner's South" takes issue with this view and the oppositions on which it rests: between the human and the animal, history and the unhistorical. Against Norman Podhoretz, who complained in the 1950s that "a genuine sense of history" is absent from Faulkner's works, Dayan argues that "the most astonishing pages in *The Hamlet* suggest a history beyond the reach of customary written history." Faulkner accesses this alternate historicity through style and subject matter, foregrounding sentience, sensation, and rural creatures and landscapes that in their strangeness and seething vitality "betoken the surfacing of suppressed histories that might or might not be told" by, to, or about the inhabitants of Frenchman's Bend, caught as they are in the turbulence of post-Reconstruction social and economic history. It is ultimately to the "shared intimacies" of Ike Snopes and his cow, Jack Houston and his hound, Armstid and Tull and their untameable Texas ponies, that we must turn, as Faulkner turned, for clues to "how we can reconstitute something of a life together" within and against a "morally disenchanted" American liberal order whose arrogance and intolerance Faulkner found inhospitable (to return to Nietzsche) "for life."

Jordan Burke takes up the much-discussed question of the philosophy of time in Faulkner and finds it to be historically inflected through and through. "'Moving Sitting Still': The Economics of Time in Faulkner's *Absalom, Absalom!*" reveals the "temporal blockages and aporias" that repeatedly surface in Faulkner's greatest historiographic fiction to be "symptoms of the fluctuating and troubled relationship between time and labor" in the modernizing US South. Faulkner's fictional antebellum planter Thomas Sutpen proves to be a historically representative figure in the awkward way he embodies without resolving the "structural contradictions" generated by his region's economic transition from "agrarian 'autonomy'" and paternalism to "[m]arket expansion, partnership with the merchant class, technological innovation, and labor efficiency." This transition was accompanied by a mutation in the lived experience of time, from the leisured quasi-"atemporality" of aristocratic slaveholders to the clock- and calendar-driven time discipline of "the Cotton Kingdom protocapitalist," with his ties to industrial rhythms and global economic flows. Sutpen's paradox, explains Burke, is that he "enlists himself as a dependent laborer in the capitalist world market so that someday he can hang in 'sunny suspension' in a precapitalist world apart," a problem that Sutpen is no more able to conceal beneath his evasive narrative tactics than Quentin Compson will be two generations later. Burke thus reveals temporality itself as a historical phenomenon, subject to the same forces that drive socioeconomic change.

The next seven essays place particular aspects of Faulkner's work in historical context. Sean McCann's "'A Promissory Note with a Trick Clause': Legend, History, and Lynch Law in *Requiem for a Nun*" finds conflicting versions of Jacksonian-era Mississippi history in the origin narrative Faulkner creates for Jefferson in the narrative prologues of his 1951 novel. In his account of the civic crisis that leads to the town's incorporation, Faulkner deviates from his primary historical source, Robert M. Coates's 1930 study, *The Outlaw Years*, to develop a "prominent legend about a transition from anarchic innocence to the burdens of civilization." Coates had told a darker story of the coming of a commercial order to the Mississippi Valley, in which the "speculative boom" of the 1830s introduced "hazard, uncertainty, ruthless exploitation, and brute repression" into the region rather than bringing anything resembling law and order. Traces of this repressed history, however, return in the text's brief references to the historical figure of John Murrell, a notorious outlaw whose crimes—real and rumored—revealed the "incipient forces of disorder" at work *within* Mississippi's "fundamentally unstable capitalist order." The prologues' "competing historiographic visions" anticipate the "rival visions of Mississippi's social order" at work in the main plot, where Gavin Stevens espouses an ethos of "civic obligation" and "paternalist racial hierarchy" that recalls his community's founding fathers, while Temple's ties to the criminal underworld, like Murrell's before her, evoke "the corrosive freedoms of the commercial marketplace."

In a richly contextualized essay, Calvin Schermerhorn tallies Faulkner's imaginative debts and contributions to a long tradition of US writing about racial slavery, a tradition that encompassed numerous "competing strands or scripts." Drawing on categories formulated by historian David W. Blight, Schermerhorn's "Faulkner and the Freedom Writers: Slavery's Narrative in Business Records from Nineteenth-Century Abolitionism to Twenty-First-Century Neoabolitionism" traces a dialectical movement from an "abolitionist script" (grounded in antebellum ex-slave narratives) that "contrasted the humanity of enslaved people with the instrumentality of paper used to mediate slave transactions," through a proslavery rhetoric that ignored economic context and ascribed paternalistic qualities to slaveholders, to an uneasy synthesis in antislavery novelists like Harriet Beecher Stowe, who decried "slavery's immoral accounting" while generally "affirm[ing] plantation paternalism." The postbellum years saw a similar cycle, as emancipationist and white supremacist scripts collided before New South writers combined elements of both into a sentimental "reconciliationist script" that won popular support and influenced many of the era's professional historians. According to Schermerhorn, Faulkner contributed to the emergence of a "civil rights script" that inaugurated a third, twentieth-century cycle of slavery representation. In *Go Down, Moses*, for instance, he redeployed the abolitionist strategy of using business records to expose slavery's abuses, fashioning the McCaslin plantation ledgers as representations of the slave past. As one of the "first white southern writers to ask what slavery did *to* southerners rather than what it did *for* them," Faulkner helped pave the way for later writers and historians committed to what Schermerhorn calls a "neoabolitionist" agenda.

Andrew B. Leiter examines Faulkner's engagement with the legacy of a controversial historical figure in "Monuments, Memory, and Faulkner's

Nathan Bedford Forrest." "Forrest's presence," writes Leiter, "permeates Faulkner's work more thoroughly than that of any other historical figure of the Civil War," the result, perhaps, of Falkner family legends that linked Forrest with "the Old Colonel," W. C. Falkner, in wartime north Mississippi. Forrest figures most explicitly in the Faulkner oeuvre in the 1943 story "My Grandmother Millard and General Bedford Forrest and the Battle of Harrykin Creek," where he makes a cameo appearance to help the Sartoris family sort out a romantic complication, but as Leiter notes, Forrest's obliquely registered history as a slave trader (developed more fully in *Go Down, Moses*), along with the exaggerated lengths he is willing to go to in support of "the sanctity of southern womanhood as central to the defense of the South," troubles the tale's "romantic façade." Interestingly, a much earlier story, the unpublished "Dull Tale," takes this critical stance further, linking Forrest's Memphis statue and public park in Nietzschean terms with the "antiquarian dreaming and vague monumentalist notions of honor" that resurface in the story's ineffectual protagonist, Gavin Blount, a figure whose Lost Cause values anticipate those of *Light in August*'s Gail Hightower. Here Faulkner enlists Forrest to critique "the impetus behind the public construction of Confederate memory and . . . the individualized memorialization of romanticized heroes."

Rebecca Bennett Clark excavates the buried labor and racial histories that simmer beneath an ostensibly comic moment in Faulkner's final novel. In "'A Well-Traveled Mudhole': Nostalgia, Labor, and Laughter in *The Reivers*," Clark resists the temptation to read the novel as an exercise in "that lowbrow historical affect we call nostalgia," finding instead "moments of cutting social criticism that reveal a keen, if conflicted, historiographic imagination." The celebrated Hell Creek Bottom episode is her Exhibit A. Viewed nostalgically by the novel's elderly narrator, Lucius Priest, who depicts the muddy crossing "as a prehistoric landscape," the morass actually proves to be a minefield of twentieth-century labor struggle, in which the poor-white mud-farmer's physical exertions resourcefully "make the land work for him in a way that actual sharecropping never had" for members of his class, while Ned McCaslin's linguistic work, his imaginative weave of anecdote, laughter, and deference, performs a verbal balancing act that voices critique, preserves dignity, and creates room to maneuver within the racial tensions that complicate the economic dynamics of the scene. In this densely layered episode, *The Reivers* "reveals the complex inner and interworkings of labor, land, and language in a South that is at once rapidly changing and, like the mud, stubbornly intractable."

W. Fitzhugh Brundage uncovers a novelist who was very much a man of his time in his concern with police brutality. "Interrogation, Torture,

and Confession in William Faulkner's *Light in August*" locates Faulkner's
seventh novel, which depicts the violent questioning of an African American detainee by the Yoknapatawpha County sheriff and his deputies,
within a national debate over custodial interrogation tactics that arose
in the years after World War I to become "a staple in American popular
culture" as Faulkner was reaching maturity as a novelist. As Brundage
demonstrates, "the third degree," as it came to be called, could be found
not only in the legal and penal spaces of the Jim Crow South but in the
nation's metropolitan police departments as well. Perhaps surprisingly,
Brundage concludes that Faulkner's interrogation scenario appears to
reflect ancient assumptions, challenged by Enlightenment thinkers but
never fully discredited, that the pain of torture can penetrate "the veil
of inscrutability" that lies between accused subjects and their interro-
gators to produce authentic testimony unclouded by "human guile" or
unreason. Faulkner thus demonstrates how "the difficulty of knowing,
the indeterminacy of truth, and the ambiguity of identity" work to elicit
and to compound the racialized violence of *Light in August*.

For Hannah Godwin the historical phenomenon under investigation is childhood. In "'Who Are You?': Modernism, Childhood, and
Historical Consciousness in Faulkner's *The Wishing Tree*," Godwin
finds an "uneasy yet potentially fruitful confluence" between modernist writing and children's literature in the only Faulkner tale penned
specifically for children. Drawing on "the Romantic reverence for the
child as transcendent and inspirational," a reverence qualified to some
degree by twentieth-century psychoanalysis and its suspicion of childhood innocence, modernist artists portrayed the child as "a vessel of consciousness" and "instinctual, intense perceptions" and thus as a source
of "defamiliarizing perspectives" that fostered artistic experimentation.
Philip Weinstein has argued in *Becoming Faulkner* that writing about
childhood in *The Sound and the Fury* ignited Faulkner's career as an
avant-garde novelist,[21] but Godwin points out that in *The Wishing Tree*,
composed the year prior to that breakthrough novel, writing *for* young
readers may have been no less important in helping Faulkner awaken
his creative potential. Moreover, Godwin observes, Faulkner's foray into
children's literature exhibits much the same "dense historical awareness
that saturates his literary output," as the author "punctuates the narrative's imaginative dream structure with key invocations of the historical
crises of the Civil War and World War I." *The Wishing Tree*'s rich mix of
fantasy and history thus "works to imbue the child reader with a sense of
historical consciousness" while recognizing her as the bearer "of a more
hopeful future."

For Conor Picken, the path from *Sanctuary* to *Requiem for a Nun*
bridges not only two decades but two distinct historical phases of

temperance reform in the United States. In "The Noble Experiment? Faulkner's Two Prohibitions," Picken argues that *Sanctuary* (1931) dramatizes the failure of the Prohibition movement "to 'cure' the American alcoholic republic and restore domestic order" in a society where liquor "was demonized as morally wrong by some" but "recklessly consumed by many." *Requiem* (1951), on the other hand, unfolds against the midcentury Sobriety movement (led by Alcoholics Anonymous), which "retooled the temperance paradigm" by approaching alcoholism "as a physiological disease rather than a disease of the will." These paradigms reflected gendered assumptions about drinking. *Sanctuary* follows Prohibition-era reform discourse in focusing on "drunken men squandering their money on liquor before returning home." If the goal of the Eighteenth Amendment was "to protect women from men and men from themselves," Temple Drake's ordeal is the "collateral damage" that results when such legal and social measures break down. *Requiem* more nearly resembles the Sobriety movement in its emphasis on the domestic fallout from problem drinking by women as well as men and on the challenges of abstention and recovery for Gowan and Temple, who struggle to stay on the wagon as they cope with family tragedy. In both novels, Picken adds, the flight into alcohol prevents the central characters from dealing meaningfully with social change—an especially damning "prohibition," indeed.

Three essays mine the history of print culture to illuminate Faulkner's career. In "Mr. Cowley's Southern Saga," Sarah E. Gardner gives us a new backstory for Malcolm Cowley's *Portable Faulkner* volume of 1946, which helped revitalize Faulkner's career. Conceived, proposed, and compiled during World War II, the volume was obliged to address two important demands of wartime publishing in the United States: to contribute to an educated citizenry, the "best defense against fascism and totalitarianism," by encouraging Americans at home and abroad to read; and to present "the nation's diversity and heterogeneity as constitutive to America's development." Enter Faulkner—but a particular version of Faulkner fashioned by Cowley: "Balzacian" rather than "Caldwellian," and national rather than strictly regional. Moreover, Cowley's construction of a chronological "saga" out of Faulkner's diffuse and diverse Yoknapatawpha materials invited readers to see in the novelist's South the milestones of American history: "European encroachment on the frontier, the repercussions of Jacksonian Indian policy, the buying and selling of human flesh, the dying away of an old order, and the attendant ills of mechanization and modernization." Though Faulkner sometimes chafed at this agenda, at one point pronouncing the volume "a new work by Cowley," in the end Cowley produced an anthology that made "Faulkner's southernness . . . crucial to the national culture-building of the 1940s."

Anna Creadick turns her attention to the reception history of Faulkner's work, focusing on what his encounters with midcentury readerships reveal not about his writings but about how they approached his work and indeed literature more generally. "Reading Faulkner's Readers: Reputation and the Postwar Reading Revolution" utilizes the recently digitized sound recordings of Faulkner's interview sessions at the University of Virginia in 1957 and 1958 as "a previously neglected archive of reader response" that documents how everyday readers experienced Faulkner as author and oeuvre. Highlighting their questions rather than Faulkner's answers, Creadick explores four distinct lines of response. Readers "engaged with cultural hierarchies," often challenging the boundaries between highbrow and lowbrow literary forms; they "enacted formalist reading strategies," marshaling their close-reading skills to pose questions about symbolism, irony, point of view, and style; they "interrogated the function of literature," querying Faulkner about reading protocols and literary value; and they exhibited a preoccupation with "matters of rank and reputation," inviting Faulkner to join them in constructing an American literary canon. In this way, Creadick demonstrates, ordinary readers "became a critical force in the making of Faulkner's literary reputation" at midcentury.

Meanwhile, in "'The Paper Old and Faded and Falling to Pieces': *Absalom, Absalom!* and the Pulping of History," Brooks E. Hefner examines how Faulkner's dramatization of the historical endeavor reflects the print culture conventions of his era. Hefner contends that *Absalom's* "fluid and flexible" relationship to history amounts to a "pulping" of the historical record, "self-consciously destroying, recycling, and repurposing" it in ways gleaned from the "popular literary production" of the 1920s and 1930s. The so-called shudder pulps, with their emphasis on terror and the occult; "hero pulps" and other modes of popular adventure fiction; *Black Mask*–school hard-boiled crime fiction; Yellow Peril narratives and other tales depicting "racialized threat[s] to sexual purity" and the domestic sphere—the novel employs all of these pulp genres to shape and sensationalize the Sutpen saga and its central figures, in what amounts to a lowbrow version of the "emplotment" process that Hayden V. White finds at work in all historical narrative.[22] What is more, argues Hefner, Quentin and Shreve's narrative method "echoes the immersive and escapist experience of pulp reading," which stresses identification over critical detachment, and the novel's thematic emphasis on "the ephemerality of history" evokes the materiality of the pulp text, published on cheap paper and thereby doomed to evanescence.

We close with a pair of essays that place Faulkner's writings in conversation with the work of professional southern historians. Natalie J. Ring

draws on her own experiences as an undergraduate American studies
major and on the career of a turn-of-the-century Harvard historian and
public intellectual to examine the cultural framing of the US South as
a national problem, a view of the region that spanned the entire twentieth century and clearly left its mark on Faulkner's imagination. "Massachusetts and Mississippi: Faulkner, History, and the Problem of the
South" takes up Faulkner's interrogation of and response to this national
discourse of regional othering in the Compson novels, *The Sound and
the Fury* and *Absalom, Absalom!*, texts which, as Ring points out, double
as Harvard novels. Quentin's brief tenure at Harvard overlaps with the
career of Albert Bushnell Hart, an important period commentator who
contributed to the national debate over the "Problem South." In a fascinating thought experiment, Ring proposes that Quentin and his roommate Shreve might have enrolled together in Hart's celebrated History
13 class, an undergraduate introduction to American political history,
during the fall 1909 semester at Harvard. There the young men would
have encountered course assignments inviting them to cultivate "a personal identification with American history" through the study of specific
"biographical subject[s]." The dormitory scenes of *Absalom* suggest that
Hart's influence may have extended beyond the classroom, as Quentin
and Shreve investigate just such a subject—and a vivid incarnation of the
Problem South—in the historical figure of Thomas Sutpen.

If Faulkner was a historian's kind of novelist, C. Vann Woodward was
among his century's most Faulknerian historians. In "'Saturated' with the
Past: William Faulkner, C. Vann Woodward, and the 'Burden' of Southern History," James C. Cobb explores how "two of the South's ablest
interpreters may have complemented, supplemented, or contradicted
each other as they examined a common time and place." Though they
never quite met, Faulkner might have recognized an imaginative fellow
traveler in Woodward: a superb storyteller combining a "determination
to challenge the past and explore its power over the present" with a
relative disinterest in the narrow facts of history. Though he steered
clear of the prismatic historical perspectivism of an *Absalom, Absalom!*
or a *Go Down, Moses*, many of Woodward's guiding themes as a historian, and some of his shortcomings as well, share common ground with
Faulkner's. Both struggled, for instance, to give African American figures
the same historical weight and agency attributed to whites, and both at
times cast a sympathetic eye on the antebellum planter class. Moreover,
Woodward drew directly on Faulkner in developing his account of what
he called the "burden of southern history": a historical experience and
consciousness among southerners that he nominated as an alternative
to white supremacy as the basis of a distinctive regional identity and the

central theme of a distinctive regional history. In this way the novelist's "genius for helping us 'know' the past as other humans experienced it, rather than as a mere collection of fact and detail," proved an invaluable touchstone for a young Arkansan with literary ambitions who became the most influential southern historian of his generation.

Faulkner's writings invite us into a world inadvertently limned by the philosopher Susan Buck-Morss, where "the central question of history's meaning cannot be asked outside of time but only in the thick of human action."[23] This means that "the way the question is posed, the methods of the inquiry, and the criteria of what counts as a legitimate answer all have political implications," as indeed they do in Faulkner's writings and the historical landscape they portray.[24] Yet in Faulkner as elsewhere, the politics that at every moment attends history is not simply, as Michel Foucault would have it, a technology of power. It is also what Otto von Bismarck once called an "art of the possible."[25] Historical thinking, argues Collingwood, reveals "how things have come to be what they are."[26] If this view appears to flirt with the sense of historical fatality that stymies so many of Faulkner's white southerners, it is actually emancipatory, opening up a space for critical agency and human freedom, since, as the Frankfurt School thinkers never tired of reminding us, things that have come to be the way they are can also come *not* to be the way they are. History may be "what hurts," in Fredric Jameson's famous formulation, but it is also, argues Mary Ann Doane, "the mark of what could have been otherwise."[27] In that recognition, that mark, lies the way to a better future, a better world, where history remains in the making, not even past.

Jay Watson
University of Mississippi

NOTES

1. Candace Waid, *The Signifying Eye: Seeing Faulkner's Art* (Athens: University of Georgia Press, 2013), 25.

2. John T. Matthews, introduction to *William Faulkner in Context*, ed. Matthews (New York: Cambridge University Press, 2015), 6n1.

3. Telephone conversation with the author, July 2, 2015.

4. See Barack Obama, "A More Perfect Union," video transcript, National Constitution Center, http://constitutioncenter.org/amoreperfectunion.

5. Ibid.

6. See Jay Watson and Jaime Harker, "The Summer of Faulkner: Oprah's Book Club, William Faulkner, and Twenty-First-Century America," *Mississippi Quarterly* 66.3 (Summer 2013): 371–74.

7. James B. Meriwether and Michael Millgate, eds., *Lion in the Garden: Interviews with William Faulkner, 1926–1962* (1968; repr., Lincoln: University of Nebraska Press, 1980), 255.

8. William Faulkner, *Absalom, Absalom!*, rev. ed. (1936; repr., New York: Vintage International, 1990), 142; emphasis removed.

9. Michel-Rolph Trouillot, *Silencing the Past: Power and the Production of History* (Boston: Beacon, 1995), 149. Subsequent references to this edition will be cited parenthetically in the text.

10. Friedrich Nietzsche, "On the Uses and Disadvantages of History for Life" (1874), in *Untimely Meditations* (1893), trans. R. J. Hollingdale (New York: Cambridge University Press, 1983), 57–123. For illuminating critical applications of Nietzsche's ideas about history to Faulkner's works, see Richard H. King, *A Southern Renaissance: The Cultural Awakening of the American South, 1930–1955* (New York: Oxford University Press, 1981), 77–145; John Lowe, "*The Unvanquished*: Faulkner's Nietzschean Skirmish with the Civil War," *Mississippi Quarterly* 46 (1993): 407–36; and Andrew B. Leiter's essay for this volume.

11. R. G. Collingwood, *The Idea of History* (1946; repr., London: Oxford University Press, 1956), 202.

12. See Carl E. Rollyson Jr., *Uses of the Past in the Novels of William Faulkner*, rev. ed. (1984; repr., San Francisco: International Scholars Publications, 1998), 106; and Georg Lukács, *The Historical Novel* (1947), trans. Hannah and Stanley Mitchell (1962; repr., Lincoln: University of Nebraska Press, 1983), 19–62. Subsequent references to Rollyson's book will be cited parenthetically in the text.

13. Michael Millgate, *Faulkner's Place* (Athens: University of Georgia Press, 1997), 5–6. Subsequent references to this edition will be cited parenthetically in the text.

14. Dominick LaCapra, "Is Everyone a *Mentalité* Case? Transference and the 'Culture' Concept," in *History and Criticism* (Ithaca, NY: Cornell University Press, 1985), 71–94.

15. Some contemporary works of historical scholarship, on the other hand, do honor the mysteries and silences that surround the past despite (or arguably because of) the historian's best efforts. For two examples that have become classics, see Simon Schama, *Dead Certainties: Unwarranted Speculations* (New York: Knopf, 1991), and Winthrop Jordan, *Tumult and Silence at Second Creek: An Inquiry into a Civil War Slave Conspiracy* (Baton Rouge: Louisiana State University Press, 1993). And for an eye-opening account of how the process of historical production actually *generates* silences in creating and authorizing facts, sources, and archives, see Trouillot, *Silencing the Past*, 26–29.

16. Joseph Blotner, ed., *Selected Letters of William Faulkner* (New York: Random House, 1977), 79.

17. Linda Hutcheon, *A Poetics of Postmodernism: History, Theory, Fiction* (New York: Routledge, 1988), 5; Brian McHale, *Postmodernist Fiction* (New York: Methuen, 1987), 10–11.

18. See for instance John T. Matthews, "*As I Lay Dying* in the Machine Age," *boundary 2* 19.1 (Spring 1992): 69–94; Matthews, "Faulkner and Proletarian Literature," in *Faulkner in Cultural Context: Faulkner and Yoknapatawpha, 1995*, ed. Donald M. Kartiganer and Ann J. Abadie (Jackson: University Press of Mississippi, 1998), 166–90; Richard Godden, *Fictions of Labor: William Faulkner and the South's Long Revolution* (New York: Cambridge University Press, 1997); Godden, *William Faulkner: An Economy of Complex Words* (Princeton, NJ: Princeton University Press, 2007); and Godden, "Mired Mediations: *As I Lay Dying*, a Horse, a Fish, Telepathy, and Economics," in *William Faulkner in the Media Ecology*, ed. Julian Murphet and Stefan Solomon (Baton Rouge: Louisiana State University Press, 2015), 238–65. I have gleaned the idea of aes-

thetic form as a carrier of "sedimented" socioeconomic residues, the empirical stuff of history, from Theodor Adorno's *Aesthetic Theory*, by way of Matthews, "*As I Lay Dying* in the Machine Age," 85–86. See also 79, 83.

19. See Lawrence M. Schwartz, *Creating Faulkner's Reputation: The Politics of Literary Criticism* (Knoxville: University of Tennessee Press, 1988); Pascale Casanova, *The World Republic of Letters* (1999), trans. M. B. DeBevoise (Cambridge, MA: Harvard University Press, 2004); and David M. Earle, "Faulkner and the Paperback Trade," in *William Faulkner in Context*, ed. John T. Matthews (New York: Cambridge University Press, 2015), 231–45.

20. Nietzsche, "On the Uses and Disadvantages of History for Life," 61.

21. Philip Weinstein, *Becoming Faulkner: The Art and Life of William Faulkner* (New York: Oxford University Press, 2010), 36–61.

22. See Hayden V. White, *Metahistory: The Historical Imagination in Nineteenth-Century Europe* (Baltimore: Johns Hopkins University Press, 1973); and *Tropics of Discourse: Essays in Cultural Criticism* (Baltimore: Johns Hopkins University Press, 1978).

23. Susan Buck-Morss, *Hegel, Haiti, and Universal History* (Pittsburgh: University of Pittsburgh Press, 2009), 109.

24. Ibid.

25. Wikiquote attributes the quotation to an 1867 interview with Friedrich Mayer von Waldeck of the *St. Petersburgische Zeitung*. See https://en.wikiquote.org/wiki/Otto_von_Bismarck.

26. R. G. Collingwood, "The Philosophy of History" (1930), in *Essays in the Philosophy of History*, ed. William Debbins (1965; repr., New York: McGraw-Hill, 1966), 124.

27. Fredric Jameson, *The Political Unconscious: Narrative as a Socially Symbolic Act* (Ithaca, NY: Cornell University Press, 1982), 102; Mary Ann Doane, *The Emergence of Cinematic Time: Modernity, Contingency, the Archive* (Cambridge, MA: Harvard University Press, 2002), 231. I encountered Doane's elegant claim as the epigraph to Peter Lurie's recent essay, "'Crossing the Junctureless Backloop of Time's Trepan': Freedom, Indexicality, and Cinematic Time in *Go Down, Moses*," in *Faulkner in the Media Ecology*, ed. Julian Murphet and Stefan Solomon (Baton Rouge: Louisiana State University Press, 2015), 216.

Note on the Conference

The forty-first Faulkner and Yoknapatawpha Conference, sponsored by the University of Mississippi in Oxford, took place Sunday, July 20, through Thursday, July 24, 2014, with more than two hundred of the author's admirers in attendance. Fifteen presentations on the theme "Faulkner and History" are collected as essays in this volume. Brief mention is made here of other conference activities.

The program began on Sunday with a reception at the University Museum for the exhibition *Blues @ Home: Mississippi's Living Blues Legends* by H. C. Porter. The exhibition was a collection of thirty portraits of Mississippi living blues legends in their at-home settings. The paintings were paired with oral histories, collected by project manager Lauchlin Fields, and heard through handheld audio devices to give insights into the storied lives of the legends. Following the reception, Wai Chee Dimock presented, "Faulkner Networked: Indigenous, Regional, Trans-Pacific," followed by James C. Cobb's keynote, "The Past Lives, but What Does It Do? William Faulkner, C. Vann Woodward, and the 'Burden' of Southern History," published in this volume as "'Saturated' with the Past: William Faulkner, C. Vann Woodward, and the 'Burden' of Southern History."

Following a buffet supper at Rowan Oak that evening, George "Pat" Patterson, mayor of Oxford, and Daniel W. Jones, chancellor of the University of Mississippi, welcomed participants, and Deborah Clarke, president of the William Faulkner Society, introduced winners of the 2014 John W. Hunt Scholarships. These fellowships, awarded to graduate students pursuing research on William Faulkner, are funded by the Faulkner Society and the *Faulkner Journal* in memory of John W. Hunt, Faulkner scholar and emeritus professor of literature at Lehigh University. James G. Thomas, Jr., the Center for the Study of Southern Culture's associate director for publications, presented the 2014 Eudora Welty Awards in Creative Writing. Jessica Garner of St. Andrew's Episcopal School in Ridgeland won first place for her story "Momma Says," and Rachel Jones, a McComb native who attends the Mississippi School for Math and Science in Columbus, won second place for her poem

"Sunday Symphony." The late Frances Patterson of Tupelo, a longtime member of the Center Advisory Committee, established and endowed the awards, which are selected through a competition held in high schools throughout Mississippi. A screening of two short films, *Raisin' Cotton*, by Emma Knowlton Lytle, and *Homeplace*, by Michael Ford, rounded out the evening.

Monday's program began with Charles A. Peek and Terrell L. Tebbetts leading the first "Teaching Faulkner" session, "Whose Faulkner and Whose History?," and a panel titled "Histories of Labor and Technology" followed, with Deborah Clarke, Sean McCann, and Rebecca Bennett Clark presenting their work. The panel "History Makes Faulkner: Manufacturing a Midcentury Reputation" followed, with Sarah E. Gardner, David M. Earle, and Anna Creadick presenting their work. The day's program also included "Digital Yoknapatawpha: A Progress Report on a Work in Progress," by Dotty Dye, Theresa M. Towner, and Stephen Railton; a keynote lecture, "Torture, Southern Violence, and Faulkner in Context" (published herein as "Interrogation, Torture, and Confession in William Faulkner's *Light in August*") by W. Fitzhugh Brundage; and papers on the topic of "History, Fiction, and Interracial Intimacies in Faulkner" presented by Lael Gold, Margaret Wrinkle, Sharony Green, and Calvin Schermerhorn. The day's activities ended with Vickie M. Cook and Wil Cook hosting Faulkner on the Fringe, an open-mike evening at Southside Gallery on the Oxford Square.

Tuesday's program included the second "Teaching Faulkner" session, "Faulknerian History," led by James B. Carothers, Theresa M. Towner, and Brian McDonald. A panel on "Thinking Literature and History Comparatively" included papers by Jason Fichtel, Esther Sánchez-Pardo, and Christopher Rieger, and was followed by a panel on "Faulkner, Modern Art, and Modern War," which included papers by Serena Blount, Randall Wilhelm, and Candace Waid. That afternoon Colin Dayan presented her lecture "Salvic Animality, or Another Look at Faulkner's South," followed by Natalie J. Ring presenting "How Faulkner Grappled with the Problem South," published here as "Massachusetts and Mississippi: Faulkner, History, and the Problem of the South." An afternoon party hosted at the Oxford-University Depot followed Ring's lecture.

Wednesday's program began with concurrent panels on "Local and Regional Histories" and "Visions of History." Presentations for the former panel included papers by Peter Froehlich, Charles Hannon, and Elizabeth Steeby. The latter panel included paper presentations by Frank P. Fury, Brooks E. Hefner, and Satoshi Kanazawa. Concurrent panels, "Faulkner in the History of Modernity" and "Faulknerian Temporalities," followed. Hannah Godwin, Sara Gabler Thomas, and

Matthew Sutton presented papers in the former, and Katherine Isabel Bondy, Jordan Burke, and George Porter Thomas presented papers in the latter. The morning ended with another set of concurrent panels: "Staging Southern Histories" and "History, Power, and Gender." Daniel Ferris, Andrew Leiter, and Kristi Rowan Humphreys presented papers in the former, and Jaclyn Crumbley Carver, Rachel Watson, and Sarah Walker presented papers in the latter. Jeremy Wells presented a lecture on "Faulkner and the Spirituals" that afternoon, and concurrent panels on "Moonshine and Magnolias: A History of Spirits in Faulkner's Mississippi" and "Deciphering Sutpen's Hundred: Ideology, Representation, and the Politics of Aesthetics in *Absalom, Absalom!*" included papers by Carrie Helms Tippen, Conor Picken, Meredith Kelling, Josh Jones, and Jennifer Gilchrist, and Mark Sursavage brought the conference presentations to a close.

Guided tours of north Mississippi, including Oxford and Lafayette County, New Albany and Ripley, and the Mississippi Delta took place on Thursday, and the conference ended with a reading and signing by Josh Weil and closing party, both at Off Square Books.

Three exhibitions were available throughout the conference. The Department of Archives and Special Collections of the university's J. D. Williams Library exhibited *William Faulkner's Books: A Bibliographic Exhibit*. The University Museum hosted the *Blues @ Home: Mississippi's Living Blues Legends* exhibition, and the University Press of Mississippi exhibited Faulkner books published by members of the Association of American University Presses.

The conference planners are grateful to all the individuals and organizations that support the Faulkner and Yoknapatawpha Conference annually. In addition to those mentioned above, we wish to thank Square Books, the City of Oxford, and the Oxford Convention and Visitors Bureau.

Faulkner and History
FAULKNER AND YOKNAPATAWPHA
2014

Faulkner Networked: Indigenous, Regional, Trans-Pacific

WAI CHEE DIMOCK

In thinking about possible new directions for Faulkner studies, one concept I would like to explore is a "network." I hope I am not simply being trendy, taking a word that describes the online phenomenology of the present moment and projecting it back to the mid-twentieth century, when the Internet did not exist. Network *is* a current term; but it is also a versatile term, bringing with it a range of issues by no means limited to the contemporary world, ways of thinking about group filiation and long-distance relationships that might help put Faulkner studies on a broader, more experimental footing.

And I should be up front about why I am proposing this approach. This essay is an attempt to reclaim Faulkner as a "regional" writer: but regional in a new sense, embracing a new set of geographical coordinates, and a new set of historical references. What brings all of these into play, I would further argue, is a psychology locally felt yet globally shareable, a sense of being somehow on the wrong side of history that different groups must have experienced at different points, when they have fought for something and fought in vain. It is not a good feeling, but some good might come of it nonetheless. It has the most potential for good, in fact, when it is oriented outward, imagined as a principle of connectivity extending beyond Mississippi, a basis for reaching out to other localities with not much else in common. This transregional arc might turn out to be one of the most enduring aspects of Faulkner's thinking about history. I would like to call this kind of regionalism a "networked" regionalism.

As you can see, I am redefining the term, giving it an updated theater of action, and using it to signal a departure from two other concepts, more often associated with Faulkner: "high modernism" on the one hand, and a kind of end-game insularity on the other. In contrast, a "networked" regionalism is a low-key, low-bar way of reaching out, and likely

3

to be sustainable for just that reason, in that it is marked neither by a steep emotional curve, by the violence of rupture, nor by a fatalistic sense of closure, by the violence of everything coming to a catastrophic end. Instead, it is a steady-state, horizontal plane, going from one locale to another, translating from one to another, making the best out of the worst, and, in the end, creating what to my mind is one of the most viable ways of being both local and not local.

Casanova and Beyond

But first, a detour, by way of Pascale Casanova's account of a "networked" Faulkner, in her hugely influential book, *The World Republic of Letters*. For Casanova, Faulkner is what he is—part of an elite global network—because he has been lauded beyond national borders, "consecrated" at the "Greenwich meridian" of the literary world, Paris.[1] What she means by "consecration" is this, a process that allows an author to

> undergo a sort of transformation—one might almost say a transmutation in the alchemical sense. The consecration of a text is the almost magical metamorphosis of an ordinary material into "gold," into absolute literary value.... Paris is not only the capital of the literary world. It is also, as a result, the gateway to the "world market of intellectual goods," as Goethe put it; the chief place of consecration in the world of literature. (125–26)

Casanova points to the translations of Faulkner into French by Maurice-Edgar Coindreau, which, she claims, contributed significantly to his worldwide recognition, culminating in the 1949 Nobel Prize in Literature. And that prize, in turn, puts Faulkner in the most exclusive of clubs, with members such as Samuel Beckett, Octavio Paz, Gabriel García Márquez, and Gao Xingjian, all Nobel laureates, all of whom had been consecrated in Paris before ascending to the very top in Stockholm.

Casanova might have a point. Still, her world republic of letters, in being so relentlessly centralized and hierarchical, might strike some of us as less a "republic" than a panopticon. Not only is there a strong presumption in favor of literature as an institutional artifact, this strong presumption also carries with it a more or less predictable outcome, giving us an operating system in which a single, unchanging metropolitan center dominates a globalized field, dominates even those texts that have no chance of ever being consecrated. Casanova's paradigm needs qualification, then, both on factual grounds—did those French translations alone catapult Faulkner to fame, and is the Greenwich meridian always Paris?—and as a conceptual template for theorizing the literary field. Especially in light of what we now know about online networks, it is worth thinking of a form of connectivity antithetical to the one she describes: at some distance from seats of power, without institutional prestige, but also without the high maintenance cost of prestige, an alternative to the high-power and highly restrictive centralized model.

Low-Bar Networks

Gilles Deleuze, Félix Guattari, and Bruno Latour are helpful in steering us in this general direction.[2] For this talk, though, I would especially like to draw on a book focusing on the Internet: *Networked: The New Social Operating System*, by Lee Rainie and Barry Wellman, a study of the way social media have reshaped our patterns of association and reshaped the ways we work, get information, and find support when we are in trouble.[3] Rainie and Wellman identify a number of phenomena most of us would recognize: new kinds of connections extended across long distances rather than based on physical proximity and the prevalence of what they call "partial membership,"[4] filiations that are intermittent rather than full time, voluntary and context based rather than institutionally given, replacing vertical certifications with horizontal exchanges. The ties that result—say, on Twitter or Facebook—are weak ties. But because their membership threshold is low, they also tend to multiply fairly easily, a downstream cascade likely to recur, interfering with any strong claim about the airtight closure of a centralized regime.

Low-bar networks of this sort, rather than giving the last word either to hierarchical institutions or to individual texts as sovereign products of single authors, call attention instead to a plethora of input channels and the continual emergence of new voices, often tangential to but not without bearing on the existing corpus. It is a field elastic and revisable, a field of second look and second chance. What results is a vibrant, crowd-sourced arena, developed over time, the collective (and by no means unified) effort of many, with no fixed trajectory and no necessary destination. Networks of this sort are impossible to supervise and impossible to stop. They suggest that any individual text is bound to fall short—in the sense that it cannot be its own sequel, its own endpoint—precisely because it is singular, the work of one pair of hands, and arrested at one particular moment in time. Falling short is less a failing than a spur to the inventiveness of others. The co-dependency that results binds any given author to any number of aspiring ones. Untried options subsequently explored, roads not taken subsequently visited—these time-delayed feedback loops

make up the improvised structures of these low-bar networks. Through
these long-distance, not necessarily recuperative, though sometimes surprisingly illuminating turns, happening as much by chance as by design,
traces of the unactualized past can be carried into the future, and ill-
defined shadows can be given alternate outlines.

I will be using low-bar networks as a conceptual tool to think about
Faulkner as an intensely local author with a sustained global outreach.
To the terms proposed by Rainie and Wellman, I would like to add two
more. The network I will be exploring is for the most part an affective
network: it has to do with forms of emotional life, what Raymond Williams in *The Country and the City* calls a "structure of feeling": not
quite a philosophy or worldview but simply a "practical consciousness
of a present kind, in a living and interrelating continuity."[5] Practical consciousness of this sort, Williams goes on to say, "cannot without loss be
reduced to belief-systems, institutions, or explicit general relationships,
though it may include all these as lived and experienced, with or without
tension."[6] Losing out is often the basis for practical consciousness of this
sort. It is a low common denominator, supporting only a weak network,
but not to be dismissed either.

Trans-Pacific Regionalism

Without further ado, then, let me turn directly to such a network in
Faulkner, linking the humiliation of the South after the Civil War to
the humiliation of Japan after World War II, an ordeal no doubt further
amplified in the minds of the defeated. Faulkner was in Nagano, Japan,
as part of the State Department's Exchange of Persons Program, the
same program that sent jazz musicians all over the world as goodwill
ambassadors. By the time he went, in August 1955, he was at a low
point himself, a confirmed alcoholic, so shaky in his general conduct that
the State Department apparently thought of cutting the tour short and
sending him home. But Faulkner evidently rallied under the challenge
of on-site adjustment to a foreign environment. For a period of ten days
he was able to meet with members of the Nagano Seminar—fifty or so
Japanese professors of American literature—every afternoon or evening,
giving talks, and interacting with them in Q&A sessions. Some of his
remarks were quite odd, not what one would expect from someone in
Japan under State Department sponsorship, such as the following, in a
talk entitled "To the Youth of Japan":

> A hundred years ago, my country, the United States, was not one economy and
> culture, but two of them, so opposed to each other that ninety-five years ago

they went to war against each other to test which one should prevail. My side, the South, lost that war, the battles of which were fought not on neutral ground in the waste of the ocean, but in our own homes, our gardens, our farms, as if Okinawa and Guadalcanal had been not islands in the distant Pacific but the precincts of Honshu and Hokkaido. Our land, our homes were invaded by a conqueror who remained after we were defeated; we were not only devastated by the battles which we lost, the conqueror spent the next ten years after our defeat and surrender despoiling us of what little war had left.[7]

As Civil War history, this was atrocious: it was one-sided, and it was reductive. Faulkner never mentioned slavery at all; the Civil War here was only a war between two incompatible regions of the United States, eternally divided by their cultural and economic differences, with one side triumphing over the other and trampling the other underfoot.

What makes this peculiar account (to say the least) more forgivable is the presence here of *two* regional contexts. The first was obviously Oxford, Mississippi, and the conduct of the Union army in 1864: "that night the town was occupied by Federal troops; two nights later, it was on fire (the Square, the stores and shops and the professional offices), gutted (the courthouse too), the blackened jagged topless jumbles of brick wall enclosing like a ruined jaw the blackened shell of the courthouse . . . and so in effect it was a whole year in advance of Appomattox."[8] The other context, perhaps even more present to Faulkner at that moment, was what Japan went through at the end of World War II. The giveaway phrase, I think, is this: "the conqueror spent the next ten years after our defeat and surrender despoiling us of what little war had left." Why ten years? Faulkner was probably thinking less about the year 1875, ten years after Appomattox, than about the year 1955, the year of the Nagano Seminar, ten years after Japan surrendered. And he seemed to know intuitively that though Allied occupation had ended formally in April 1952, the emotional ramifications of defeat would persist long after. For the Japanese in 1955, what most struck a responsive chord from Faulkner's account of the American Civil War was no doubt this: that in every war there was going to be a losing side, an existential condition known only to those who have been subjected to it. Reaching out to his Japanese audience on just that basis, Faulkner's regionalism was now both rooted and extended: based in Oxford, Mississippi, but ending up with new filiations thousands of miles away. Familiar names such as Appomattox now give way to four others: Okinawa, Guadalcanal, Honshu, Hokkaido. Significantly, these were not the best-known names, not the two epicenters—Hiroshima and Nagasaki—but names far more ordinary, bringing to mind no spectacular destruction, only the steady-state, across-the-board condition of having been brought low.

It was a deliberate choice on Faulkner's part. Regional cities were in fact the reference points for him, rather than cosmopolitan cities that towered above others, like London and Paris. In his meeting with the citizens of Nagano, while trying to map his fictional world for this Japanese audience, he came up with this comparison between two pairs of cities: "My country lies between New Orleans and Memphis. New Orleans is the big, important city that in my country is like Tokyo here. That is, Nagano would be Memphis, Tokyo would be New Orleans, because Tokyo is the larger city. My country would be between Nagano and Tokyo. They were important in my work only because they were the big cities—the life in my land, the land I know, is country, it is farmland."[9]

This, in and of itself, seems to me a regional manifesto. New Orleans is the counterpart of Tokyo only on a very special map, one that leaves out New York, Chicago, and Los Angeles. And that seemed to be the point. Even though New York had been a reference point for Faulkner elsewhere, say, in *The Sound and the Fury*, and even though he knew Los Angeles well from his stint as a screenwriter in Hollywood, for this particular audience he wanted New Orleans to set the standard for a metropolitan center. And it was with New Orleans as the standard that he could then reach out to the next level, to Memphis. But even this was too major a city for him. His country was nondescript farm country, he said, offering what seemed to be agrarianism in the most traditional sense.

And yet, even as this was being put forward, two other cities, Tokyo and Nagano, were also very much in the picture. This cross-mapping, linking the cartography of an intimately known South to that of an unknown Asia, was something that Faulkner did fairly consistently throughout his stay in Japan. Rather than settling comfortably into some tried-and-tested binaries—North versus South, city versus country—his world was now far more volatile, at once extended and ill defined, a world in which unfamiliar names, perhaps seen together for the first time, produced fault lines as well as lines of filiation, giving us a sense of history far less predictable than the earlier, North-as-conqueror-and-South-as-victim script.

Varieties of Losing

Such a world produced new contexts for old enmities and grievances, to the point where even "winning" and "losing" began to shed their customary character, taking on new meanings. There is no better example of this than Faulkner's musings on the conduct of war—specifically, the conduct of the occupying forces—at the same meeting with the citizens of Nagano, when this question came from the floor:

The scene of soldiers drinking liquor which appears in the beginning of the book *Soldier's* [*sic*] *Pay* made me recall an occurrence which arose just after the end of the Pacific war. When I was standing on one of the platforms at Nagoya, some American soldiers came along and forcibly held my neck, making me drink whisky. They then passed the bottle among themselves, drinking from the same bottle that I had drunk from. Since considerable time has elapsed since the time that *Soldier's* [*sic*] *Pay* was written of, and since things are quite peaceful now, I don't imagine that such things happen nowadays. Could you tell me whether such scenes can be seen?"[10]

The remark is interesting for at least three reasons. First, the Faulkner canon in Japan was surprisingly broad: not just on this occasion, but throughout the entire ten days, references were made not just to the standard-bearers, *The Sound and the Fury*, *Light in August*, and *Absalom, Absalom!*, but also to works such as *The Wild Palms*, *Intruder in the Dust*, and here, *Soldiers' Pay*. Second, Faulkner was right about the basis for emotional connection between postbellum South and Japan in 1955: it was exactly this shared sense of humiliation that this Japanese reader would pick up on and respond to. Finally, perhaps more interesting still was the response Faulkner came up with, the explanation that he offered for why these American soldiers would behave in that way:

I wouldn't say that that is typical of American soldiers. If I said that was typical, I'd say that it is probably typical of all soldiers, that in this gentleman's case, these were young men who had never been this far from home before—they were in a strange country, they had been fighting in combat—suddenly combat was over, they were free of being afraid, and so they lost control temporarily. They wouldn't act like that always every time—it was the relief that anyone who has been a soldier and knows what it is to be fighting—when he gets over being in fighting, he's really not accountable for what he might do.[11]

This has to be one of the most counterintuitive accounts of the effect of war: focusing not on the out-of-control behavior of soldiers while the fighting is in process, but their out-of-control behavior once the fighting is over. The relaxing of extreme fear could have an adverse effect also not calculable. Whether or not we agree with this theory, it seems clear that, with Japan in the foreground, Faulkner was suddenly able to see military occupation in a different light, replacing the erstwhile conquerors with a vulnerable group of young men away from home for the first time, barely making it through and undone by the very burden of winning.

This was what Faulkner learned in Japan, learned from suddenly finding himself on the winning side. That unwonted position threw into relief a psychological truth no one would have suspected: there are no victors in war. No one wins, since winning is never an option. We all lose one way or another: whether militarily, in a public surrender; or psychologically, in a mental unraveling. All of us end up being undone by war, thrown off-kilter by it. This ironic twist—that winners do not in fact win—makes the imagined connection between Faulkner and his Japanese audience not just a fantasy on his part, but a fantasy perhaps with some truth. Perhaps there is indeed a low common denominator to war, in that it permits only varieties of losing. That irony, afflicting all of us, also points to the possibility of a further common ground, something like a nontragic sequel to World War II, and perhaps all wars, a leveling out at the absolute low point, with a hint of an upturn.

Nontragic Sequels

That hint is all we could hope for, Faulkner said, for there is no way to deny the catastrophe of war, no way to erase the two atomic bombs: "We can't go back to a condition in which there were no wars, in which there was no bomb. We got to accept that bomb and do something about it, eliminate that bomb, eliminate the war, not retrograde to a condition before it exists."[12] History is linear in the sense that it is made up of a series of irrevocable acts, but it is not the case that each of those acts marks a dead end, a point of no return. On the contrary, it is the in-progress and updatable nature of the narrative that gives Faulkner hope. In response to an observation from a Tokyo audience, that there were new literary movements in postwar Japan, new poetry being written, Faulkner has this to say: "I think what is primarily responsible for that sort of alternation in the sound, the style, the shape of work, is disaster. I think I said before that it's hard to believe, but disaster seems to be good for people. If they are too successful too long, something dies, it dries up, and then they have to collapse with their own weight, which has happened with so many empires."[13]

Defeat as the spur to experimentation: this is the low-bar starting point for a sequel to World War II. The example of Japan suggests that a similar narrative might be unfolding in the United States as well. Could it be that, here too, some glimmer of the non-traumatic could come out of the trauma of slavery, the trauma of the Civil War? Faulkner would like to think so. This is what he offers in *Absalom, Absalom!*, a low point where things bottom out, also marking a point where a utopian counternarrative might begin. Here it takes the form of a minimal connectivity among three women—two white and one black—trying their best to survive, and succeeding because they have managed to eke out an aggregate life, not a real partnership, but enough of one to keep them going:

> not as two white women and a negress, not as three negroes or three white, not even as three women, but merely as three creatures who still possessed the need to eat but took no pleasure in it, the need to sleep but from no joy in weariness or regeneration. . . . We grew and tended and harvested with our own hands the food we ate, made and worked that garden just as we cooked and ate the food which came out of it: with no distinction among the three of us of age or color. . . . It was as though we were one being, interchangeable and indiscriminate.[14]

This is the regionalism that rises from the ashes of defeat to give us a glimpse of the world as it could be, a threadbare world, it is true, but one where blacks and whites could commingle, interchangeable and indiscriminate. This is the utopian counternarrative Faulkner had imagined back in 1936. Could we take the experience of Japan as a parallel development, an affirmation?

A cautionary word from historians is helpful here. Cooperation between black and white women based on shared economic hardship was indeed one outcome of the Civil War; however, as Drew Gilpin Faust and Thavolia Glymph have noted, such partnership was relatively rare, since the uneasy coexistence between black and white women was driven less by fondness or tolerance than by fear, with many mistresses reverting to or perhaps even developing new ways of managing their slaves.[15] The harsh treatment of blacks after Reconstruction was not an unprecedented turn of events but a continuation of the racial oppression that occurred before and during the Civil War, practiced by white women no less than white men. However tempting it is to imagine an interracial peace based on scarcity and flourishing on the axis of gender, the practice was limited. Faulkner's utopian hope might have been just that: a utopian hope.

Making Up Indians

Still, the example of the Japanese, defeated not so long ago but already on the mend, seemed to have come as a spur to Faulkner to imagine a parallel story, applicable not only to slavery and the Civil War but also to the other trauma: the banishment of indigenous peoples, most

immediately, the Choctaw and Chickasaw in Mississippi. Asked about
the origin of the word Yoknapatawpha, Faulkner said:

> Yes, it's a Chickasaw Indian word. They were the Indians that we dispossessed
> in my country. That word means "water flowing slow through the flatland,"
> which to me was a pleasant image, though the word in Chickasaw might be
> pleasanter to a Chickasaw ear than to our ear, but that's the meaning of it.[16]

The dispossession of Indians need not have come up at all for a question
on etymology. Faulkner seemed to have gone out of his way to bring it
up, perhaps to show that *this* catastrophe could also now be looked in
the eye. Perhaps his novels and stories, in giving this word extended
life, scarcely imaginable when it was only a Chickasaw word, could be a
form of reparation? Encompassing the whole of his fictional world, the
Chickasaw word is as good a starting point as any for a utopian interracial
narrative, a nontragic sequel to New World genocide, as peaceful and
steadfast as "water flowing slow through the flatland."

Oddly, even as Faulkner put forth this theory, some doubt seemed
already to have occurred to him, giving him pause and making him add
the odd qualification that the sound of "Yoknapatawpha" might be pleas-
anter to a Chickasaw ear than to his own. Peace might not translate
easily between Anglos and Indians, just as it does not between blacks
and whites. The alienness of the word *Yoknapatawpha* is only the most
obvious sign of the often insurmountable barriers among humans. And
nowhere are those barriers harder to ignore than in Japan. Indeed,
simply being there, and needing to explain not only the word *Yoknapatawpha* and what happened to the Chickasaw but who they were to
begin with, seemed to have brought home to Faulkner the sharp reality
of cultural differences. Was he ever any closer to the Chickasaw than he
was to the Japanese, and how steadfast was his dedication to them?

The self-conscious gesture in Japan, in 1955, recalling a defeated
but honored people, was in fact a relatively recent development in
Faulkner, the endpoint of a long evolutionary process, significantly different from earlier iterations but not altogether resolving some of the
troubling issues they raised. Native Americans in late Faulkner, say in
Requiem for a Nun (1951), were indeed much like those invoked and
mourned in Japan. *Requiem* begins by observing that "the settlement
had the records; even the simple dispossession of Indians begot in time
a minuscule of archive."[17] It repeats that word, "dispossess," in a long-
drawn-out parenthetical aside as it recounts the bickering over whether
the town should be called "Jefferson" or "Habersham"—the latter name,
from the old doctor, founder of the town, and "friend of old Issetibbeha, the Chickasaw chief (the motherless Habersham boy, now a man

of twenty-five, married one of Issetibbeha's grand-daughters and in the thirties emigrated to Oklahoma with his wife's dispossessed people)."[18] The sentence is lopsided, like the equally lopsided fight between the Chickasaw and the US government: "Habersham" loses out in more senses than one. What the name signifies—friendship with Native Americans and continued landholding by them—was the road not taken by a nation with an official policy of Indian Removal, a nation whose Founding Fathers numbered Thomas Jefferson but not Indians.

Requiem for a Nun is in many ways the high-water mark for this sense of Native Americans as "dispossessed," despoiled of what was rightfully theirs. And yet, Faulkner's sympathies cannot be said to be entirely on their side. In act 3, "The Jail," he recounts the fateful day when Mohataha, the Chickasaw matriarch, came "to set her capital X on the paper which ratified the dispossession of her people forever," doing so while "seated in a rocking chair beneath a French parasol held by a Negro slave girl," a figure "grotesque and regal, bizarre and moribund, like obsolescence's self riding off the stage enthroned on its own obsolete catafalque."[19] This is not the first time those two words, "dispossessed" and "obsolete," are intertwined to describe a doomed people, slaveholding, with inflated egos, destined to die out in their effete ignorance. This is the refrain throughout *Requiem for a Nun*: "the obsolete and the dispossessed, dispossessed by those who were dispossessed in turn because they were obsolete."[20]

These two are also the operative words in *Go Down, Moses* (1942), especially in "The Bear," although in that earlier work Faulkner is much less interested in dispossession as a historical fact than as a spiritual malaise, afflicting anyone who gets it into his head that he can own the land, buy or sell or bequeath it. The big woods, we are told as soon as the story opens, are "bigger and older than any recorded document:—of white man fatuous enough to believe he had bought any fragment of it, of Indian ruthless enough to pretend that any fragment of it had been his to convey."[21]

"Fatuous" whites and "ruthless" Indians are almost equal partners here, with Ikkemotubbe, the Chickasaw chief, and Ike's grandfather, L. Q. C. McCaslin, being equally culpable and equally deluded: "because it was never old Ikkemotubbe's to sell to Grandfather for bequeathment and repudiation. Because it was never Ikkemotubbe's fathers' fathers' to bequeath Ikkemotubbe to sell to Grandfather or any man because on the instant when Ikkemotubbe discovered, realised, that he could sell it for money, on that instant it ceased ever to have been his forever."[22]

Dispossession in "The Bear" is simply a providential judgment, a curse incurred by Anglos and Indians both. Rather than being the outcome of a federal policy, written in a legal document and signing away the right to vast tracts of Native lands, it operates here by an entirely different syntax—"Dispossessed of Eden. Dispossessed of Canaan"— a syntax that judges those who sell even more harshly than those who buy.[23] L. Q. C. McCaslin is merely "fatuous"; it is Ikkemotubbe who is "ruthless."

That startling adjective, "ruthless," out of the blue here, seems to have been carried over from an earlier phase of Faulkner, especially from stories such as "Red Leaves" and "A Justice," where it would have been entirely fitting. In "A Justice," Ikkemotubbe—"not born to be the Man [the chief], because [his] mother's brother was the Man, and the Man had a son of his own, as well as a brother"—takes to calling himself "Doom," from the expression, "Du homme" [sic] that he has picked up in New Orleans from his French companion.[24] Armed with a little "gold box of New Orleans salt"[25] on his return, he does indeed spell doom: beginning with a puppy brought along for demonstration, then making quick work of the Man and his son, sparing the brother only because the latter, seeing what happens, has covered his head with a blanket and taken himself out of the line of succession.

That succession is just about to take place in "Red Leaves." Like "A Justice," this story is also about ruthlessness of a sort, though coming here not from Moketubbe, Issetibbeha's son and heir, who is obese and lethargic, "diseased with flesh," not much of a schemer.[26] Ruthlessness inheres, rather, in the tribe as a whole, in their low-energy but unrelenting pursuit and capture of a black slave, who has run away to escape being buried alive with Issetibbeha, his old master.

How credible is this portrait of Native Americans? "Red Leaves" has been challenged on multiple fronts, not least the burial practices of Native Americans in Mississippi.[27] Faulkner, when asked by a contemporary local historian "where he got his Indians," had famously replied, "I made them up."[28] In a letter to Scribner's accompanying the submission of "Red Leaves," he had also said: "So here is another story. Few people know that Miss. Indians owned slaves; that's why I suggest you all buy it. Not because it is a good story; you can find lots of good stories. It's because I need the money."[29] Faulkner's financial needs might indeed have been dire, since he had just bought a wreck of a house (later named Rowan Oak). And the muckraking impulse, to show that whites were not the only slaveholders, might indeed have been irresistible.[30] Whatever the reason, historical accuracy could not be said to be his top priority, which is why the names and identities of individuals and even of whole tribes could be switched from story to story. Native Americans, identified as Chickasaws in Requiem for a Nun, had started out in the early stories as Choctaws. As Robert Dale Parker and Robert Woods Sayre have pointed out, Native Americans in early Faulkner were figments of his imagination, grotesque "projections and introjections" of the slaveholding South: archaic, degenerate, and doomed.[31] With the effete Moketubbe setting the tone, the other two Indians in "Red Leaves" are also "burgher-like" and "paunchy," one wearing an "enameled snuff box" in his ear, and both receding into "a certain blurred serenity like carved heads on a ruined wall in Siam or Sumatra, looming out of a mist."[32] These fictional Indians have nothing to do with the Native populations who had stayed on in Mississippi after the Treaty of Dancing Rabbit Creek in 1830, after even the Second Choctaw Removal of 1903, struggling to safeguard their communal holdings against land frauds and the influx of white settlers, protecting the livelihood of small subsistence farmers, while debating citizenship rights.[33]

Gerald Vizenor, Jim Barnes, Lucien Stryk, in Progress

What to do with this lacuna in Faulkner, this substitution of actual Native Americans with ones of his own making? As it turns out, a weak network—extending minimally but with some regularity across the Pacific—does offer a connectivity of sorts between Faulkner and the Indians outside the bounds of his imagination. For historical reasons that warrant a full-length study in itself, many Native authors have felt specially drawn to Japan, much like Faulkner. Gerald Vizenor, posted there in 1953 with the occupation forces, was so taken with the haiku form that he wrote haiku for the rest of his life.[34] The overlapping traumas of the atomic bomb and New World genocide, meanwhile, were such that, in 2003, he found himself writing a novel, *Hiroshima Bugi*, featuring a character, Ronin, whose "nightmare lasted sixty years," a composite ghost from the past haunting the present: "I am dead, the one who shatters nuclear peace. Some of my deaths have been reported in obituaries around the world. Dead Amerika indian, hafu peace boy out to sea, was the report of my second death at the orphanage. I am forever an orphan, a tatari of the ruins."[35] Is peace ever possible for such a composite ghost, peace that is not a travesty, an insult to the memory of the dead? Vizenor writes, "peace is untrue by nature, a counterfeit of nations" (16). And there "is no more treacherous a peace than the nuclear commerce of the Peace Memorial Museum in Hiroshima" (16), with feel-good messages emblazoned on every souvenir T-shirt: "No More Hiroshima, August 6, 1945" (17) and "Hiroshima Loves Peace." Against such phoniness, the only truth is the tatari, "spirits of retribution and vengeance, a curse of kami" (25). This is what the Japanese believe in: "the tatari of the dead, that is, the vengeance of people who had been killed, or killed themselves, after being falsely accused or unfairly treated." The *tatari* will "persecute its enemies, strike at the innocent in passing," and stop at nothing.

Here is a response of sorts, not specifically directed at Faulkner, but devastating all the same. It does not have to be the absolute last word, however. I would like to temper its finality with an in-progress network, adding to Vizenor's unappeasable voice a different voice from two poems by the Choctaw-Welsh poet, Jim Barnes: one, a direct response to Faulkner, carefully staged, and the other, not intended as a response at all, but, in its trans-Pacific arc and its many accidental echoes, as good a response as any.

In "The Only Photograph of Quentin at Harvard," Barnes begins and ends with pairs of hands and a book:

On the far left, at the edge,
a pair of hands holds
an open book.

At the right-hand bottom corner
a pair of shoes hangs
pegged to the wall,

the soles outward and soiled.
At the end of a word Shreve laces
his hands in his lap.

Central, across the checkered table,
Quentin counts the silence in his throat
below a half-

curtained bookcase. A mirror
reflects pictures pyramided
up a wall.

The one window is draped in white
gauze. Time is stilled
forever

in a hushed tone of sand.
The hands are about
to turn a page.[36]

The photo is of course apocryphal—there could be no photo of a fictional character—though the scene here could easily have come from either *The Sound and the Fury* or *Absalom, Absalom!*, more likely the latter, given the tenor of the composition. Everything is in pairs here: the shoes, the pictures (thanks to the mirror), and the two friends, one lapsing into silence and the other about to speak, with their hands cross-stitched in their gesture of expectancy. This is a Quentin not alone, not in despair, a Quentin literally and metaphorically with an open book.

Without being asked to, Jim Barnes has come up with a nontragic sequel. It cannot undo the tragedy already in the script, but while the open book remains open, and while the companionship lasts, that ending can be momentarily put off. A sustaining companionship is also what Barnes highlights in a poem featuring not a photograph but a postcard— "After a Postcard from Stryk in Japan"—its very structure of sending and receiving already affirming the tie between two friends:

> *Lucien, all*
> *the green river,*
> *falling*
> *green beneath*
> *the green bridge,*
>
> *all*
> *the green houses,*
> *their windows*
> *opening light*
> *onto the river*
>
> *falling*
> *now beyond*
> *the green bridge*
> *into the green sky,*
>
> *and now*
>   *all*
>   *quiet*
> *the green night blossoms*[37]

The "Lucien" in question is Lucien Stryk, poet and translator of Zen poetry, born in Poland, professor for more than thirty years at Northern Illinois University, with a lifelong attachment to the haiku of Issa and Bashō, and visiting Japan often to teach at Niigata University and Yamaguchi University.³⁸ In this postcard, there is no hint of the atomic bombs, and no hint of any catastrophe anywhere in the world (though elsewhere, notably in the poem "Choctaw Cemetery," Barnes has been pointed about the infant mortality and hardship among Native people: "Familiar glyphs: / *ushi holitopa* / The dates: / short years").³⁹ Instead, the postcard, like the apocryphal photo of Quentin, celebrates the life-giving force of continuity across different experiential registers: the green bridge mirroring the green river, the houses and the sky mirroring both, making even the night green.

This is what Faulkner was hoping to find in the word *Yoknapatawpha*—"water flowing slow through the flatland"—a peace probably impossible to achieve when the victims of the atomic bombs and indigenous dispossession are squarely in the foreground, but now offered him, obliquely and unexpectedly, as a gift from Japan, a joint gift from Lucien Stryk and Jim Barnes. A trans-Pacific network does not always work this sort of wonder, but sometimes it does.

What links together the indigenous populations of the Americas and the Japanese in their Pacific home is a structure of feeling, an emotional bond with water as a visual and auditory rhythm, intimately woven into the fabric of everyday life. Few of us have a connection to water in this way. And yet, in the twenty-first century, a century of climate change, with more floods, more droughts, rising sea levels, and the acidification of the ocean, such an emotional bond with water might be the very thing that we need. Reaching back to the Native Americans, and reaching out to Japan, Faulkner's networked regionalism is one place to begin.

NOTES

1. Pascale Casanova, *The World Republic of Letters*, trans. M. B. DeBevoise (Cambridge, MA: Harvard University Press, 2007), 87. Subsequent references to this edition will appear parenthetically in the text.

2. Gilles Deleuze and Félix Guattari, *A Thousand Plateaus*, trans. Brian Massumi (Minneapolis: University of Minnesota Press, 1987); Bruno Latour, *Reassembling the Social: An Introduction to Actor-Network Theory* (New York: Oxford University Press, 2005).

3. Lee Rainie and Barry Wellman, *Networked: The New Social Operating System* (Cambridge, MA: MIT Press, 2012).

4. Ibid., 39.

5. Raymond Williams, *The Country and the City* (London: Chatto and Windus, 1973), 132.

6. Ibid.

7. Robert A. Jelliffe, ed., *Faulkner at Nagano* (Tokyo: Kenkyusha, 1956), 185.

8. William Faulkner, *Requiem for a Nun* (New York: Random House, 1951), 232–33.

9. Jelliffe, *Faulkner at Nagano*, 139–40.

10. Ibid., 141.

11. Ibid., 141–42.

12. Ibid., 78.

13. Ibid., 37–38.

14. William Faulkner, *Absalom, Absalom!* (1936; New York: Vintage, 1972), 155.

15. Drew Gilpin Faust, *Mothers of Invention: Women of the Slaveholding South during the Civil War* (Chapel Hill: University of North Carolina Press, 1996); Thavolia Glymph, *Out of the House of Bondage: The Transformation of the Plantation Household* (Cambridge, UK: Cambridge University Press, 2008).

16. Jelliffe, *Faulkner at Nagano,* 82.

17. Faulkner, *Requiem,* 3.

18. Ibid., 8.

19. Ibid., 216–17.

20. Ibid., 101. Here Faulkner invokes not only the Chickasaw but also the "nameless though recorded predecessors" they had in turn displaced: "the wild Algonquian, Chickasaw and Choctaw and Natchez and Pascagoula" (ibid.).

21. William Faulkner, *Go Down, Moses* (New York: Random House, 1942), 191.

22. Ibid., 256–57.

23. Ibid., 258.

24. William Faulkner, "A Justice," in *Collected Stories of William Faulkner,* (1950; repr., New York: Vintage, 1995), 346.

25. Ibid., 345.

26. William Faulkner, "Red Leaves," in *Collected Stories,* 321.

27. For a good summary of the controversies, see Gene M. Moore, "Faulkner's Incorrect Indians?" *Faulkner Journal* 18 (Fall 2002–Spring 2003): 1–3. For a detailed critique, see Howard Horsford, "Faulkner's (Mostly) Unreal Indians in Early Mississippi History," *American Literature* 64 (1992): 311–30.

28. Lewis M. Dabney, *The Indians of Yoknapatawpha: History and Literature* (Baton Rouge: Louisiana State University Press, 1974), 11.

29. Joseph Blotner, ed., *Selected Letters of William Faulkner* (New York: Random House, 1977), 46–47.

30. Faulkner was on solid historical ground here: slaveholding was a common practice among Native Americans: "The Cherokees had the most slaves, with 1,600 before removal and about 2,500 in 1860. The Choctaw planters had the next highest number of slaves, with about 500 before removal and 2,350 in 1860. The Creek held 902 slaves in 1832 and 1,532 in 1860, while the Chickasaw had the fewest slaves—several hundred near removal and about 1,000 in 1860. The free Chickasaw population, however, was less than one-fourth the size of the Cherokee population, so the per capita slaveholding among the Chickasaw was relatively higher." See Duane Champagne, *Social Order and Political Change: Constitutional Governments among the Cherokee, the Choctaw, the Chickasaw, and the Creek* (Stanford, CA: Stanford University Press, 1992), 176–77.

31. Robert Dale Parker, "Red Slippers and Cottonmouth Moccasins: White Anxieties in Faulkner's Indian Stories," *Faulkner Journal* 18 (Fall 2002–Spring 2003): 81. See also Robert Woods Sayre, "Faulkner's Indians and the Romantic Vision," *Faulkner Journal* 18 (Fall 2002–Spring 2003): 33–49.

32. Faulkner, "Red Leaves," 313.

33. Daniel H. Usner, "American Indians on the Cotton Frontier: Changing Economic Relations with Citizens and Slaves in the Mississippi Territory," *Journal of American History* 72 (1985): 297–317; and Samuel J. Wells and Roseanna Tubby, eds., *After Removal: The Choctaw in Mississippi* (Jackson: University Press of Mississippi, 1986).

34. Vizenor's haiku poems are collected in *Raising the Moon Vine* (1964); *Empty Swings* (1967); *Matsushima: Pine Islands Collected Haiku* (1984); and *Favor of Crows: New and Collected Haiku* (2014).

35. Gerald Vizenor, *Hiroshima Bugi: Atomu 57* (Lincoln: University of Nebraska Press, 2003), 16–17. Hereafter cited parenthetically.

36. Jim Barnes, *On a Wing of the Sun: Three Volumes of Poetry* (Urbana: University of Illinois Press, 2001), 45.

37. Ibid., 56.

38. As editor and translator, Stryk published *World of the Buddha: An Introduction to Buddhist Literature* (1968), *Zen Poems of China and Japan: The Crane's Bill* (1973), and, with Takashi Ikemoto, *The Penguin Book of Zen Poetry* (1977), which won the Islands and Continents Translation Award and the Society of Midland Authors Poetry Award. His other translations include *Bird of Time: Haiku of Bashō* (1983), *Triumph of the Sparrow: Zen Poems of Shinkichi Takahashi* (1986), and *The Dumpling Field: Haiku of Issa* (1991), with Noboru Fujiwara.

39. Barnes, *On a Wing of the Sun*, 123.

Salvific Animality, or Another Look at Faulkner's South

Colin Dayan

Ten years ago, when I drove down from Nashville, passing Memphis and coming into Mississippi for the very first time, I felt that here was an opportunity to blend the personal with the scholarly. During this visit and the reengagement with William Faulkner, I began to think through what matters most to me about the South—and about history, about what gets remembered and why. Bear with me, then, as I take you back in time and into the one novel by Faulkner I had not seriously considered before, *The Hamlet*.[1]

I was thirteen in 1963 when Martin Luther King wrote his letter from the Birmingham jail, when four girls died in the Sixteenth Street Baptist Church bombing there, when Kennedy was assassinated in Dallas and Ngo Dinh Diem in Saigon. Malcolm X suffered Elijah Muhammad's discipline of public silence after X described Kennedy's murder as a case of "the chickens coming home to roost." In Atlanta, "the city too busy to hate," Lester Maddox took up iron skillets and ax handles at his Pickrick Restaurant to block "colored folk" from entry. My father's friend Charlie Leb (born Lebedin) dragged the Reverend Ashton Jones by his feet, across the floor, and out the door of his restaurant at 66 Lucky Street.

Facing what remains to some extent an irretrievable past, Faulkner takes the remnants of a history ignored or denigrated and turns the dead archive into a live and changeable landscape. The "little lost village, nameless, without grace, forsaken" of *The Hamlet* is ground and impetus for many of the processes that shaped the post–Reconstruction South.[2] His South is a place finally without consolation.

In that broken patch of rich river-bottom country lying twenty miles southeast of Jefferson, he asks that we open ourselves imaginatively to the natural world. That locale is "inextricable from the creatures who inhabit it, whose lives and labor shape, and were always shaped by the land."[3] The writing at its most extreme demands a radical change in

perspective, beyond the resources of rational inquiry. It invites a knowledge that has everything to do with sentience, an unprecedented attentiveness to the sensual world. In exhuming what is truly harrowing, and
equivocal, about humans—and human sociality—he returns, time and
again, to nature, or, more precisely, to what I'm calling *animality*. I ask
how Faulkner's most vexing asides or unreadable detours become the
necessary prompts to an attentiveness that is crucial to his ethics, and to
the kind of historical response that it demands.

Now a brief caveat here: in writing for years about the legal history
and practice of slavery and imprisonment in the Americas, I learned
that the idea of the beast or—to quote the natural historian of Jamaica,
Edward Long—"the senseless icon of the human"[4] was a category best
avoided. After all, in racist taxonomies or natural histories of the Caribbean and the American South, categorical thinking ushered in taxonomic
boundaries that not only separated humans from animals but also generated new ideas about what was to count as human. These new taxonomies depended on the rank of animal to embody the slave, a fiction of
law that became a moral truth: a fantastic amalgam of human, animal,
and inanimate thing. Such racist fantasies could locate "a guinea-negro"
in the same category as "learned horses, learned and even talking dogs."[5]

It is natural, then, to sense the danger of such juxtapositions. But
in my recent work I want to trace a form of ethics that moves beyond
dehumanization and beyond the anthropocentric worldview that sup-
ports it. Instead, I focus on the oscillation between categories usually
kept separate, especially in mainstream thought: between human and
nonhuman animals.

Ike's cow

"They walk in splendor" (175). From dawn until night, we move through
a landscape suffused with the "head: shoulders: hips," the "trotting legs"
of a man whose body slowly approaches his beloved. It is a cow he seeks.
"She stands as he left her, tethered, chewing." But what a cow she is. Part
of what Faulkner describes as "[t]he shifting shimmer of incessant leaves,"
she gains a palpability so weighty that she appears transcendent, buoyed
up out of this world, with "a quality of illusion as insubstantial as the prone
negative" of Ike's breathless approach. But, no, she is more even than that:
a blanched shadow, in Faulkner's words, as "one blond touch stipulates
and affirms both a weight and mass out of the flowing shadow-maze." It
is Ike's touch that changes shadow into flesh: "a hand's breadth of contact
shapes her solid and whole out of the infinity of hope. He squats beside

her and begins to draw the teats" (172). The phantasmal becomes incarnate, as definitive and weighty as a force of nature, which, of course, the cow is. How could we have been lured into thinking otherwise?

> Then he would hear her, coming down the creekside in the mist. It would not be after one hour, two hours, three; the dawn would be empty, the moment and she would not be, then he would hear her and he would lie drenched in the wet grass, serene and one and indivisible in joy, listening to her approach. He would smell her; the whole mist reeked with her; the same malleate hands of mist which drew along his prone drenched flanks palped her pearled barrel too and shaped them both somewhere in immediate time, already married. He would not move . . . smelling and even tasting the rich, slow, warm barn-reek milk-reek, the flowing immemorial female, hearing the slow planting and the plopping suck of each deliberate cloven mud-spreading hoof, invisible still in the mist loud with its hymeneal choristers. (157)

Cleanth Brooks in *William Faulkner: First Encounters* presents Ike to his readers: "we have in Ike a character who presses humanity to its farthest limits."[6] But Faulkner troubles any easy definition of the term "humanity." The experience of reading "The Long Summer," book 3 of *The Hamlet*, is purely corporeal—a surfeit of matter so extreme that it becomes preternatural: a supernatural that is natural to the nth degree. Refusing to reduce living characters into dead myths, Faulkner makes Ike's love real. This reality is found in what might seem to defy it. No ambrosia of the gods here. After saving his cow from the fire, he receives her gift, "the violent relaxing of her fear-constricted bowels" (164).

Instead of turning Ike or the cow into mythic characters—even the mention of Juno is only a prompt to move beyond the solace of myth—Faulkner brings out something else in the union. Whatever is defiled can be exalted. It all depends on the strength of the affections. As I hope to show, Faulkner's troubling of human entitlement depends on a radical way of looking at the natural. And he leaves no doubt about the wanton injury and casual cruelty of humankind, with preconceptions as delusional as they are damaging.

Ike and his cow together consume what the reasonable and cultivated among us—and Faulkner's critics—identify as trash or dirt or waste: when *The Hamlet* was published, Frank Brookhauser in the *Philadelphia Inquirer* called it the "lower depths," "some hitherto unprinted nastiness," and John Selby in the *Charlotte Observer* called Faulkner's characters "sluggish, dirty, and worthless."[7] A few years before, Louis Kronenberger in the *Nation* had condemned Faulkner for "exploring the most polluted streams and malarial swamps of the subhuman spirit."[8]

Indeed, for one critic, the story of Ike's infatuation with the cow is an "exercise in horror."[9] But in these pages, even the shared consumption of "hulls and meal, and oats and raw corn and silage and pig-swill" (172) is nothing short of sacramental. Their communion over what Faulkner will call "the mammalian attar" (176) becomes something like a hint of grace in a belittered world. Faulkner challenges us to look again at dirt and muck, to think again about the "things" which, in his words, "the weary long record of shibboleth and superstition had taught his upright kind to call filth" (172–73).

The reciprocal vulnerability does not merely turn human into animal but also turns physicality into spirituality. It is grasped in Ike's sentience, his way of knowing the cow: "he could hear her; it is as though he can see her—the warm breath visible among the tearing roots of grass" (170). Not even Eula Varner is endowed with such fullness of life. Indeed, she most often seems more like an inanimate object, as still as the chairs on which she sits, static in her idleness. Even her face is described as "unseeing and expressionless," a "mask-face" (339). With Eula, Faulkner riffs on the verbal reservoir of terms for capacious sexuality, what Labove describes as "rich mind- and will-sapping fluid softness" (97). But we cannot help feeling that this woman is not only doomed but dead and hollowed out, nothing more than a receptacle for the projections of men. Whatever is mammalian in these descriptions seems overwrought, even parodic, especially when read against the quiet beauty and warm breath of the cow, so responsive to Ike's presence.

The exacerbation of life in the love between Ike and the cow reveals what is most telling about their encounters. Animality or animalism becomes something other than what we think. For it is not something vague and grand called "humanity" that interests Faulkner and inspires his most stunning if disconcerting writing so much as the stuff of the senses. The experience of such relational, alive, and unsettling life forecloses a history of disregard, and confronts the loss in what remains: "monuments of a people's heedless greed" (163).

What society deems unfit or expendable, Faulkner reclaims. It is not, therefore, a matter of considering folks who are nothing more than animals but an effort to upend such judgment wherever it occurs. To be an animal in *The Hamlet* is not what we assume. The care depicted in Ike's sojourn with his bovine beloved is an animal's, not a human's care. These pages are traversed with evidence of his toil to excavate what has been lost. In one sense, Faulkner writes for this reason alone: to make his sentences the habitat for that unearthing.

In order to exhume and put back into history whatever had been ignored or denied, Faulkner surrenders his prose to the *excrescence*. He reminds us that this past can only be told by depending on, even while buckling under, the conceptual force of the superfluous. It is not just a matter of accumulating the shards found in the wake of insignificant lives, but something more risky. Every detail of the encounter between the idiot and the cow adds to a textured, disquieting atmosphere that both entices and repels the reader.

Perhaps this is how life insists on being remembered, felt, and known. Faulkner compels us to risk losing ourselves in what is beyond our ken. He writes in order to sharpen our appetite for seeing and knowing. The hypothetical matters most. Faulkner stirs up uncertainty, a kind of murkiness, no matter how specific the pile-up of details or how sharp the images. He invokes, though tentatively, a reservoir of economy and power on which all creatures draw but from which most of us have learned to cut ourselves off completely. This is not a mythical world, pace George Marion O'Donnell, but rather a terrain that makes us think and feel and sense more abundantly than we normally think and feel and sense.[10]

What kind of world resists domestication? It is not easy to write this cosmos into being. It is even more difficult to read pages that resist what we admire as most humanizing. The burden of *The Hamlet* is to find beauty in the muck. Faulkner wants us to obey the terms of his characters' delicate epiphanies and take seriously the magic found in the hardest matter. He dissolves distinctions so that all kinds of things, living and dead, persons and property, are put into relation. This is something more virulent than "magical realism," though Gabriel García Márquez declared *The Hamlet* "the best novel of South America ever written."[11]

Houston's Hound

Whenever Faulkner found himself uncomfortable or bored, he turned to dogs. In *Becoming Faulkner* Philip Weinstein recounts the time when Faulkner found himself in the Hollywood studio of Sam Marx. Led to the projection room so that he could see some footage of a film with Wallace Beery, whom Faulkner claimed he did not know, he refused to look at the screen. Instead, he turned to the office boy and asked, "Do you own a dog?" And when he answered no, Faulkner replied, "Every boy should have a dog."[12] To talk about dogs, whether terrier, treeing feist, or hound, was a way to stay alive in the ersatz civility of the culture-mongers. Faulkner found ways to feel the dirt and hear the breath of animals, a way of living so in excess of the customary and apparently so oblivious to good tidings that it discomfited both his critics and his admirers.

Late in *The Hamlet*, the sewing-machine salesman, raconteur, and sometime voice of conscience, Ratliff, opposes the effects of Flem's machinations—his auction of wild spotted ponies and their dizzying escape—with a turn to creaturely vulnerability. In the face of the lawsuits brought against Flem and Eck Snopes by Armstid and Tull, respectively, in their futile attempt to redeem something from the loss of their horses, Ratliff articulates a kind of ethics, somewhat cold but unabashedly candid. It is reducible to no moral code and conformable to no doctrinal purity. It lies outside the parameters of either bartering or charity. Instead of replacing the last bit of cash Armstid has paid for one of the spotted horses, Ratliff turns to the mysteries of what Herman Melville, in a review of Nathaniel Hawthorne's *Mosses from an Old Manse*, called "spiritual truth."[13] Even though the context is horse-trading, Ratliff registers something beneath—or outside of—intention, reason, and calculation:

> I wasn't protecting a Snopes from Snopeses; I wasn't even protecting a people from a Snopes. I was protecting something that wasn't even a people, that wasn't nothing but something that dont want nothing but to walk and feel the sun and wouldn't know how to hurt no man even if it would and wouldn't want to even if it could, just like I wouldn't stand by and see you steal a meat-bone from a dog. (301)

What are dogs? What are people? It might seem that these questions are easily answered, even when the bounds between supposed opposites are most threatened. Yet there remains something equivocal about assumptions about human and animal, about the role of reason in making us who we are. Throughout *The Hamlet*, the killing of animals is never without effects on the life of humans. And nowhere does that yoke become so clear as in the tangle of mind and motive gathered in the relation between Jack Houston and the unnamed hound, that "regal dog" (64), alert and grave, whose baying Faulkner describes as more like a shout.

Words like *body* and *spirit*, *human* and *nonhuman* sit uneasily in their customary positions. No longer contradictory, they are intermeshed one in the other in the heat of an engagement shared equally by men and dogs, a nuanced and particular passion. In the novelistic entanglement of Mink Snopes and Houston's hound, Faulkner makes the ordinary something marvelous. It is a reality more ample than the divine. On one hand, what first seems ordinary soon manifests a spectral vitality. On the other, though characterized as a ghost story, this dog is never simply a ghost. He is too palpable, too real, to be cordoned off somewhere in the beyond. The enmeshing of man and hound requires that we suspend our beliefs, put aside our craving for final answers, and learn to live in a place where neither luck nor fatality has any meaning.

What does have meaning? Following Faulkner's lead, I ask that we become curious about the most inauspicious objects. Moreover, I want to retrieve for our reading of Faulkner "animality" not merely as a counter to the world of the human but as an inextricable part of it. Writing in 1941 about the "Snopes World" in the *Kenyon Review*, Robert Penn Warren praises O'Donnell's "Faulkner's Mythology" and invokes his opposition between "humanism and naturalism," and/or "animalism," but then he cautiously responds to and blurs such a dichotomy, setting out the terms of contrast on a continuum: "Flem does not stand, it seems to me, as 'naturalism or animalism' in the terms of the contrast; he stands outside the scale which runs from the idiot to Houston, from groping animalism to a secret poetry; in his cunning, he stands beyond appetite, passion, pride, fidelity, exploiting all those things."[14]

Houston is never without his hound, and the hound is never without Houston—not even in death. The juxtaposition of dead body, howling dog, and a breathless Mink reinforces animal sensuality so that it could almost be said that the embodied sentience of these pages is only fully revealed in what lies beyond human life. We are also asked to see the mysterious life of objects, for instance, the gun butt that knocks Mink's shoulder, the tree malignly rotten, and "the tangle of foul and sweating wood" (212). Houston's body, once dead, takes its life from "the shell of a once-tremendous pin oak" (213). Corpse and wood become dislodged from the plot that swirls around them, galvanizing our experience of a landscape that is indistinguishable from a gun shooting, hooves thundering, frogs grunting, dogs howling.

This writing delivers insights to the senses in ways that skirt and even evade expressive communication. We are to take in what precedes understanding, like the hound that witnesses what is indecipherable but also indispensable. It is as if Faulkner presses us to see, through the dog's attentiveness, something that might otherwise escape us. Like the tryst between the idiot and the cow, this entanglement unleashes intelligibility beyond the human world, beyond the claims of reasonableness. It has nothing to do with sentiment, but everything to do with experiencing what it might mean to feel sufficiently.

This novel remains haunted by its own excess, as if the words themselves have their closest analogue in something like the haunt and howl of the dog that tracks Mink and abides with Houston. Readers are made to drift from the realm of a precarious human into what we call "nature" and back again. Faulkner demands, especially when his animals appear—whether loyal dogs, wild horses, or transmogrified cows—that we confront a language that churns out the degraded and despised excess of its own operation.

Dangerous Horses

What kind of redemption was possible for the cast-offs left behind in the waste after the Civil War? Farms mortgaged, monies due, bills consigned, notes transferred, deficits tallied, and exchanges thwarted punctuate the lives of Frenchmen's Bend. Redemption is not a matter of fact or faith. It is something unreal, for even if it can be measured, the measure is incalculable. Measure itself is dubious: the debt cannot be paid and no one, except for Flem, can purchase back what has been lost. Only his debts are satisfied. No one else seems to get what is due or owed.

There is no recompense for Armstid, who bought and then promptly lost his horse in "The Peasants," the final section of *The Hamlet*. What seems to be Faulkner's greatest concern is the spectacle of law moving from a structure of norms and rights to a process of history. This history is old and musty, even obsolete, like the Old South itself. But its remnants still matter, especially when the poor and dispossessed make claims on the powerful—in this case, Flem Snopes and his money-making tricks with a band of wild Texas horses, bound together with barbed wire, until they break free, racing through barns, bridges, even a house: "They went up the road in a body, treading the moon-blanched dust in the tremulous April night murmurous with the moving of sap and the wet bursting of burgeoning leaf and bud and constant with the thin and urgent cries and the brief and fading bursts of galloping hooves" (287).

In the lawsuit scene, Faulkner returns to the chaos of English common law, digs through the layers, and exhumes its deposits as the working materials of his fiction. One can never be sure if an old law is dead or alive. When the peasants come to claim their due, the justice of the peace belabors the law of occupation and possession, ownership and creature liability. The medieval fiction of the deodand comes alive in these pages. Not only could objects kill, but they could also cause death with a vitality and menace normally thought to be the capacity of persons, not things.

We know that Faulkner understood not only how objects lived but also how they enticed and wreaked havoc on the lives of persons. Caddy's drawers dirty with mud; Eula's bench, warm to the touch; the husk of a pin oak, crumbling beneath Mink's weight. In his short story "The Hound," in part incorporated into *The Hamlet*, Faulkner embodies the experience of nonhuman animals in the portrayal of a nature gone wild and hostile as if in answer to Houston's murder. In "the dark wall of the jungle," Mink stumbles and falls in a terrain gone "treacherous with slime and creepers and bramble." They "possessed," as Faulkner puts it, "the perversity of inanimate things." And behind it all, the sound, the "bell-like and mournful" howling—a sound that will not stop.[15]

Whether inanimate (a tree or the wheel of a cart) or animate (a horse or dog), these entities were once believed to possess an evil will. They were, as I said, "deodand," meaning "what must be given to God" (*Deo dandum*). As I've written previously elsewhere, "Whether beasts, slaves, or things, they had to be surrendered in recompense for blood casually shed. Vengeance must be wreaked upon the object before the dead could lie in peace. In English law this peculiar practice centered on forfeiture of the offending object not to the victim or his kin but to the Crown. Any personal chattel that caused the death of any *reasonable* creature was believed to carry homicidal taint and malicious influence. In these deaths by misadventure, the sword, cart, tree, dog, or horse that in legal language '*moved to the death*' of a person would be surrendered to the king as expiatory offering by the owner of the wrong-doing thing."[16]

In *The Hamlet*, the justice explains the law to Mrs. Tull:

> "The law says that when a man owns a creature which he knows to be dangerous and if that creature is restrained and restricted from the public commons by a pen or enclosure capable of restraining and restricting it, if a man enter that pen or enclosure, whether he knows the creature in it is dangerous or not dangerous, then that man has committed trespass and the owner of that creature is not liable. But if that creature known to him to be dangerous ceases to be restrained by that suitable pen or enclosure, either by accident or design and either with or without the owner's knowledge, then that owner is liable. That's the law." (308)

Even the characterization of the horse as "dangerous" is legally nonbinding, although that denial flies in the face of reality: an overturned and wrecked wagon, a husband knocked unconscious and off his feet, become nothing more than elements in a yarn as futile as it is compelling. Since no owner is present, since no one in that courtroom possessed the horse, and since no one in the room has anything in writing—no bill of sale or deed—then no one is liable for any loss. "So I get nothing . . . and I get nothing," Mrs. Tull says (310).

The law has the power to put what is obvious in doubt, to make the facts pass from sight, lost in fragments of legality that turn real harm into imaginary complaint. In the words of Jeremy Bentham, who wrangled throughout his life with law's unreality: "Look to the letter, you find nonsense—look beyond the letter, you find nothing."[17]

The only way that Tull and Armstid can receive restitution is through the nonhuman entity. No human can make good on the barter. "The law says," the justice explains, "that when a suit for damages is brought against the owner of an animal which has committed damage or injury, if the owner of the animal cant or wont assume liability, the injured or damaged party shall find recompense in the body of the animal" (310). In the body of the animal: that is where Faulkner wants us to be, where his writing aims to take us.

Reading this last section of *The Hamlet* is excruciating—excoriating in the sense of being nailed to a prose of meat and blood. The prose is the animality. I do not mean that the prose conveys "animality," but rather that it is alive in its task of being a language bent upon eschewing the script of civility. These pages are not easy to read, but they are not difficult in the contrived repetition and stylistic affront of the inward-turning rendition of memory in *Absalom, Absalom!* But in *The Hamlet*, we as readers are not so much possessed as pushed away by the pile-up of incidents and things. That is the breath and fury and flexing of life at the edges in the extremity of its force, just as if the words were running and stamping and rearing up on the page.

I adduce violence and violation as the animating force of this writing. It violates the readers' cognitive capacity and their assumptions. It asks for something else, something that is not of the mind but instead reeks of the body, while making the sensory overload so excessive that it gives us the only spirituality that matters. Can you find God in a slab of meat? That is the question.

No matter how much Faulkner relies on the stuff of spiritual life, he grapples with a language capacious enough to be both "myth or meat," to recall Richard Gray's lovely coupling in his *Life of William Faulkner*.[18] Such composition registers fully the perceptions of the external world, even as it urges on readers a visceral unease, as if changing us physically, forcing us into de facto submersions of the good taste and propriety Faulkner disqualifies. Again, the burden of his craft is not to describe but rather to intensify the perceptual environment. Compelled to give us what words might be if they were nothing more and nothing less than the breath of an animal—human or nonhuman—he writes as if words could attain to the rhythm of an experience where anything like certainty is always gratuitous, where we move in a slightly obscure way toward a knowledge that is always tattered at the edges.

What Faulkner offers us in *The Hamlet* is the passionate, grieving, and exacting impartiality of fiction, handled with seeming effortlessness. I quote his rendition of Eula Varner and Hoake McCarron's buggy rides, described at the time of their last meeting—in sight of the boys—who had before watched, waited, and lusted for Eula. And now, on this night, the boys attack them. Faulkner suggests an unseen and commonplace immensity behind the violence and beyond what is seen and heard. Held between something animate and inanimate, we are led into an unexpected prospect of thought and action:

> The long return through night-time roads across the mooned or unmooned sleeping land, the mare's feet like slow silk in the dust as a horse moves when the reins are wrapped about the upright whip in its dashboard socket, the fords into which the unguided mare would step gingerly down and stop unchidden and drink, nuzzling and blowing among the broken reflection of stars, raising its dripping muzzle and maybe drinking again or maybe just blowing into the water as a thirst-quenched horse will. (129–30)

In the extraordinary compression of this passage—the sensation of the mare that is like a horse (and, of course, this simile also blurs in an indistinctness that imitates the movement of consciousness)—the reader's senses are quickened by words that emerge heavy, even if as vacillating, as the radiant, wet, and celestial movement of the animal they describe.

Whose Justice?

There is a fight on in this country, and it matters greatly to our future. To take the journey with Ike or Houston or Mink, crude or unpalatable as that might appear, is to know how we can reconstitute something of a life together. In the tension of our disagreements and hatreds, we might begin to share a narrative as discontinuous as it is embattled. That is what Faulkner teaches us. The experience of reading *The Hamlet* disables our sense of privilege and its unerring cruelty. Because, you see, enlightenment and intolerance are often intertwined: the most high-minded sentiments are tainted with self-regard. These paradoxes lie at the heart of the American liberal tradition, as Faulkner understood it. What does conscience look like, he asks, here at the boundaries of humanity, or let me go further, at the edge of a cherished humanism? I mean to yoke our consciousness to what Reinhold Niebuhr—not too happily—called "the easy conscience of modern man."[19]

Is there some mode of apprehension that would find no place in a self-congratulatory and liberal enlightenment? In his 1954 review of

A Fable, Norman Podhoretz complained, "As far as Yoknapatawpha
is concerned, the Enlightenment might just as well have never been.
The qualities of reasonableness, moderation, compromise, tolerance,
sober choice . . . no more exist for Faulkner than plain ordinary folks
do." For Podhoretz, a "genuine sense of history" is lacking, just as is the
capacity for ideas. To feel is not to think. Instead of understanding the
world, according to Podhoretz, Faulkner wants only "to feel deeply and
to transcribe what he felt and saw."[20] Yet the most astonishing pages in
The Hamlet suggest a history beyond the reach of customary written
history. It is this perspectival, indeed sensory phenomenon, shifting and
elusive, that Podhoretz disdains. The "creekside mist," "the waking life
of grasses," "the steady booming of the frogs," "coiling buzzards on the
sky" betoken the surfacing of suppressed histories that might or might
not be told, and Faulkner risks giving his writing over to the continued
force of such histories, forceful because of their suppression.

What matters ultimately is how the division between the worthy and
the worthless is enforced. A phantasm of animality haunts the patrolled
boundaries between what is proper to the human and what is proper
to the animal. Faulkner deliberately blurs these bounds. Human and
animal attributes are mixed in a landscape of intercommunicability that
might more accurately be thought of as a transubstantiation of attributes,
as the "grave blue-ticked Walker hound" (61) shares Houston's identity,
and vice versa. Houston speaks to the dog, ordering him to go after Ike,
and the dog speaks too: "the dog shouted"—the dog shouts "Boo!" (159).
Once Houston is killed, becomes part of rotted tree and earth marrow,
the hound remains, though howling now, moored there, animated by
some sense of steadfastness that is sufficient—and powerful enough to
seal Mink's fate.

To put it another way, and perhaps more precisely: in reading *The
Hamlet* the oppositional limits between humans and animals—and other
subjectivities that inhabit the world (meteorological phenomena, plants,
occasionally even objects and artifacts)—are confounded, as are the
human-centered determinations of the just and the unjust, the worthy
and the worthless, the binaries upon which the rigorous purity of these
limits rests. This is not a philosophical inquiry. I do not attempt to define
how and where we draw the line between humans and animals. Rather,
I am trying to contribute to the understanding of how, where, and why
human beings, often quite arbitrarily, devise, formulate, and apply lines
separating human and animal or deliberately blur those lines.

In a morally disenchanted world, daily cruelty and casual violence
accompany the call for order, the need for security. Reading Faulkner

demands a radical change in perspective. He sets out to test the limits of decency, common sense, and even, at times, "good" writing. Words no longer mean what we assume. They lead us into a feeling that is not sympathy or sentiment but something much less comforting, more acute and unsettling: a way into the crud, not out of it.

"Reasonable consensus" and "civility" engage me, unsettled as I am by the prospect of divisions (not only of subject but also of genre) that allow the continued dispossession of those creatures—human and nonhuman alike—who remain outside the circle of grace, delivered to subjection without recourse. We are living in a time of extinctions, a systematic disposal of creatures deemed threatening or unfit. Faulkner teaches us compassion, an exceptional tenderness, and not just for other humans and their lost relation to animals but also for the fast-disappearing wilderness. At the University of Virginia in 1959, Faulkner lamented the loss, and calling for feeling, he inspirited the earth with sentience:

> What the writer's asking is compassion. . . . It's to have compassion for the anguish that the wilderness itself may have felt by being ruthlessly destroyed by axes, by men who simply wanted to make that earth grow something they could sell for a profit, which brought into it a condition based on an evil like human bondage. . . . [The big woods] were obsolete and had to go. But that's no need to not feel compassion for them simply because they were obsolete.[21]

There is a world out there, neglected or abhorred by many. It lies deep in our culture. It is the habitat of spirits and animals, not men. There is always something outside the human world. And there is another kind of love, something close to attachment and awe. We sense it when Ike cushions deep into the flesh of his cow. Or when Houston heels his dog, which remains "puzzled and gravely alert" in response to Houston's fury (177). Not the same kind of love as that of an elite who lives in the world of sentimental entrapment, where teacup dogs can fit in your palm and barking dogs can be silenced with a simple operation.

Perhaps as Catherine says in Truffaut's *Jules and Jim*, one must "reinvent" the word "love."[22] Faulkner teaches us how that word needs to be exhumed, not just remade. Experiencing such love—which is, finally, nothing other than compassion according to St. Paul—means to be taken out of our comfort zone and pushed beyond what can be simply comprehended. Something about skin and heart and heat and closeness more intense than what can be easily borne. The shared intimacies of animals, human or no, plants, things out of the earth and down from the sky—and everything in between—set the terms for Faulkner's insistence on a creaturely experience that upsets the sensible, the reasonable, the moral order of things—and the mean and monopolizing spirit that such legitimacy masks.

NOTES

1. I want to thank Michael Kreyling for his on-target suggestions about further reading on *The Hamlet*.

2. William Faulkner, *The Hamlet*, in *The Snopes Trilogy* (New York: Modern Library, 2012), 140. Subsequent references to this edition of the novel will be cited parenthetically in the text.

3. I am grateful to my graduate student Petal Samuel's brilliant phrasing from her forthcoming essay about Melville's *Pierre*, "The Landscape Has Its Language."

4. Edward Long, *The History of Jamaica; or, General Survey of the Antient and Modern State of That Island: With Reflections on Its Situation, Settlements, Inhabitants* (London: Printed for T. Lowndes, 1774), 371.

5. Ibid., 375.

6. Cleanth Brooks, *William Faulkner: First Encounters* (New Haven, CT: Yale University Press, 1983), 99.

7. See M. Thomas Inge, *William Faulkner: The Contemporary Reviews* (Cambridge, UK: Cambridge University Press, 1995), 215, 218.

8. Louis Kronenberger, "Faulkner's Dismal Swamp," *Nation* 146, February 19, 1938, 212.

9. See Inge, *William Faulkner*, 219.

10. George Marion O'Donnell, "Faulkner's Mythology," *Kenyon Review* 1, no. 3 (1939): 285–99.

11. Gabriel García Márquez qtd. in William Kennedy, *Riding the Yellow Trolley Car: Selected Nonfiction* (New York: Viking Penguin, 1993), 261.

12. Philip Weinstein, *Becoming Faulkner: The Art and Life of William Faulkner* (New York: Oxford University Press, 2010), 186.

13. Herman Melville, "Hawthorne and His Mosses," in *The Portable Melville*, ed. Jay Leyda (New York: Viking Press, 1952), 408.

14. Robert Penn Warren, "The Snopes World," in *William Faulkner: The Critical Heritage*, ed. John Bassett (London: Routledge, 1997), 261.

15. William Faulkner, "The Hound," in *Uncollected Stories of William Faulkner*, ed. Joseph Blotner (New York: Vintage Books, 1997), 154.

16. For a fuller discussion of the deodand, see Colin Dayan, *The Law Is a White Dog: How Legal Rituals Make and Unmake Persons* (Princeton, NJ: Princeton University Press, 2011), 127–30.

17. Jeremy Bentham, "Government by Generalization," in *English Prose: Eighteenth Century*, ed. Sir Henry Craik (London: Macmillan and Co., 1911), 536.

18. Richard J. Gray, *The Life of William Faulkner: A Critical Biography* (Oxford: Blackwell, 1994), 259.

19. Reinhold Niebuhr, "The Easy Conscience of Modern Man," in *The Nature and Destiny of Man: A Christian Interpretation* (Louisville, KY: Westminister John Knox Press, 1996), 93–96.

20. Norman Podhoretz, "Faulkner in the 50s," in *William Faulkner: Critical Assessments*, vol. 4, ed. Henry Claridge (Robertsbridge, East Sussex, UK: Helm Information, 1999), 86–87.

21. Frederick L. Gwynn and Joseph L. Blotner, eds., *Faulkner in the University: Class Conferences at the University of Virginia 1957–1958* (Charlottesville: University Press of Virginia, 1959), 277.

22. *Jules and Jim*, directed by François Truffant (1962; New York: The Criterion Collection, 2005), DVD.

"Moving Sitting Still": The Economics of Time in Faulkner's *Absalom, Absalom!*

Jordan Burke

> I never could come out even with the bell, and the released
> surging of feet moving already, feeling earth in the scuffed floor,
> and the day like a pane of glass struck a light, sharp blow, and my
> insides would move, sitting still. Moving sitting still.
> —Quentin Compson, *The Sound and the Fury*

Ever since Jean-Paul Sartre published his classic essay "On *The Sound and the Fury*," Faulkner's philosophy of time has been a topic of perennial concern for critics. Justifiably so, for time is something that many of Faulkner's characters fight against. Witness Quentin bleeding after breaking the glass cover on his inherited watch, or Thomas Sutpen returning from the Civil War to wage a new war "against the ponderable weight of the changed new time itself."[1] To say that these efforts to combat or stay the measured motion of clock time cause Faulkner's characters to live in a state of temporal suspension is not to say anything new. Sartre refers to Quentin's experience of time as one of "frozen speed," without a "*Being-toward*."[2] Cleanth Brooks characterizes Quentin as "freezing into permanence one fleeting moment of the past."[3] And Édouard Glissant writes that Faulkner's characters more generally are "people prey to . . . a suspension of being, a stasis," people whose failure to accommodate exogenous cultural and economic intrusions is figured in their immobility, inwardness, and incestuousness.[4]

In this essay I explore the way in which the temporal blockages and aporias commonly identified in *Absalom, Absalom!* are symptoms of the fluctuating and troubled relationship between time and labor in the American South during the nineteenth and early twentieth centuries. Through Thomas Sutpen and his descendants, Faulkner builds a web connecting time, narrative practice, and historical process, one which reflects both the changing socioeconomic milieu of the US South and the evolving narrative strategies employed by the plantocracy to reverse and refuse change. Sutpen serves as the primary figure for a hybridized and internally contradictory economy transitioning from agrarian "autonomy" to capitalist dependence and, concurrently, from a paternalist atemporality to the work rhythms more commonly associated with the industrial North. He is the Janus-faced symbol of the late-antebellum South, the admixture of the slave-owning aristocrat and the Cotton Kingdom protocapitalist. And in order to disguise the conflicting demands of his "split identity," Sutpen cultivates techniques of narrative obfuscation that Quentin Compson eventually inherits, techniques that enable him to embalm an obsolete paternalist and precapitalist temporal structure by rendering the Haitian Revolution, the Civil War, and the ascendance of a hegemonic capitalist time-discipline "unthinkable" in Michel-Rolph Trouillot's sense of the word.[5]

Transitions, Contradictions, Capitalisms

In their revolutionary study of the southern economy, *Time on the Cross*, William Fogel and Stanley Engerman attempted to dispel "romantic" notions of the antebellum South as a world somehow beyond the reach of industrial capitalism by arguing precisely the opposite: that capitalism was a constitutive feature of the plantocracy.[6] Responding to historians like Eugene Genovese, who held that plantation "society, in its spirit and fundamental direction, represented the antithesis of capitalism, however many compromises it had to make," Fogel and Engerman used quantitative analyses of the antebellum economy to demystify paternalist ideologies, which only seemed hostile to capitalism.[7] "Paternalism is not intrinsically antagonistic to capitalist enterprise," they write, "for there is considerable evidence that slaveowners were hard, calculating businessmen who priced slaves, and their assets, with as much shrewdness as could be expected of any northern capitalist" (Fogel and Engerman, 73). They go on to demonstrate that as slaveholders began cultivating land in the Old West in the early nineteenth century to accommodate the growing global demand for cotton, they developed efficient management strategies, specialized labor forces, incentive systems, and work rhythms that resembled the industrial factories of the North, simultaneously increasing ties of dependency to the world market and entrenching capitalist principles in what has historically been seen as a noncapitalist, relatively autonomous economy.

While Carolyn Porter transposes Fogel and Engerman's work onto a reading of *Absalom, Absalom!*—she claims that through Sutpen, Faulkner "reveals the explosive consequences of understanding the slaveowning planter for the capitalist entrepreneur he was"—recent developments in southern historiography complicate the binary capitalist-precapitalist debate and invite more gradational readings both of Sutpen's generation and of Faulkner's South.[8] Rather than conceiving of the transition to capitalism as a cataclysmic and uniform event (one largely unaffected by political, cultural, and regional particularities), global comparative studies have led economists to understand the process as polymorphic. Hence Rebecca Jean Emigh observes that "transitions to capitalisms are highly local and gradual affairs, with different outcomes in different places, influenced by politics and culture."[9] In keeping with the work of Emigh and other "third-wave" theorists of economic transition, Tom Downey's regional survey of the evolution of an antebellum merchant class, the rise of railroads and cotton factories, and the development of cotton as a cash crop in response to the demands of British textile mills distills a sense of "a [southern] society in transition, where established and intruding features overlap and interact."[10] The South's transition to capitalism, as Downey illustrates in his study of the southern interior, necessarily entailed contradiction, concession, and equivocation: there are no pure agrarians, nor are there pure capitalists in his southern diorama. For market revolutions involve their subjects in complex patterns of ideological and economic negotiation, even collusion.

Faulkner's rendering of Sutpen is similarly stereoscopic. If, as Ramón Saldívar has contended, Sutpen stands "as a figure of the internally conflicted nature of class and racial relations in the antebellum South," he also stands as a figure of the structural contradictions plaguing a transitioning antebellum economy.[11] Sutpen is first exposed to the socioeconomic realities of the South after moving to a Virginia plantation as a boy who "had never even heard of, never imagined, a place, a land divided neatly up and actually owned by men who did nothing but ride over it on fine horses or sit in fine clothes on the galleries of big houses while other people worked for them" (Faulkner, *Absalom*, 179). He quickly perceives the mechanics of the social hierarchy he has entered into: the practice of dividing property, the prestige that material ownership affords, the leisure enjoyed by slaveholders. And he quickly decides that he will use any means necessary to supplant the established aristocracy. "So to combat them," he tells Quentin's grandfather, "you have got to have what they have that made them do what he did. You got to have land and niggers and a fine house to combat them with" (192). His decision to move to Haiti in 1823 marks the beginning of his "combat" with the older class of landed elite, but it also marks his first fatal step toward dependency on the world market: "What I learned was that there was a place called the West Indies to which poor men went in ships and became rich, it didn't matter how, so long as that man was clever and courageous" (195). At this point, Sutpen is ignorant of the implications of his decisions. He has only learned to do anything necessary to achieve his desired socioeconomic end: that is, to have land, slaves, a plantation, a son, and to lie all day in the master's "barrel stave hammock" (184). But the beginnings of the paradox underlying his "design" are already apparent: Sutpen enlists himself as a dependent laborer in the capitalist world market so that someday he can hang in "sunny suspension" in a precapitalist world apart (58).

As Sutpen establishes himself in Yoknapatawpha, the disjunction between his economic system and his agrarian dreams only intensifies. "In the beginning," Sutpen is much like the "younger sons of Virginia and Carolina planters" driving "wagons laden with slaves and indigo seedlings" who converge on the Mississippi frontier in Faulkner's essay "Mississippi."[12] Both are of a new generation of planters, remarkably different from the easygoing gentility that a younger Sutpen encounters when he and his family move to the Tidewater plantation. Their mode of farming, made possible by Colonel Sartoris, who "opened the local cottonfields to Europe by building his connecting line up to the main railroad," takes place on a much larger, industrial scale (Faulkner, "Mississippi," 20). Within two years Sutpen becomes "the biggest single landowner and cotton-planter in the county" (Faulkner, *Absalom*, 56), having essentially stolen ten-by-ten square miles of land from Ikkemotube (compare this to the Compsons' one-by-one plot of land). To go along with his land, he builds the biggest house in the county. He hires not on the basis of friendship but of profitability; hence, his overseer is "the son of that same sheriff who had arrested him" (57). And he marries his wife to "patent" (39) and consolidate "the shape and substance of . . . respectability" (31). At the same time, he begins developing ties to the local elite, forming a business friendship with General Compson, who loans him the seed for his first cotton crop. The partnership that Sutpen initiates between the presiding and ascendant classes signals an ideological and economic shift in Yoknapatawpha County away from the world where "planter and yeoman shared visions of local sufficiency," as Allan Kulikoff might put it, and toward a new plantation society, characterized, according to Susanna Delfino, by "more rational and exploitative management" practices that began "wiping away the last vestiges of a paternalist plantation system."[13] This "new society" that Sutpen helps create is one in which the "Cotton King" marries the merchant's daughter.

Impossible Temporalities and Unthinkable Histories

Market expansion, partnership with the merchant class, technological innovation, and labor efficiency are the principles at the base of Sutpen's plantation. And in terms of time, his design is entirely dependent on the calendar and the clock. "Perhaps a man builds for his future in more ways than one," he tells General Compson, "builds not only toward the body which will be his tomorrow or next year, but toward actions and the subsequent irrevocable courses of resultant action which his weak senses and intellect cannot foresee" (Faulkner, *Absalom*, 196). Here he is referring not to his downfall, which he has not foreseen, but to the completion of a design he cannot fully imagine. And in order to complete the design in time, within the scope of the "years" allotted to him, he adds, "I should need . . . money in considerable quantities and in the quite immediate future" (ibid.). Money and efficient use of time are thus connected in Sutpen's economic imagination even before he moves to Haiti: his nascent capitalist code is one of efficient accumulation.

In his essay "Economies of Time," James Booth observes, "All major servile classes have been characterized, according to Marx, by the fact that their bound time yielded surplus or free time, whether for their leisured masters or for the creation of surplus value."[14] This idea is as old as Homer, Aristotle, and Hesiod, each of whom observes that slaves serve as laboring surrogates for their masters, generating temporal surplus, or freedom, that the master can then convert into leisure (Booth, 7). From the beginning that is Sutpen's goal: to become a master and thereby to exempt himself from the obligations of "labor time." Booth might call the kind of temporality Sutpen seeks "classical" and fundamentally precapitalist, categorically distinct from what E. P. Thompson identifies as the "time-discipline" of every "mature capitalist society," where "all time must be consumed, marketed, put to use."[15] It is the classical idea of time that Sutpen uses his capital to infuse into the Hundred and that each member of his family consequently lives within. Hence, Ellen "seemed to have encompassed time. She postulated the elapsed years during which no honeymoon nor any change had taken place, out of which the (now) five faces looked with a sort of lifeless and perennial bloom like painted portraits hung in a vacuum" (Faulkner, *Absalom*, 59). Judith and Henry are held "distended and light and iridescent with steady breathing in that fairy balloon-vacuum" (255–56). And the antebellum Hundred itself is "like a lake welling from quiet springs into a quiet valley and spreading, rising almost imperceptibly and in which the four members of it floated in sunny suspension" (58). Yet as the Cotton Kingdom planter he is, Sutpen's means of achieving this precapitalist temporality directly controvert his end goal. He is bound by the forward motion of his design, and yet his ultimate hope is to extricate himself from any sort of motion. He is dependent on the world market for cotton, and yet he seeks the temporal independence of the antebellum planter. Ultimately, in Sutpen Faulkner *conflates* the two distinct economies of time that Booth summarizes in his essay: "Marx's political economy of time," Booth writes, "raises again the question of real wealth: whether it ought to be considered as hours embodied in things, governed by the laws of the market and, above all, economic efficiency, or (so far as is possible) as free time under human control and used for freely chosen purposes" (Booth, 23). Complicating this temporal binary, through Sutpen and his Hundred Faulkner projects an image of the mutual imbrication of Booth's two temporalities—an image changing with the shifting soil of the antebellum world.

Historian Mark M. Smith identifies a restructuring of temporal experience taking place in the progressively capitalist order of the antebellum South that mirrors Sutpen's own. While slaveholders began to use the clock to regulate slave labor, to increase efficiency, and thereby to justify their economic system by demonstrating its ability to conform itself to "modern" conceptions of clock-regulated productivity, the clock conversely began to govern the masters. Smith argues that clock-regulation of the slave population, which "germinated" in the 1830s,

> reinforced among masters a time discipline, an internal sense of time that commanded that they act in accordance with the clock. For slaves, clock time was important but, during the antebellum period at least, it was not internalized. . . . Masters, however, had much earlier become enslaved by a power they themselves had helped create for the purposes of furthering their profits and their mastery.[16]

While Genovese identifies the temporal contradictions that slaves reckoned with as they transfused a "quasi-industrial [time] discipline" into a world where "the rhythm of work followed seasonal fluctuations," Smith here highlights a contiguous, yet more fundamental shift in the economic structure of the plantocracy.[17] For as the fabric of plantation time unraveled and the chronograph took a permanent place on slaveholders' mantels, the clock gradually gained "mastery of masters."

Sutpen suspends recognition of the implications of this fundamental paradox in his narrative of Haiti. As a number of critics have noted, his move to Haiti is historically anachronistic.[18] After the slave revolts ended with the defeat of Napoleon's army in 1804, the Haitian people declared their independence from France and the end of slavery. This was accompanied by the disenfranchisement of white colonists, who were no longer allowed to own land or to hold political office.[19] But not only does Sutpen claim to have "subdued" the slaves during an 1827 uprising on the plantation he oversaw in Haiti, he also tells Quentin's grandfather that he gained possession of that plantation by marrying the owner's daughter. Neither of those actions is historically feasible. Sutpen's Haitian narrative exists in symbolic opposition to the actual events of history: Haiti's liberation, after all, marked the destruction and reversal of the racial hierarchy Sutpen claims to have preserved during his time there and thus represented Smith's "mastery of the masters."

Using Hegel's master-slave dialectic as a guide, Richard Godden explains Sutpen's mis-narration as an act of "counterrevolution" by which he suppresses awareness that his body is produced by, and therefore dependent on, black labor. "Sutpen can raise the Hundred," Godden argues, "because, having experienced slavery as the suppression of revolution, he can . . . displace his knowledge that the master's mastery depends upon the body and the consciousness of the bound man."[20] Yet what Godden here labels Sutpen's "suppression of revolution" can be better understood not in terms of physical domination but in terms of the manipulation of narrative time. Just as Faulkner's readers identify Sutpen's Haiti as anachronistic, opposed to, or ignorant of the events of history, Quentin's grandfather has difficulty believing the tale because it does not make chronological sense: "the getting there from Virginia" was imaginable "because that did infer time . . . while the other, the getting from the fields into the barricaded house, seemed to have occurred with a sort of violent abrogation . . . a very condensation of time which was the gauge of its own violence" (Faulkner, *Absalom*, 201). The trouble for General Compson is not believing Sutpen's claim to have traveled to Haiti but rather accepting the fact that Sutpen's narrative of Haiti entails the abrogation of sequential time. The scrutiny and skepticism that he directs toward Sutpen's story suggests that he suspects, if he does not in fact know, that it is flawed. Perhaps that is why he characterizes Sutpen's Haiti as the site of "incredible paradox" (202), a "little lost island beneath its down-cupped bowl" (204) that is suspended in a temporal "vacuum into which no help could come."

Yet not only does General Compson listen silently and eagerly to Sutpen's anachronistic narration, he also hands it down to successive generations for replication and revision. In doing so, he mimics the antebellum South's behavior toward the Haitian Revolution. Alfred Hunt writes that "the specter of St. Domingue was primary in the minds of southerners," because it portended the eventual destruction of the southern labor hierarchy.[21] Hence, after 1804, "Southerners relied upon exclusion, of émigrés and slaves and of attitudes they deemed hostile to slavery, as a way to protect their social system" (Hunt, 114). Trouillot elaborates upon the scope and longevity of these exclusionary tactics in his study of Haiti, history, and power. He posits that after 1804 the West cultivated "formulas of erasure" and "banalization" in an attempt to avoid recognizing the way in which the Haitian Revolution discomposed Enlightenment political theories and ontological hierarchies: countries refused to acknowledge Haiti as an independent political entity; historians left Haiti out of their texts; slaveholders used the instability of the Haitian economy in anti-abolitionist arguments (Trouillot, 96). And what emerged from these various methods of dissent and denial was "a particular bundle of silences" that ensured that "[the] revolution that was unthinkable became a non-event" (27, 98).

What Faulkner explores in Sutpen's mis-narration—what Compson perpetuates in his retelling—is a consanguine yet more active form of silence. It is a silence that stops the flow of time and that not only erases but reverses the events of history. Sutpen's tale is about the resilience of the slave-owning way of life. Yet in order to create a feasible story of that way of life, he must change the constitution of time, holding Haiti in the same changeless "vacuum" that Ellen inhabits on the Hundred.[22] The threat that he attempts to stave off with his fictional narrative of Haiti is awareness that the master will become the slave, both in the Haitian context and in the economic context of the American South. In temporal terms, this last form of slavery is not the same as Godden's Hegelian idea of dependence on the black body: it is slavery to a capitalist clock. Yet the dissonance of Sutpen's narrative project is audible in the very name he uses to identify that "little lost island" under his dominion. "It is in this act of writing one's own name—Haiti—that the former master is reduced to a bag of body parts," writes Sibylle Fischer, for "like the resignification of all inhabitants of the new state as black, regardless of skin color, the renaming of Saint Domingue signals a violent break with the colonial past and a symbolic erasure of colonialism and colonial slavery."[23] "Haiti," as both a historical coordinate and a rudimentary name for emancipation, is a word that invades Sutpen's and the South's atemporal narrative space, like a drum in the jungle auguring an unthinkable revolution.

Rupturing Silences

Although the Civil War promises the end of the slave system in *Absalom, Absalom!*, and of the narrative barricade that Sutpen builds, Quentin Compson sustains Sutpen's narrative practices and temporal code. Like

Sutpen mis-narrating Haitian history, Quentin attempts to soften the contradictions inherent in Sutpen's story through a fictional account of Bon. Yet if Sutpen's fiction of Haiti preserves a form of time that depends upon the distinction between master and slave, precapitalist and capitalist, then Quentin's contribution to the novel's historiography—Bon's miscegenated body—only embeds failure deeper into Sutpen's design. For as an embodied collapse of the master-slave hierarchy, Bon is also emblematic of the paradoxical confluence of the two temporalities Sutpen pretends to have kept separate. In spite of the fact that his own body is a harbinger of the disappearance of precapitalist time, Quentin and Shreve's Bon shares Ellen, Henry, and Judith's experience of living inside what Rosa calls that *"cocoon-like and complementary shell"* (Faulkner, *Absalom*, 111). Hence, as Bon steps onto the steamboat at the beginning of his journey to Mississippi, he watches "all motion cease, the boat suspended immobile and without progress from the stars themselves" (250). It is not the steamboat that is suspended in this scene, but rather Bon's perception of movement, of chronology. Just as Sutpen builds the "cocoon" or "vacuum" in which his family hangs, Bon's mother and her lawyer-accomplice have done the same for Bon. Yet as his mother "grooms" him in a space outside of time, where there exists no first cause (no father) and no apparent connection between money and efficiency, her lawyer sits in his chair graphing Sutpen's net worth. What becomes apparent is that mother and lawyer will use Bon to defeat and subjugate Sutpen. Hence Bon is "so much rich and rotting dirt . . . a chart with colored pins stuck into it like generals have in campaigns" (241). The parallels between the Civil War and the battle being waged here are clear. As the symbol of Sutpen's failure, Bon is the vehicle for Sutpen's destruction and the instrument of his (Bon's) own doom: he models the idea of temporal suspension as it is found in the plantation environment, attests bodily to its contradictive economics, and destroys himself by unwittingly pursuing its interests. And behind this tragic war is the shrewd capitalist, the closest thing to a divine being that Quentin and Shreve can imagine.

What is really being litigated in the Civil War, "that probation, that suspension," and in the clash between Bon and Henry, is the nature of economic time (267). Bon would embrace the new time and with it the death of the plantation system: *"the irrevocable repudiation of the old heredity and training and the acceptance of eternal damnation"* (277). But Henry cannot accept the economic failure of the plantation that the Civil War enacts (the loss of the old time), nor can he surrender the *"illusions that he* [Sutpen] *begot"* (revealed in Bon's contradictive body), which he posits are *"a part of you like your bones and flesh and memory"* (ibid.). The shot that Rosa calls the *"sharp and final clap-to of a door between us and all that was . . . a forever crystallised instant in imponderable time"* (127) leaves Henry free from envisioning the traumatic implications of the new time, but thereby forever dead to the world that is. After Henry kills Bon, and with him the possibility of accepting the capitalist world that Bon's victory would have exposed, he remains in a state of perpetual temporal miscarriage. He has preserved the integrity of the plantation, as Sutpen does with his narrative of Haiti, but the very guarantee of his failure is embedded in his victory: the paradox making the old time possible dies, and with it Henry's future.

For Quentin, narration is a way of justifying Henry's murder of Bon and, on a broader scale, the code of the antebellum South. Yet his concern with love and race only hides the more fundamental labor contradictions behind Henry and Bon's war. These contradictions compose the rope tying Sutpen's narrative of Haiti to Quentin's narrative of Henry's fall. In Sutpen's case, narration allows the illusion of the timeless plantation to continue. But the same is not true for Quentin and Henry: both of them, paired by Faulkner as Quentin-Henry at one point, are aware of the *"illusions that he begot"* and in that sense their acts of refusal are defenses of the indefensible. After all, the Civil War has destroyed the possibility of the plantation, with its honorable coating, and it has intensified the conflicts already inherent in the South's economic transition. The world of the postbellum South was one in which "categorical uncertainty" prevailed: entirely novel forms of economic and social exchange emerged as former slaves and slaveholders improvised strategies for surviving in the ruins of the plantocracy.[24] As Martin Ruef observes, it was a world with an emancipated labor class whose "[s]ocial networks" and newfound agency "served as a key impetus to mobilization toward alternative organizational arrangements" (129). And so what Sutpen has available to him in the post-Haiti Mississippi context, where the division between master and slave remains intact, Quentin and Henry do not. When Henry kills Bon and claims allegiance to his father's code, he is also killing himself, cursing himself to hang suspended in a forty-four-year loop that ends in the burning of the house whose integrity he sought to defend. And in narrating, Quentin likewise creates for himself a "tomblike" room (Faulkner, *Absalom*, 240), which even though it is "snow-sealed" (243) cannot quite keep out the "melodious" bells of the clock tower ringing faintly every hour, ringing the sound of his subjugation.

If the process of narration causes Quentin's body to merge with Henry's, the novel's final scene does have him—on a fundamental level—blending into Sutpen, suggesting that we are witnessing both an avatar of Sutpen shivering in a Harvard dormitory and, earlier, an iteration of Quentin sweating inside a Haitian barricade. Deborah N. Cohn similarly suggests that as Quentin and Shreve immerse themselves in their narration, they commune not just with Henry and Bon, but also with Sutpen himself: in them, she concludes, "the truth of history becomes immanent, and the past once again immediately present."[25] But Faulkner is doing much more here than rehearsing his apothegm, "The past is never dead. It's not even past."[26] He is blending the narratives—and their attendant silences—that southern history has inscribed upon Haiti and Mississippi in order to reveal and critique the temporal paradoxes and repressive historiographies that Sutpen, Quentin, and the South have produced. It is no accident that the stillness of Quentin's dormitory is ruptured by the sound of a bell keeping time outside, just as "the air" in Sutpen's barricade is "throbbing and trembling with the drums and the chanting" of the Haitian uprising (Faulkner, *Absalom*, 204). In both instances, domestic spaces serve as analogues for the narrative enclosures that their residents have created: they fail to dam the rhythmic push of historical and industrial time, to suppress the realities of defeat and dependency. Thus while "privileged Southerners of the Compson caste found refuge . . . in a language that displayed historical realities without granting them visibility," as John T. Matthews argues, Quentin's narration allows Faulkner to indicate that such refuges, both physical and semantic, prove incommensurate to the task set before them.[27]

Mastering Time

What Faulkner captures in *Absalom, Absalom!* is not so simple as victory over the new form of time that troubles Sutpen, that is infused in Bon, and that finally destroys the plantation's illusion of temporal freedom. It is closer to what Horace, one of Mr. Compson's beloved poets, understood centuries before the clock subjugated the South: "for slaves are of two kinds—vicarial some, / The others equal; so it is at home, / I am your slave, and thou my master art; / But elsewhere you are slave and play your part / As others pull the strings."[28] Those "others" ensure the market dependence of every character in *Absalom, Absalom!*: they are a part of Sutpen's system before he can even name them, and they send Quentin to Harvard under the guise of fulfilling his "mothers dream" (Faulkner, *Sound*, 178). They even supersede Mr. Compson, who sits in his office reading the classics of "classical" time as the Snopeses take over the town his family helped found.

Subjugation within an industrializing economy where machines are masters—where the chronometer is a universal supervisor—is the danger threatening Sutpen and Quentin as they walk backward into the New South. But it is also a danger that Faulkner deployed his art to combat. As he proclaimed in a 1955 interview, "[man] has created machinery to be his slave but his danger is that he will become the slave of that machine he has created. He will have to conquer that slavery."[29] Seen in a certain light, *Absalom, Absalom!* is the story of the South's failed attempt to conquer time and with it the realities of a new economic and temporal order, to master machinery. But while it is a record of failure, it is also an emblem of an artist's command of narrative machinery and of time itself. Perhaps that is why Faulkner unreservedly claimed that "time can be shaped quite a bit by the artist" and that "man is never time's slave."[30] For ultimately, Faulkner is the deity standing over Yoknapatawpha, whose mastery is emblematized in Sutpen's and Quentin's failure. It is his voice that speaks most insistently in the silences and paradoxes of their narratives, in the gaps they refuse to fill. And it is his voice that deconstructs the myth of the South by both commandeering and undermining the narrative strategies of Yoknapatawpha's dispossessed progeny. The story that Faulkner tells in *Absalom, Absalom!* is the story his characters do not.

NOTES

William Faulkner, *The Sound and the Fury*, rev. ed. (1929; repr., New York: Vintage International, 1990), 88. Subsequent references to this edition will appear parenthetically in the text.

1. William Faulkner, *Absalom, Absalom!*, rev. ed. (1936; repr., New York: Vintage International, 1990), 130; emphasis removed. Subsequent references to this edition will appear parenthetically in the text.

2. Jean-Paul Sartre, *Critical Essays*, trans. Chris Turner (London: Seagull Books, 2010), 108, 119. Sartre is referencing Heidegger in this instance.

3. Cleanth Brooks, *William Faulkner: The Yoknapatawpha Country* (New Haven, CT: Yale University Press, 1963), 331.

4. Édouard Glissant, *Faulkner, Mississippi*, trans. Barbara Lewis and Thomas C. Spear (New York: Farrar, Straus and Giroux, 1999), 22.

5. Hosam Aboul-Ela also refers to a technique of splitting and twinning in *Absalom, Absalom!*, which he argues gives the novel a circularity that undermines teleological and inherently "Western" understandings of history. See Aboul-Ela, *Other South: Faulkner, Coloniality, and the Mariátegui Tradition* (Pittsburgh: University of Pittsburgh Press, 2007), 152. Michel-Rolph Trouillot's study of the Haitian Revolution, particularly his conception of "unthinkability" and "silence," is central to my argument overall. He writes, "The unthinkable is that which one cannot conceive within the range of possible alternatives, that which perverts all answers because it defies the terms under which the ques-

tions were phrased. In that sense, the Haitian Revolution was unthinkable in its time: it challenged the very framework within which proponents and opponents had examined race, colonialism, and slavery in the Americas." See Trouillot, *Silencing the Past: Power and the Production of History* (Boston: Beacon Press, 1995), 83. Subsequent references to this edition will appear parenthetically in the text.

6. Robert William Fogel and Stanley L. Engerman, *Time on the Cross: The Economics of American Negro Slavery* (Boston: Little, Brown, 1974), 77. Subsequent references to this edition will appear parenthetically in the text.

7. Eugene Genovese, *The Political Economy of Slavery: Studies in the Economy and Society of the Slave South* (New York: Random House, 1965), 23.

8. Carolyn Porter, *Seeing and Being: The Plight of the Participant Observer in Emerson, James, Adams, and Faulkner* (Middletown, CT: Wesleyan University Press, 1981), 222.

9. Rebecca Jean Emigh, "The Great Debates: Transitions to Capitalisms," in *Remaking Modernity: Politics, History, and Sociology*, ed. Julia Adams et al. (Durham, NC: Duke University Press, 2005), 379.

10. Tom Downey, *Planting a Capitalist South: Masters, Merchants, and Manufacturers in the Southern Interior, 1790–1860* (Baton Rouge: Louisiana State University Press, 2006), 4–5. See especially chapter 3, on the rise of an antebellum merchant class.

11. Ramón Saldívar, "Looking for a Master Plan: Faulkner, Paredes, and the Colonial and Postcolonial Subject," *The Cambridge Companion to William Faulkner*, ed. Philip M. Weinstein (Cambridge, UK: Cambridge University Press, 1995), 118.

12. I borrow this otherwise biblical phrase from Faulkner's essay on Mississippi found in William Faulkner, *Essays, Speeches, and Public Letters*, ed. James B. Meriwether (New York: Random House, 1966), 13-14. The essay is entitled "Mississippi" and is a mixture of Mississippi history and the fictional history of Yoknapatawpha. Subsequent references to this edition will appear parenthetically in the text.

13. Allan Kulikoff, *The Agrarian Origins of American Capitalism* (Charlottesville: University Press of Virginia, 1992), 35; Susanna Delfino, "The Idea of Southern Economic Backwardness: A Comparative View of the United States and Italy," in *Global Perspectives on Industrial Transformation in the American South*, ed. Delfino and Michele Gillespie (Columbia: University of Missouri Press, 2005), 112. For a perspective similar to Delfino's, see Stanley Engerman, *Slavery, Emancipation, and Freedom: Comparative Perspectives* (Baton Rouge: Louisiana State University Press, 2007). Engerman writes that "the slave economy was rather adaptable to innovations in transport and production, such as the cotton gin, canals, the steamboat, and the railroad, and was able to benefit from various technical and organizational innovations" (29).

Alan L. Olmstead and Paul W. Rhode argue that along with the industrialization of the cotton industry, the development of seed technology actually led to heightened picking efficiency. See Olmstead and Rhode, "Productivity, Growth, and the Regional Dynamics of Antebellum Southern Development," in *Economic Evolution and Revolution in Historical Time*, ed. Rhode et al. (Stanford, CA: Stanford Economics and Finance, 2011). Hence when Sutpen's observers superstitiously posit that "he had found some way to juggle the cotton market itself and so get more per bale for his cotton than honest men could" (Faulkner, *Absalom*, 56) or that "the wild niggers which he had brought there had the power to actually conjure more cotton per acre from the soil than any tame ones had ever done," they may unknowingly be referring to a technological revolution (56). Faulkner himself was aware of the change in seed technology: he writes in his essay "Mississippi" of a "Mexican cotton seed" that "changed the whole face of Mississippi" (14).

14. James Booth, "Economies of Time: On the Idea of Time in Marx's Political Economy," *Political Theory* 19 (1991): 7–27. Subsequent references to this edition will appear parenthetically in the text.

15. E. P. Thompson, "Time, Work-Discipline, and Industrial Capitalism," *Past and Present* 38 (1967): 91.

16. Mark M. Smith, *Mastered by the Clock: Time, Slavery, and Freedom in the American South* (Chapel Hill: University of North Carolina Press, 1997), 15.

17. Eugene Genovese, *Roll, Jordan, Roll: The World the Slaves Made* (New York: Pantheon Books, 1974), 293.

18. In addition to Richard Godden's and George Handley's arguments, which I later address, Hosam Aboul-Ela explains Faulkner's "mistake" by suggesting that Sutpen and his narrators are working "to conceal the historical dynamics of the colonial economy that enriches him while he is in the West Indies" (149). John T. Matthews argues that the anachronism reflects Haiti's reversion back to prerevolutionary attitudes toward race, as a result of the Rural Code, which was instituted in 1826. See Matthews, "Recalling the West Indies: From Yoknapatawpha to Haiti and Back," *American Literary History* 16 (2004): 253. And, most recently, Michael Kreyling claims that Sutpen's narrative is actually proleptic, not anachronistic: it prefigures the United States' colonization of Haiti in the early twentieth century. See Michael Kreyling, *The South That Wasn't There: Postsouthern Memory and History* (Baton Rouge: Louisiana State University Press, 2010), 133.

19. For an account of the Haitian Revolution and its aftereffects, see Robert Debs Heinl Jr. and Nancy Gordon Heinl, *Written in Blood: The Story of the Haitian People, 1492–1971* (Boston: Houghton Mifflin Company, 1978), chapters 4 and 5. For a classic, though somewhat dated, history of the same, see C. L. R. James, *The Black Jacobins: Toussaint L'Ouverture and the San Domingo Revolution* (New York: Vintage Books, 1963), especially chapter 13.

20. Richard Godden, *Fictions of Labor: William Faulkner and the South's Long Revolution* (Cambridge, UK: Cambridge University Press, 1997), 63. Susan Buck-Morss offers a helpful historical analysis of Hegel's relationship to Haiti, arguing that Hegel's master-slave dialectic was inspired by the events of the Haitian Revolution. See Buck-Morss, "Hegel and Haiti," *Critical Inquiry* 26 (2000): 821–65.

21. Alfred N. Hunt, *Haiti's Influence on Antebellum America: Slumbering Volcano in the Caribbean* (Baton Rouge: Louisiana State University Press, 1988), 130. Subsequent references to this edition will appear parenthetically in the text.

22. George B. Handley makes a similar claim, but one directed toward "imperialism" more generally: "for Faulkner it [anachronism] is the product (consciously or not) of the empire's objectifying gaze that symbolically orders time and marginalizes people. Imperialism does not operate according to strict chronology, as other writers and critics have assumed, but rather relies on a tacit ahistoricism." See Handley, *Postslavery Literatures in the Americas: Family Portraits in Black and White* (Charlottesville: University Press of Virginia, 2000), 137.

23. Sibylle Fischer, *Modernity Disavowed: Haiti and the Cultures of Slavery in the Age of Revolution* (Durham, NC: Duke University Press, 2004), 202, 242.

24. Martin Ruef, *Between Slavery and Capitalism: The Legacy of Emancipation in the American South* (Princeton, NJ: Princeton University Press, 2014), 9–10. Subsequent references to this edition will appear parenthetically in the text.

25. Deborah N. Cohn, *History and Memory in the Two Souths: Recent Southern and Spanish American Fiction* (Nashville, TN: Vanderbilt University Press, 1999), 76.

26. William Faulkner, *Requiem for a Nun* (New York: Random House, 1951), 92.

27. Matthews, "Recalling the West Indies," 257.

28. Horace, *Satires, Epistles, and Odes*, trans. John Benson Rose (London: Dorrell & Son, 1869), 75.

29. James B. Meriwether and Michael Millgate, eds., *Lion in the Garden: Interviews with William Faulkner 1926–1962* (1968; repr., Lincoln: University of Nebraska Press, 1980), 200.

30. Ibid., 70.

"A Promissory Note with a Trick Clause": Legend, History, and Lynch Law in *Requiem for a Nun*

SEAN MCCANN

Where did the city of Jefferson, Mississippi, come from? *Requiem for a Nun*—arguably Faulkner's most historiographic novel—provides one compelling answer. In the three extended prose narratives that introduce the hybrid text's dramatic "acts," Faulkner gives us a grand vision of the emergence of Mississippi from the primal muck, the foundation of Jefferson as an incorporated town, and the city and region's increasing assimilation into the national culture of the United States. As the novel's most attentive critics have noted, together the three prose narratives amount to a foundation myth to justify the origins and destiny of Faulkner's world and to place it in counterpoint to the directions that Faulkner feared were evident in the emergence of postwar mass culture.[1]

Although each of the two succeeding prose narratives develops and elaborates these concerns, the crucial issues are dramatized most memorably in "The Courthouse," the novel's first preface. There Faulkner introduces an event returned to repeatedly over the course of the novel: the creation of Jefferson's municipal institutions out of a moment of "civic crisis" in the life of the frontier settlement that preceded the town.[2] This crisis was occasioned, we are told, when "the progenitors of the Jefferson city fathers" (15) acted to prevent the "lynching" (13) of a crew of "Natchez Trace bandits" (4) who had been captured by a group of drunk militiamen after a Fourth of July picnic. To prevent violence, Jefferson's founders—Compson, Peabody, and Ratcliffe—conspire to lock the bandits in the town jail and spike the militiamen's whiskey with laudanum. Despite these creative efforts, however, the "the law-and-order party" (16) awakes the next day to discover that the bandits have dismantled a wall of the jail and made off in the night. Their escape turns out to be a seminal event. The bandits leave with a highly symbolic

lock—a legacy of the Revolutionary past that has been carried to the
Mississippi frontier from Carolina by Alec Holston, one of the original pioneers of the settlement. Confronted by the disappearance of this
symbol of patrimonial authority, the settlement's leading figures agree to
replace it with the new civic organization symbolized by the courthouse.[3]
In the process, they are amazed to find themselves transformed from
settlers to citizens and burghers. As the lock undergoes a "transubstantiation into the Yoknapatawpha County courthouse" (9), the settlement
is transformed from frontier outpost to urban civilization. "Overnight
it would become a town without having been a village" (4). Further, its
leading figures become new men. "Something happened to them," the
novel tells us to indicate their own experience of wonder (30). They have
become, Faulkner's narrator tells us, a "prototype not only of the town
council . . . but of the Chamber of Commerce" (14).

What "The Courthouse" provides Faulkner's Yoknapatawpha, as
Don H. Doyle notes, is a fable of "civic genesis."[4] The tale is, in other
words, an example of perhaps the core myth in the ideology of liberal
democracy: the story of the social contract.[5] The progenitors of Jefferson have come together to impose "rationality" (16) on "the fantastic
and the terrifying and the bizarre" elements of the Mississippi frontier
(18). Implicit in the creation of Jefferson, furthermore, is a rich series
of analogous displacements: of the lawless world of the frontier by a
new constitutional order; of a former loose confederation of settlements
by the ultimate authority of the United States; of the rule of fathers by
the reign of brothers; of the multiethnic world of the frontier by Indian
removal and white hegemony; of wilderness and wild game by cleared
land and settled society; of a world composed almost entirely of men to a
newly "uxorious" urban civilization (48). Most importantly, in Faulkner's
telling, these developments all lead to what will become the dominant
forces in the development of Mississippi: the rise of the cotton plantation and the arrival of mass slavery. No sooner has the town of Jefferson
been formed, we are told, than a mysterious stranger named Sutpen
appears, "bringing with him thirty-odd men slaves" and a French archi-
tect (37).

As elements in *Requiem*'s fable of social contract, all these features of
modernization are cast by Faulkner, as Noel Polk observes, as elements
of a binary transition in which the founding fathers of Jefferson appear
to step at once from the timeless realm of folktale and legend into the
tragically timebound world of history, the temporal realm indicated by
"the ding dong of time and doom" that resounds from the courthouse
bell.[6] The price of this transition, the novel suggests, is a set of enduring problems. In exchange for wealth, power, and the "dream" of civic

life (107), the people of Jefferson must accept the persistent tension between public purposes and commercial interests; the enduring necessity of law and constraint; and the entanglement of its Enlightenment visions of self-government with the reality of chattel slavery. Those who refuse this contract, or who are denied the chance to enter it—Mohataha, Louis Grenier, Dr. Habersham and his son—are rewarded with obsolescence. "A hundred years later," we are told, Grenier "will have vanished, his name and his blood too, leaving nothing but . . . a little lost paintless crossroads store" (33). Those who accept the social contract, by contrast, find a place in the "thin durable continuity" of the town's history (250)—a fate underscored by the fact that the names Compson, Peabody, and Ratcliffe will remain persistent elements in the chronicles of Yoknapatawpha long after Grenier is recalled only as the Frenchman.

Grand as this narrative of social transformation is, however, it has left Faulkner's readers with at least one big question. Just what does this story of social contract have to do with what appears to be the novel's main concern: the confrontation of Temple Drake Stevens with the looming execution of her "sister in sin," Nancy Mannigoe (158)? Why did Faulkner feel the need to provide his readers with a deep history of the foundation of Jefferson in order to frame the central enigmas in the novel: the questions of why Nancy kills Temple's child and of how Temple should respond to that murder and to Nancy's subsequent trial and execution? And what vantage does Faulkner's fable of social contract provide on the novel's only slightly more distant concerns: the transformation of Mississippi and the United States more generally in the mid-twentieth century by the continued extension of federal power and by the increasing reach and consolidation of national commercial and media markets?

These are important problems, but they should lead us to further questions as well. For if, as virtually every reader of the novel has acknowledged, Nancy's crime is mysterious, in truth, no less so is Faulkner's story of the founding of Jefferson. Consider some obvious questions: Who were the bandits? Why exactly were they in danger? Why did the law-and-order party led by Jason Lycurgus Compson wish to protect them? And how plausible was it that men like Compson would actually make such efforts to prevent lynching in the first place?

On these questions, Faulkner's novel is nearly—although not completely—silent. And that silence has been largely repeated by the novel's critics, who have mainly followed Faulkner's lead in viewing the jailbreak as a moment of civic genesis in which the differentiations of law and civilization are created *ab initio*. That is not surprising. For after all, Faulkner's fable provides a compelling account of the remaking of

Mississippi in the 1830s—of the rapid transformation that occurred as Indian removal opened the way to a booming real estate market and to the metastasis of cotton farming and the mass importation of slaves. "One day someone brought a curious seed into the land," we are told in the second prose narrative, "The Golden Dome," "and now vast fields of white . . . were effacing, thrusting back the wilderness" (103). On closer inspection, however, Faulkner's foundation narrative can also be recognized as a strong misreading of the past and, more particularly, of the very materials that Faulkner drew on to construct his story. Indeed, repeatedly over the course of the novel, if subtly, Faulkner himself draws attention to that misreading.

Requiem casts its story of the jailbreak at Jefferson as a product of "legend" (5). But in truth, Faulkner almost certainly got the main elements for his story from The Outlaw Years (1930), Robert M. Coates's popular history of criminal activity on the antebellum Natchez Trace.[7] Coates, a New Yorker and Yale graduate who had moved in Dadaist circles in Paris and pursued a career as an avant-garde novelist in the twenties, came to the subject of Mississippi's "land pirates" at the recommendation of his friend Malcolm Cowley.[8] His vivid and brisk narrative, constructed out of his reading in nineteenth-century memoirs and dime novels, offered a romantic account of the outlawry that supposedly flourished on the margins of the expanding commercial civilization it mirrored. Faulkner read Coates, we can be confident, not only because The Outlaw Years appears in his library but because in a number of respects, Requiem draws directly from Coates's book.[9] In particular, Requiem refers repeatedly to the series of grand outlaws whose campaigns of crime provide the spine of Coates's narrative—the Harpe brothers, Joseph Hare, Samuel Mason, and, most important, John Murrell. These are the figures from whose criminal bands, Faulkner tells us, his anonymous bandits must have come.

Yet Faulkner's depiction of those criminals departs intriguingly from the image presented by Coates, who casts his several outsize criminals as a mirror of the progressive settlement and rationalization of the Mississippi River valley. For Coates, that is, the Harpes, Hare, Mason, and Murrell are viewed as distinct and successive tribunes of the frontier underworld, and their criminal schemes, which grow progressively in sophistication, take advantage of, and thus reflect, the expanding agencies of commercial civilization that remade the Mississippi River valley in the early nineteenth century. The narrative begins with the disorganized banditry exemplified by the Harpe brothers, rises through the incipient criminal networks seen in the criminal careers of Hare and Mason, and culminates in a grand vision of conspiracy described in Murrell's alleged reign of terror in the 1830s. Faulkner, by contrast, radically foreshortens Coates's narrative. Rather than *The Outlaw Years*'s gallery of progressive criminal types, Faulkner gives us a generalized portrait of evocative outlawry. His bandits, *Requiem* tell us, come from "the old tradition of Mason or Hare or Harpe" (223). They have been transformed, in short, from distinct indexes of social modernization to a single image of a fabled past.

Or rather, *sometimes* Faulkner provides this kind of simplified image. At other moments, he undercuts it. When first describing the anonymous bandits, for example, *Requiem*'s narrator slyly introduces the epistemology of history into the framework of legend and fable. The narrator tells us that "legend" would come to affirm that "two of the bandits were the Harpes themselves" (5). But this "was impossible, since the Harpes and even the last of Mason's ruffians were dead . . . by this time, and the robbers would have had to belong to John Murrel's [*sic*] organization—if they needed to belong to any at all other than the simple fraternity of rapine." In this sentence, the Harpes are assimilated to the evocative terrain of legend. Murrell's organization, which is introduced seemingly as an afterthought, is implicitly differentiated out as a subject of history. In keeping with this ambivalent depiction, moreover, Faulkner's narrative appears to go out of its way repeatedly to both invoke and avoid Murrell's name. What might it be, then, that "legend" hopes to avoid in maintaining the "impossible" hope that the bandits were the Harpe brothers rather than members of Murrell's organization?

As it happens, relatively little can be said for certain about the actual historical person John Murrell. In all likelihood, Murrell was a petty criminal who engaged without great success in the crimes of fraud, robbery, assault, and slave theft that were profitable amid the rapidly growing commercial networks of the Jacksonian era. But the historical Murrell was himself displaced by a far more powerful fantasy image of the man as terrifying master criminal—in Coates's retelling, a "Napoleon of the outlaws" (17). That fantasy image flourished, with significant consequences, in the frontier Southwest of the 1830s and then entered into the annals of nineteenth-century popular culture, from which it would be subsequently resuscitated by Coates's *Outlaw Years*. In invoking that fantasy image as he repeatedly does, Faulkner calls on a vision of criminal terror that spoke powerfully to white Mississippians in the 1830s and that persisted in fiction and popular memory as a threat of the anarchic peril that once haunted the slaveholding South. But in doing so, Faulkner also creates some significant problems for the dominant narrative that *Requiem for a Nun* otherwise presents.

As the historian Joshua Rothman has shown, the popular image of the demonic Murrell can be traced largely to the creative artistry of one writer—an ambitious and reckless man named Virgil Stewart who traveled through Georgia, Tennessee, Alabama, and Mississippi in the 1830s in pursuit of wealth and social advancement.[10] Stewart was, that is, a man not unlike Thomas Sutpen or, for that matter, Jason Lycurgus Compson—a migrant and a man on the make who sought to exploit the opportunities opened by the booming Southwest frontier. It was Stewart, who in his effort to ingratiate himself with potential wealthy patrons in Madison County, Tennessee, hunted Murrell and plotted his arrest when the latter was suspected of slave stealing. In response to charges that he himself was a thief and a purveyor of fraud, Stewart went on to promote the grandiose image of Murrell that implanted itself in the imaginations of his contemporaries.

To create that demonic image, Stewart likely drew on inchoate rumors of dark conspiracy and obscure criminality already circulating through the frontier Southwest. Mississippi in the 1830s was a region in the midst of a real estate bonanza and of the upheaval that usually surrounds sudden, easy access to highly valuable resources. Following Indian removal, millions of acres of Choctaw and Chickasaw lands were being auctioned off by the federal government, whereupon they were typically purchased by conglomerates of investors, resold, and turned into vast plantations whose enormous output of cotton could then be shipped off at great profit to England for industrial production. Financial interests were flooding the region with tides of capital, and wildcat banks were springing up to offer the often unreliable currency that allowed the region's commercial markets to expand. Great fortunes were made seemingly overnight, and thriving services in gambling and prostitution flourished in the cities of Natchez, Vicksburg, Memphis, and New Orleans, where the profits of the emerging cotton kingdom were concentrated. Most important, the rapid expansion of cotton farming called forth a vast interstate traffic in slaves that brought thousands of human commodities into Mississippi and made them highly profitable objects of investment, sale, exploitation, and theft.[11]

Such feverish conditions made the frontier Southwest welcoming territory for bold and ambitious men with significant resources behind them; it was also an ideal terrain for thieves, con men, counterfeiters, and fraudsters. As Rothman writes, Mississippi in the 1830s was gripped by "a culture of speculation" characterized by instability and predation.[12] "The institutions or customs that might have instilled civility and order were weak or nonexistent, and appearances were often deceptive, allowing the brash, the crafty, the venal, and the predatory to thrive."[13] In particular, the region's vast interstate slave trade enabled the rise of the new criminal enterprise of slave theft, in which once petty criminals like John Murrell could hope to make easy money by stealing, transporting, and reselling human beings.

For Murrell's captor Virgil Stewart, those same conditions created an opportunity to exploit inarticulate but potent popular fears. As Rothman explains, when Stewart was called upon to clear his own name, this ambitious but now desperate man worked to salvage his reputation by crafting a narrative that exploited the rumors of crime and insurrection that swirled through the frontier Southwest. But Stewart also infused those fears with his own resentment toward a social order that promised equality and opportunity to all white men while effectively reserving power and opportunity for a small and self-protective class of wealthy landowners and their allies among financial elites. Writing under the name Augustus Q. Walton, Stewart published a pamphlet that imagined Murrell as a criminal mastermind determined to bring an illegitimate society to ruin.[14] In the vision Stewart offered, Murrell was a brilliant entrepreneur whose mastery of the obscure codes of the law and keen managerial abilities enabled him to accomplish a precipitous rise, from assault to slave theft to the creation of a vast criminal syndicate—or "Mystic Confederacy"—with some four hundred members (Coates, 239). Murrell's ultimate aim, Stewart informed his readers, was to foment a mass slave uprising in Mississippi. The resulting panic and chaos would permit his conspiracy to empty the banks and bring low the established society he loathed. "With his army of slaves behind him," Murrell "would sweep in bloody and destructive fury through the country," Coates writes, summarizing Stewart's apocalyptic vision, "pillaging, sacking, burning, looting—until 'all but his own girt' had indeed been killed" (240).

The Murrell imagined by Stewart, in short, combined the figure of an anarchic lord of misrule with the image of an apocalyptic revolutionary. In the mode later popularized by Conan Doyle's Professor Moriarty or Batman's Joker, this fictional Murrell exploited the skills and resources (intelligence, education, enterprise, managerial organization) that were rewarded by a rapidly growing commercial society, employing them to malevolent ends that threatened an unjust social order with fateful retribution.[15] Indeed, as historians like Walter Johnson and David J. Libby have pointed out along with Rothman, the Murrell depicted by Stewart was a brilliantly fashioned image of antebellum Mississippi's deepest fears—about social mobility and disorder; about the instability of a booming capitalist economy and the opacity of long-distance commercial networks; above all about slave insurrection and the newly emergent challenge of abolitionism.

Perhaps not surprisingly, Stewart's literary creation had significant real-world effects. In the summer of 1835, amid a national wave of popular violence, Stewart's pamphlet provided a catalyst that set off fears of slave rebellion in Livingston, Mississippi, and a vigilante campaign against "gamblers" in Vicksburg, along with echoing disturbances throughout the South. The disturbances, ultimately grouped together in popular memory as "the Murrell excitement," led to the murder of probably two dozen slaves and the extralegal execution of nearly twenty white men, along with a campaign to control vice and to regulate the informal commercial markets of a tumultuous frontier society. The white deaths made the events a scandal and provoked a heated national debate, in the course of which the ideology of "lynch law" and its role in preserving slavery and racial supremacy came to be lastingly defined by both abolitionist and Whig critics of mob violence and by its southern defenders.[16]

Nearly all of this history is discussed at length in Coates's *Outlaw Years*. But Murrell appears in only provocatively marginal ways in *Requiem*. The seminal jailbreak in Faulkner's novel, which leads to the founding of Jefferson, appears to draw directly from the feature of the Murrell excitement that the nineteenth-century public found most sensational, the popular hysteria, culminating in the lynching of five gamblers, that broke out in Vicksburg in July 1835, following disturbances among militiamen at a rowdy Independence Day barbecue. Less directly, Nancy Mannigoe's crime may be inspired by the event that, as Coates notes, prompted the first wave of panic in Madison County, Mississippi, when the mistress of a plantation believed she overheard a slave nurse discussing plans to murder the master's infant child. More generally, Murrell's name pops up several times in Faulkner's narrative, always in ways that indicate that his image does not quite fit into the story the narrative intends mainly to tell.

It is not hard to conceive reasons for that awkward fit. For, taken seriously, the popular anxiety that blossomed in the Murrell excitement of the 1830s casts doubt on every element of the fable of social contract presented by *Requiem*. In its dominant mode, Faulkner's narrative gives us a simple, binary structure in which, as Noel Polk notes, the anarchy and innocence of the frontier are replaced by the tragic burdens of civilization.[17] Seen from this view, the unnamed criminals who escape the settlement jail are members of what Faulkner calls "the simple fraternity of rapine." They are, that is, versions of Eric Hobsbawm's "social bandits"—primitive rebels who resist the incorporation of their terrain by the imperial forces of capital and centralized authority.[18] They are in this mode, as Faulkner tells us, the "ghost, pariah and proscribed" (103) of the displaced "pioneer" (102).

As members of what Faulkner appropriately calls Murrell's "organization," however, the bandits have an entirely different aspect, no longer suggesting a romantic exterior to modern civilization but something like an interior double to it. As Coates puts it, Murrell's alleged reign of crime could only seem possible in a world where "the conception of man's abstract civic duties had been formalized" and in which the elaboration of law "and finance" made "legal dishonesty" profitable (204). The vision of Murrell invented by Stewart and passed on by Coates, in other words, suggested that anarchy and banditry were not primitive legacies that lingered beyond the borders of civilized society. They were, rather, incipient forces of disorder always brewing within a fundamentally unstable capitalist order.

By the same token, Coates's portrait of Murrell suggests a different account of Mississippi's development than the one Faulkner's narrative appears to prefer. In the dominant story told by *Requiem*, the cotton economy and mass slavery *follow* from the establishment of legal order and thus appear as a kind of unfortunate symptom of civilization. From this perspective, that is, banditry and mass slavery appear as trade-offs. In establishing law and order, and bringing criminal violence under control, Jason Compson and his allies unwittingly pave the way for northern Mississippi to enter a global economy in which slavery and plantation agriculture will be rewarded. "Men's mouths were full of law and order, all men's mouths were round with the sound of money," Faulkner tells us of the "new time" that is created in Mississippi: "one vast single net of commerce webbed and veined the mid-continent's fluvial embracement" (104).

The story told by Coates, however, casts Mississippi history in a somewhat different light. From this far more plausible perspective, the cotton economy and mass slavery did not follow the development of civilized order; they drove it. And, indeed, in marginal details, Faulkner's narrative acknowledges all the elements of the land rush that dominated Mississippi's economy in the 1830s and the ruthless exploitation that accompanied it. From *Requiem*'s first page, in fact, Faulkner refers to the "dispossession of Indians" (3), and, listing the "archive" of documents that precedes the founding of Jefferson, he alludes to the frontier region's feverish culture of speculation and its reliance on the mass slave trade:

> [a] sheaf of land grants and patents and transfers and deeds . . . and bills of sale for slaves, and counting-house lists of spurious currency and exchange rates, and liens and mortgages, and listed rewards for escaped or stolen Negroes and other livestock. (3)

Even before Jefferson was founded, in short, the settlement that preceded it was less a realm of frontier innocence than a world of predation, speculation, and instability. Despite both the civic "dream" Faulkner's narrative announces and the nostalgia for the "eupeptic" (103) days of the timeless past that complements that dream, the details that appear in the text's margins suggest that a continuity of venal exploitation runs through Jefferson's history from its beginnings.

By the same token, the story told by Coates in his account of the Murrell excitement is frankly incompatible with Faulkner's vision of Jason Lycurgus Compson and his confederates as a "law-and-order party" that, in the impulse to restrain vigilante justice, reluctantly creates a new political order. Historically, large planters of frontier Mississippi like Compson were not, as Faulkner suggests, opponents of lynching. Rather, as the Murrell excitement made particularly clear, Mississippi's planter class and the aspirants who hoped to join it created a regime in which legal authority and extralegal violence were not antagonistic but complementary forces.[19] Melded by the ideology of white supremacy, they operated together to submit a roiling and fractious world to elite control and to keep a ruthless social order in place. Coates's narrative—which casts lynching in precisely the mode of its orthodox defenders, as an expression of the sovereign will of a collective people—is clear and emphatic about this point. As *The Outlaw Years* correctly reports, the vigilance committees that carried out campaigns of popular justice in Madison County and Vicksburg in 1835 were not faceless mobs but formal organizations headed by pillars of their communities and, in Madison, by the owners of large and middling plantations.[20]

Such men were fearful about the threat of slave insurrection, of course, an anxiety made especially forceful by the recent Nat Turner uprising in Virginia. But they were perhaps equally troubled by the threat posed by white men who appeared insufficiently committed to defending slavery and maintaining white supremacy. They thus trained their wrath on the lower-class milieu of workers and itinerants—gamblers, steam doctors, flatboat men and dockworkers, clerks and manual laborers, prostitutes, and barkeepers—whose place at the margins of their communities revealed the disturbingly ragged edge of the region's capitalist transformation.[21] In Coates's description, this was the world whose seething energies Murrell set loose: a "straggling uproarious population of brothels and gambling houses" (279) that "blustered up and down the streets" (278) only finally to be repressed by the "good citizens."

Faulkner himself perhaps hints at the similarity of these "good citizens" to his own town fathers in giving the leader of Jefferson's progenitors the middle name Lycurgus after the Spartan lawgiver. For in the narrative provided by Coates, just as for the original defenders of Mississippi's vigilantes, the state's 1835 wave of lynching was understood not as popular hysteria or as uncontrolled mob violence but rather as the carefully and justly applied tool of an estimable civilizing order. "Groups of men bound themselves together in summary authority," Coates writes, in testament to the civic spirit of the vigilance committees (298). "And the immediate results were tremendous. . . . [L]aw had broken the back of lawlessness" (300).

In short, what *Requiem's* brief and ambivalent references to John Murrell highlight is the fact that Faulkner's novel implicitly presents its readers with not one but at least two competing historical narratives of Mississippi's development. In its marginal details, the text acknowledges Jefferson's origins amid a speculative boom characterized by hazard, uncertainty, ruthless exploitation, and brute repression. But the novel displaces that undeveloped account of the past with a more prominent legend about a transition from anarchic innocence to the burdens of civilization, a narrative that both justifies and obscures the region's history of expropriation and racial domination.

The distinction between these competing historiographic visions is important because something very much like their conflict appears to be at issue in the "acts" that provide *Requiem's* dramatic present. As Noel Polk plausibly contends, those parts of Faulkner's narrative depict something more than the spiritual trial of Temple Drake Stevens. They represent more particularly a battle between Temple and Gavin Stevens in which Stevens strives relentlessly to compel Temple to accept the authority he represents and to expunge the embarrassment she has brought to his family name. "Stevens is not at all out to 'save' Temple," Polk claims, "but rather to crucify her."[22] Seen in the light of the competing back-stories of Jefferson's past, however, this campaign can be described in broader terms. The battle between Stevens and Temple is a struggle between a vision of civic obligation that rests on powerful norms of racial and gender hierarchy and a challenge to those norms whose very indifference to the pretenses of conventional morality threatens to reveal Mississippi's social order as a cynical and predatory regime. If Gavin Stevens is, in effect, an heir to Jason Lycurgus Compson, then Temple Drake presents him with the shadow of John Murrell.

Importantly, *Requiem* is not silent on the significance of racial supremacy to the model of civic obligation that Gavin Stevens represents. In the third of the novel's prefaces, Faulkner describes Jefferson's jail, casting it as an emblem of the deep history of the town and, in this respect, as a counterforce to the banality of mass culture. The "hollow inverted air . . . of radio" (244) and the "corpse-glare of fluorescent light" links "Chicago and Kansas City and Boston and Philadelphia" (243–44), the preface laments, "bathing the sons and daughters of men and women, Negro and

white" alike (244). By contrast, the jail provides a reminder of a nearly
forgotten legacy of coercion and of an accompanying ideology of civic
paternalism:

> Only the old citizens knew the jail any more, not old people but old citizens:
> men and women old not in years but in the constancy of the town . . . who still
> insisted on . . . handymen who had to be taken out of hock on the mornings after
> Saturday nights and holidays . . . servants, housemen and gardeners and handy-
> men, who would be extracted the next morning by their white folks. (250–51)

Such old citizens (all of them, of course, assumed to be white) presumably take for granted what Temple observes about the black hands she
sees at the windows of the jail: that they are "shaped . . . to the handles of
the plows and axes and hoes, and the mops and brooms and the rockers
of white folks' cradles, until even the steel bars fitted them without alarm
or anguish" (197).[23]

When, in the culmination of his campaign, Gavin arranges for Temple's visit to the jail in *Requiem*'s final act, he is also effectively recruiting
her to a racial fantasy in which black labor and white paternal care are
joined by civic obligation and racial hierarchy. In Gavin's understanding, Temple's past speaks of an inclination to disregard this fantasy. She
has spent time in a Memphis criminal underworld reminiscent of the
dangers once represented by John Murrell, and in her experience of
that ethnically indeterminate realm, she has "haggle[d], traffic[ked]"
with corruption (129). In her encounter with Popeye Vitelli, moreover,
Temple has been tainted by a subhuman "hybrid" (145) who raises at
once the threat of the racial Under Man ("He should have been crushed
somehow under a . . . boot, like a spider," Gavin remarks) and an image
of aristocratic decadence ("He was a gourmet, a sybarite . . . of that
age of princely despots" [146]).[24] In both respects, Popeye exemplifies a
profound threat to the model of civic paternalism that Gavin represents.

That threat is raised again when Temple has the opportunity to flee
Jefferson with her would-be blackmailer, Pete, another emissary from
Popeye's underworld. As Stevens views him, Pete presents—as Murrell
once did—a model of ruthless acquisitiveness that makes him appear
a natural figure for an amoral commercial market. A man "so hard and
ruthless, so impeccable in amorality, as to have a kind of integrity" (171),
Pete also appears the epitome of mass culture in his resemblance to "the
general conception of a college man, or a successful young automobile or
appliance salesman" (174). The peril is presented in yet another form in
the image of the cynical "whore morality" that Nancy Mannigoe exemplifies *before* she becomes the murderer of Temple's unnamed infant

daughter (184). As Temple recalls, Nancy "made her debut into the public life of her native city while lying in the gutter with a white man trying
to kick her teeth or at least her voice back down her throat" (121). She is,
in this respect, a stubbornly abject reminder of the features of the commercial market that Mississippi elites like Jason Lycurgus Compson once
sought to control. She undermines Gavin Stevens's pretenses to obligation and paternal benevolence with a reminder that his civic fantasy rests
on the reality of a different public order, one governed by amoral desire
and cynical exploitation.

Just as *Requiem*'s prefaces provide two accounts of Mississippi's history, then, the novel's present action dramatizes the struggle between two
rival visions of Mississippi's social order: between the "old" citizenship
and its fantasy of a paternalist racial hierarchy and the ruthless integrity
of a predatory marketplace. Nearly every aspect of the novel's dramatic
"acts" reflects this conflict. Thus, all that distinguishes Gowan Stevens
from Pete is that he has permitted himself to suffer the burdens that
Faulkner suggests those atop Jefferson's racial hierarchy must endure.
Gowan is "almost a type," we are told (53)—one of the sort who graduate
from "the best colleges" (54) and who are employed in "cotton futures,
or stocks, or bonds." Only "tragedy" has made his "face . . . a little different." Similarly, Temple, in her desire to avoid the burdens Gavin thrusts
upon her, would like to call on the terms of the commercial market to
view herself as an autonomous agent who can cancel debts and free
herself of the claims of the past. "Why cant you buy back your own sins
with your own agony?" she asks (277). But in the novel's most famous
line—"The past is never dead"—Gavin is present to deny this hope (92).
"The past," he informs us, is not a cancellable debt but "something like
a promissory note with a trick clause" (162). On this account, as Temple
comes to realize, its claims can never be redeemed: "now it can go on,
tomorrow and tomorrow and tomorrow" (210).

Following the same logic, *Requiem* makes clear that Mississippi's
racial order permits Nancy Mannigoe to appear in only two possible
modes. She can represent the "whore morality" that she does on the
streets of Jefferson and accept the abjection and social death that accompany that role. "In the eyes of the law," Gavin Stevens asserts, Nancy
Manigault "is already dead" even before her execution (82)—a condition that Temple claims for herself, as well, when she claims to share
with Nancy a "whore morality." "Temple Drake is dead," she repeatedly
asserts of herself (92, 93).[25] Alternately, Nancy can accede to the paternalist vision Gavin Stevens encourages her to adopt and appropriately
presents to her in the jail. There he outlines for Nancy an extraordinary
vision of the afterlife: "The harp, the raiment, the singing, may not be for

Nancy Mannigoe. . . . But there's still the work to be done—the washing
and sweeping, maybe even the children to be tended and fed" (279).
Gavin has already urged Temple to trade an implicitly soulless version of
personal freedom for an eternal sense of sin and obligation. So, too, does
he offer Nancy a deal to replace the social death of prostitution with the
promise of eternal life. She may have this deal, he implies, so long as she
accepts that even in Heaven she will fill a servile position.

In short, the drama presented by *Requiem*'s acts stages not only a
story of sin and redemption but a battle between the corrosive freedoms of the commercial marketplace and a local social order organized
by a paternalist vision of white supremacy. Gavin Stevens, like Jason
Lycurgus Compson before him, aspires to view that battle in terms of a
contest between irresponsibility and civic obligation, between disorder
and benevolent authority. But the figure of John Murrell is present in
Faulkner's narrative to trouble that gratifying picture and to suggest the
extent to which Jefferson's civic dream rested (and still rests) on a reality
of brute repression. Appropriately, in the novel's final scenes, Faulkner
introduces a jailer whose kind treatment of Temple reveals the moral
triviality of paternalist benevolence and its ultimate dependence not just
on coercion but on a social order maintained by extralegal violence and
racial terror. The jailer, like his friend and ally Gavin, is "gentle and com-
passionate and kind" (268). In this respect, Temple notes, he resembles
"the member of the mob who holds up the whole ceremony for seconds
or even minutes while he dislodges a family of bugs or lizards from the
log he is about to put on the fire" (268). What can this astonishing line
tell us but that at the core of Jefferson's civic dream lies a reality so
fundamental as to seem almost unworthy of notice? Everything rests on
lynch law.

                              NOTES

1. See especially Leigh Ann Duck, *The Nation's Region: Southern Modernism,
Segregation, and US Nationalism* (Athens: University of Georgia Press, 2002), 219–32;
Barbara Ladd, "'Philosophers and Other Gynecologists': Women and the Polity in
Requiem for a Nun," *Mississippi Quarterly* 52.3 (1999): 483–501; Spencer Morrison,
"*Requiem*'s Ruins: Unmaking and Making in Cold War Faulkner," *American Literature*
85.2 (2013): 303–34; Noel Polk, *Faulkner's "Requiem for a Nun": A Critical Study*
(Bloomington: Indiana University Press, 1981); Jay Watson, "Dangerous Return: The
Narratives of Jurisgenesis in Faulkner's *Requiem for a Nun*," *Modern Fiction Studies* 60.1
(2014): 108–37; and Steven Weisenburger, "Faulkner in Baghdad, Bush in Hadleyburg:
Race, Nation, and Sovereign Violence," *American Literary History* 18.4 (2006): 739–71.

2. William Faulkner, *Requiem for a Nun* (New York: Random House, 1951), 22.
Subsequent references to this edition will be cited parenthetically in the text.

3. The lock, which belongs to Alec Holston, "the grandfather in the settlement," has been used by the community to establish its authority over the mail pouch (a leather bag, slit "under each jaw of the opening" and secured by the lock) delivered by the carrier for the US mail. In these respects, it is an emblem of private ownership and of patriarchal authority, as it is of the political independence of the settlement in a weakly federalist political order: "the old lock was not even a symbol of security: it was a gesture of salutation, of free men to free men, of civilization to civilization," from Mississippi "to Washington: of respect without servility, allegiance without abasement to the government which they had helped to found . . . still free to withdraw from it at any moment" (12). Faulkner's narrative implies that all these conditions are traded for the new order established with the founding of the town.

4. Don H. Doyle, *Faulkner's County: The Historical Roots of Yoknapatawpha* (Chapel Hill: University of North Carolina Press, 2001), 65.

5. On the social contract as a myth of liberal society, see Northrop Frye, "Varieties of Literary Utopias," *Daedalus* 94.2 (Spring 1965): 323–47. As a story of how white men, in creating a political community, displace ostensibly pre-political Native Americans, Faulkner's tale is more specifically a version of what Carole Pateman and Charles Mills identify as "the settler contract." See Pateman and Mills, *Contract and Domination* (Malden, MA: Polity Press, 2013), 35–78.

6. Polk, *Faulkner's "Requiem for a Nun,"* 21–22.

7. Robert M. Coates, *The Outlaw Years: The History of the Land Pirates of the Natchez Trace* (New York: Literary Guild of America, 1930).

8. See Mathilde Roza, *Following Strangers: The Life and Literary Works of Robert M. Coates* (Columbia: University of South Carolina Press, 2011).

9. Joseph Blotner, *William Faulkner's Library: A Catalogue* (Charlottesville: University Press of Virginia, 1964), 23.

10. Joshua Rothman, *Flush Times and Fever Dreams: A Story of Capitalism and Slavery in the Age of Jackson* (Athens: University of Georgia Press, 2012). On the broader significance of the image of Murrell and the events surrounding him, see also Ann Fabian, *Card Sharps and Bucket Shops: Gambling in Nineteenth-Century America* (New York: Routledge, 1999), 28–38; Kenneth S. Greenberg, *Honor and Slavery* (Princeton, NJ: Princeton University Press, 1997), 135–45; David Grimsted, *American Mobbing, 1828–1862: Toward Civil War* (New York: Oxford University Press, 1998), 144–54; Walter Johnson, *River of Dark Dreams: Slavery and Empire in the Cotton Kingdom* (Cambridge, MA: Harvard University Press, 2013), 46–72; David J. Libby, *Slavery and Frontier Mississippi* (Jackson: University Press of Mississippi, 2004), 101–18; and Richard Slotkin, *The Fatal Environment: The Myth of the Frontier in the Age of Industrialization* (1985; repr., Norman: University of Oklahoma Press, 1998), 133–37. On Murrell's appearance in literary texts in particular, including *Requiem*, see Dianne C. Luce, "John A. Murrell and the Imaginations of Simms and Faulkner," *William Gilmore Simms and the American Frontier*, ed. John Caldwell Guilds and Caroline Collins (Athens: University of Georgia Press, 1997), 237–57, and Thomas Ruys Smith, "Independence Day, 1835: The John A. Murrell Conspiracy and the Lynching of the Vicksburg Gamblers in Literature," *Mississippi Quarterly* 59.1–2 (2005): 129–60.

11. Over the first half of the 1830s, the slave population of the state grew by some 250 percent. By the middle years of the decade, Mississippi was a black majority state. Growth in the slave population was particularly rapid in the frontier regions in the central and northern parts of the state, where the Choctaw and Chickasaw cessions made land newly available. By 1837 at least 30 percent of Lafayette County's population would be slaves. See Rothman, *Flush Times and Fever Dreams,* 10 and *passim*; Libby, *Slavery and Frontier Mississippi,* 77 and *passim*; and Johnson, *River of Dark Dreams,* 1–17 and *passim*.

12. Rothman, *Flush Times and Fever Dreams*, 6.

13. Ibid., 9. See also Johnson, *River of Dark Dreams*, 1–72 and *passim*, and Libby, *Slavery and Frontier Mississippi*, 37–78.

14. Stewart's narrative became still more influential when it was adapted by H. R. Howard and republished with Harper Bros. the subsequent year, in a version that was reprinted multiple times, including as a dime-novel-type narrative in the widely circulated cheap publication *The National Police Gazette*.

15. Subsequent adaptations of Stewart's narrative made this point clear by prefacing Murrell's biography with a phrenological analysis that identified Murrell's main qualities as "Energy," "Acquisitiveness," "Self-Esteem," and "Firmness," along with "great power of application." "His notorious rascality does not depend so much on a bad Phrenological organization, as upon the wrong direction of his mind when young." O. S. Fowler qtd. in H. R. Howard, *The Life and Adventures of John A. Murrell, the Great Western Land Pirate* (New York: H. Long & Bro., 1847), iv.

16. See Ashraf Rushdy, *American Lynching* (New Haven, CT: Yale University Press, 2012), 28–38; and Christopher Waldrep, *The Many Faces of Judge Lynch: Extralegal Violence and Punishment in America* (New York: Palgrave Macmillan, 2002), 27–48.

17. Polk, *Faulkner's "Requiem for a Nun,"* 20–52.

18. Eric Hobsbawm, *Bandits* (New York: Delacorte Press, 1969), 33 and *passim*.

19. Grimsted, *American Mobbing*, 85–180.

20. Ibid., 146–48.

21. Johnson, *River of Dark Dreams*, 70–72; see also Fabian, *Card Sharps and Bucket Shops*, 36–38.

22. Polk, *Faulkner's "Requiem for a Nun,"* xiii.

23. Appropriately, describing the jail, Temple recalls the story of Rider from "Pantaloon in Black"—one of the rare instances in Faulkner's work where he acknowledges not only the southern practice of lynching but its complementary relation to Jefferson's legal order. See Faulkner, *Requiem for a Nun*, 198–99.

24. On Popeye as a version of the "Under Man" prominent in the transatlantic racial discourse of the 1920s and 1930s, see Bram Dijkstra, *Evil Sisters: The Threat of Female Sexuality and the Cult of Manhood* (New York: Knopf, 1996), 381–91. Interestingly, Gavin Stevens's racial animus in this passage suggests that he refuses to relinquish elements of anti-Italian and anti-immigrant bigotry that many of his contemporaries among southern elites were moving rapidly away from in the postwar years. See Robert L. Fleegler, "Theodore G. Bilbo and the Decline of Public Racism," *Journal of Mississippi History* 68 (2006): 1–27.

25. Not surprisingly, Gavin expects that this status will mean for Temple something close to what it has meant for Nancy. He predicts that, should Temple flee with Pete, he will "simply black her eyes and knock a few teeth out and fling her into the gutter" (171).

Faulkner and the Freedom Writers: Slavery's Narrative in Business Records from Nineteenth-Century Abolitionism to Twenty-First-Century Neoabolitionism

CALVIN SCHERMERHORN

In *Go Down, Moses* (1942) William Faulkner dramatizes a central contradiction of American slavery—turning people into property—and the culture of impunity that arose from it. Faulkner engaged seriously with historical debates and the theories of race and culture that underlay them, influencing a conversation about the American past and racial slavery. In "The Bear," Ike McCaslin discovers in a ledger that his inheritance was born of a brutal business, one that made the family estate a landscape of sexual violence. He repudiates his legacy and denounces the Slave South. Though wrapped in humor and irony and conveyed using the author's peculiar accent and language, Faulkner's novel draws from a rich narrative tradition composed of competing strands or scripts that he used to critique not only the prevailing historiography but a celebration of the Old South most evident in Margaret Mitchell's *Gone with the Wind* (1936; screenplay, 1939).[1]

In doing so, Faulkner retrieved and modified elements of an abolitionist script that used business records to shine a light on an ugly social landscape obscured by moonlight and magnolias. Nineteenth-century abolitionists highlighted the destructive aspects of slavery using dry business records that reversed the fortunes of flesh-and-blood subjects, a script southern regionalists and proslavery writers negated by elaborating an organic social order that supposedly defined slavery. Antislavery novelists drew from both scripts, producing in the 1850s a commercially successful sentimental synthesis. Following the Civil War, slavery's competing scripts reemerged in a three-way struggle. An emancipationist script calling attention to the need for black freedom competed with a white supremacist script celebrating the Lost Cause and whitewashing the slavery business. By the end of Reconstruction in the late 1870s,

New South writers began softening the hard core of the white supremacist script, incorporating sentimental elements of the antislavery script to produce a national literature that bears striking resemblance to what historian David Blight terms a reconciliationist script.[2] Reconciliation celebrated white sacrifice during the Civil War, downplayed slavery's legacy, denied the legitimacy of black freedom, and endorsed a benevolent white supremacy that was supposedly part of an organic social order. By the early twentieth century, historians had professionalized, and mainstream historians gave scholarly authentication to the reconciliationist script. Dissenters ranged from novelists like Arna Bontemps and Frances Gaither to historians like Carter Woodson and sociologists like E. Franklin Frazier, who fashioned a civil rights script, retrieving black abolitionist voices.

By taking up the historian's craft in *Go Down, Moses* Faulkner contributed to that civil rights script while critiquing the prevailing historiography on slavery. Faulkner was not politically aligned with the emerging civil rights movement, but Faulkner did contribute to a tradition of historical storytelling that has its roots in ex-slave autobiography and was used to powerful effect later in the twentieth century. Novelists explored enslaved people's perspectives in the 1960s, developing a neoabolitionist script in the process. In that schema Faulkner contributed more to a civil rights script than he has been credited with, influencing a range of novelists from Toni Morrison to Margaret Wrinkle, whose *Wash* (2013) exemplifies a neoabolitionist script of historical storytelling with Faulknerian overtones.[3] This essay contextualizes and explores the interplay of historical narrative and imaginative literature, surveying the historiography to which Faulkner and later writers contributed.

A Civil War of Slavery Scripts

Abolitionists harnessed the moral power of literature to condemn an urgent moral problem and expose the economic power of enslavers. Ex-slave autobiographers contrasted the humanity of enslaved people with the instrumentality of paper used to mediate slave transactions. Some of the earliest called attention to the paper that transmitted legal ownership, laying bare the market that was the defining feature of slavery in the early republic. Therein the trope of the talking book was featured less often and less prominently than talk of transactions.[4] In *A Narrative of Some Remarkable Incidents in the Life of Solomon Bayley* (1825), Delaware native Solomon Bayley recalled bargaining for his wife's freedom, the owner agreeing to her manumission upon payment,

promising "me a bill of sale to empower me to free her." After Bayley
paid two-thirds of the asking price, the owner balked and threatened to
"take her away." Although enslaved, Bayley dealt with his wife's owner
as a businessman. He had proof of the manumission agreement in the
shape of "receipts for all the money I had paid him, but no bill of sale or
freedom."[5] In Bayley's narrative, paper documents represent the owner's
power to sever ties of blood, love, and kinship, and Bayley's own claims
as a husband and father were inscribed on similar instruments.

As the abolitionist script developed in the 1840s, ex-slave autobiographers theorized the nexus that linked enslaved people and debt instruments. In *The Fugitive Blacksmith* (1849), Maryland native James W. C.
Pennington contended that "the being of slavery, its soul and body, lives
and moves in the chattel principle, the property principle, the bill of sale
principle."[6] Pennington narrates the scene of an enslaved woman named
Rachel, who attracted the unwanted attention of one of the sons of her
owner. Her rape preceded her sale, the owner using the slave market
to make his son's sins vanish. The sale completed, Pennington recalls,
"That same son who had degraded her, and who was the cause of her
being sold, acted as salesman, and bill of salesman," his sexual violence
sanitized and transmuted into a transaction he notarized, his impunity
sealed with his honorable signature. Sexual violence and slave sales are
close on a continuum, Pennington argues, which was an inevitable if not
planned outcome of the chattel principle.[7]

Turnabouts inscribed on paper had become a trope in ex-slave autobiography by the 1850s. Solomon Northup gave perhaps the fullest expression of the power of debt instruments, ledgers, and official records as
instruments of reversals of fortune. At the start of Northup's twelve-
year nightmare odyssey he encounters an enslaved woman, Eliza, while
confined in a Washington, DC, jail. She had been promised manumission, but when taken to Washington, Eliza found out that "the paper
that was executed was a bill of sale," Northup testified.[8] "The hope of
years was blasted in a moment."[9] Yet, the emancipatory potential of the
printed word pervades the narrative. Fundamentally, *Twelve Years a
Slave* concurs with the abolitionist understanding that slavery was subject to legal termination. The rule of law, abolitionists held, exemplified
by the stroke of an executive's pen or the seals of a constitutional convention could end slavery. On a small scale, gaining literacy was thus a
step toward freedom. Frederick Douglass's acquisition of literacy was
paradigmatic of his emergence from slavery, but more prosaically and
more practically, forged papers quietly released him from bondage as he
passed through Maryland's slave security checkpoints. Northup's gam-
bit for freedom relied on a letter and a near-miraculous response that

included a particularly intricate set of legal maneuvers, each requiring paper documentation. And his captors knew the liberating potential of the truth attested to on paper. Owner Edwin Epps warned Northup that if he "caught me with a book, or with pen and ink, he would give me a hundred lashes."[10] The liberating letter was eventually sent, and the captive was redeemed. But justice eluded Northup. In the trial of the slave trader who bought Northup from his kidnappers, records of the transaction had vanished, likely destroyed when their existence could implicate the trader. Northup gained freedom but lost justice; the absence of a record of his sale prevented his captors from being held to account.[11] Yet a slavery business so ostensibly sharp became obscure in the novels of white southerners.

White southern regionalists represented a ruling race and a ruling faction in the American republic, and as a group they disputed abolitionists' accounts of slavery and the business principles that underlay them, contending instead that slavery's paper trail led to the well-managed organic households centered on plantations. George Tucker's *The Valley of Shenandoah; or, Memories of the Graysons* (1824) was an early novel that developed the theme of slaveholding paternalism. Threatened with bankruptcy after the death of her husband, Mrs. Grayson instructs her attorney to sell the bondspersons at auction to satisfy the debts of the estate. The slave, the author explains, is "a member of a sort of patriarchal family: but when hoisted up to public sale, where every man has a right to purchase him . . . the delusion vanishes, and he feels the bitterness of his lot, and his utter insignificance as a member of civilized society."[12] But the dramatic tension of the auction block is diffused when Mrs. Grayson decides to balance the moral account books at the expense of her estate. She and other whites adjust sales to preserve kinship and emotional ties even against economic self-interest. Those bound for Georgia do so with family intact, Mrs. Grayson "[writing] down the names of those who preferred staying behind, and taking the chance of a good master in Virginia, rather than the certainty of a good one in Georgia."[13] Business is subordinated to human ties, which was the opposite of ex-bondspersons' memories of how slavery worked.

In the early nineteenth century, white novelists depicting the South registered unease with slavery but struggled to keep bills of sale from featuring prominently. Sarah J. Hale's *Northwood; or, Life North and South* (1827) features a Liberian colonization scheme by a slaveholder who educated his slaves and protected them from sale. "I have opened an account with all of my field hands, over twenty-one years of age," the owner contends. "Each has a daily allotted task; for every hour of over-work, I pay a stipulated sum; this is returned to me and credited to the individual."[14] While earning freedom each bondsman learns the virtue of thrift, and the ledger keeps a moral account. Marylander John Pendleton Kennedy prescribed slave reform in *Swallow Barn* (1832) and recommended "infusing into it something of a feudal character."[15] On the Virginia plantation he imagined in *Swallow Barn*, life in the Quarter was bucolic, the bondspeople troubled solely by their own misdeeds. Scott Romine contends that Kennedy's plantation pastoral landscape aligns "nature and social ritual against the ideological pressures of the outside world," eluding historical context.[16] Neither investment input nor agricultural output is discussed, separating the plantation from the political economy of the early republic. That world is premised on black dependence and white benevolence.

As abolitionists deepened their critique of the chattel principle, a proslavery script became highly articulated, authors shaking off Hale and Kennedy's hesitations and conceding little to the chorus of ex-slave autobiographers pointing to the underbelly of slavery in the seeming ubiquity of bills of sale, slave mortgage documents, and letters of conveyance.[17] William Gilmore Simms masterfully elaborated slaveholding paternalism, weaving enslaved people's fealty into a tenacious narrative of South Carolina's colonial past and the national founding in *The Partisan* (1835), *The Yemassee: A Romance of Carolina* (1835), and *The Kinsmen* (1841).[18]

Not all southern regionalists shared Simms's proslavery script. In *The Flush Times of Alabama and Mississippi* (1853), Joseph Glover Baldwin hyperbolizes slavery's terrors in the booming 1830s Cotton Kingdom, where credit was as cheap as African Americans' lives. To calm fears of slave insurrection, slave owners reportedly contributed sacrificial enslaved victims whose public execution would teach would-be rebels the price of revolt. But in a paradise of self-seeking slaveholders even such a grim levy inspired evasion. "Instead of throwing in one of his own negroes, as an honest ruffian would have done," jurist Sam Hele tells an astonished interlocutor, "he threw in yellow Tom, a free negro; another threw in an estate negro, and reported him dead in the inventory; while Squire Bill Measly painted an Indian black and threw him in, and hung him for one of his Pocahontas negroes, as he called some of his half-breed stock."[19] Baldwin was not indicting slavery so much as the blood-stained and greed-soaked Black Belt cotton frontier—including Lafayette County, Mississippi, the model for Faulkner's fictional Yoknapatawpha—contrasting the region with his native Virginia. "In the old country, a jolly Virginian, starting the business of free living on a capital of a plantation, and fifty or sixty negroes, might reasonably calculate, if no ill luck befell him, by the aid of a usurer, and the occasional sale of a negro or two, to hold out without declared insolvency, until a green old age."[20] Baldwin obscured Pennington's chattel principle with hyperbole while Kennedy and Simms denied it with pastoralism and the romance of the American founding.

White antislavery novelists, notable for the proportion of female authors in their ranks, brilliantly thrust the thorny issue of slavery into the center of American social discourse in the 1850s. Moreover, some of the first African American novelists borrowed elements of both the abolitionist and proslavery scripts to elaborate the contrast between the ostensible paternalism of slaveholders and the business of slavery on which they relied to maintain social position. Antislavery novels developed the theme of slavery's immoral accounting in the 1850s, borrowing from African American autobiography. Yet they affirmed plantation paternalism while disputing the benevolence of particular slaveholders. Harriet Beecher Stowe's sensational *Uncle Tom's Cabin* (1852) includes a scene in which a bondswoman disputes her transfer of ownership, to which slave trader Dan Haley responds, "this yer's the bill of sale, and there's your master's name to it; and I paid down good solid cash for it, too, I can tell you . . . !"[21] Within the novel, however, slaveholding paternalism survived both the slave market and the death of Uncle Tom. George Shelby arrives at Simon Legree's Louisiana plantation in a tragic attempt to recover the bondsman his father had sold. Tom's sale proves to have been tragic, but the emotional bonds between Tom and benevolent whites hold fast. The human relationships framed by sentiment bind the characters more profoundly and enduringly than the business transactions unbind them. Borrowings from multiple genres enriched antislavery novels. Emily Clemens Pierson made the bill of sale the catalyst for a reversal in *Cousin Franck's Household* (1852). "He had a bill of sale, which he handed to Mrs. S. Rachel knew that it was all over with her—that she was destined for the Southern market, and fell senseless on the floor."[22] Literature scholar Sterling Brown termed *Cousin Franck's Household* "*Swallow Barn* in reverse."[23] The novel unfolded an extensive denunciation of slavery using the voices of nearly every character type in southern fiction, the antislavery voices being as sympathetic, principled, and credible as the proslavery voices were vapid, stolid, and untrustworthy.

Disputing the reliability of white paternalism, African American fiction writers placed the slavery business at the center rather than the periphery of their novels. In what is arguably the first African American novel, *Clotel; or, The President's Daughter* (1853), William Wells Brown represents Horatio Green attending the slave auction where Currer and her daughters Clotel and Althesa are cried off, "a blank bank check in his pocket, awaiting with impatience to enter the list as a bidder for the beautiful slave."[24] Despite an attempt to use the slave market to recover Clotel, the family is split up in the auction rooms of Richmond. As in African American autobiography, acts of sale embody reversals of fortune for Clotel, her sister Althesa, and their mother, Currer, an enslaved former concubine of Thomas Jefferson. After the sale a slave trader carts off the protagonists and sells them to slaveholders in southern cities along the Mississippi River like Natchez, New Orleans, and Vicksburg. Frank Webb's *The Garies and Their Friends* (1857) explores the effects of slavery and the ideology of race yet strips away the romantic racialism of antislavery novels and the racist romanticism of anti-*Tom* novels. Webb borrowed much from William Makepeace Thackeray and Charles Dickens (and Stowe wrote a preface), but he crafted the dramatic tension out of the reality of the slave market in a manner redolent of ex-slave autobiography.

Despite their literary achievement, Brown's and Webb's novels were unavailable to American audiences, and other early African American novelists like Martin R. Delany and Harriet E. Wilson were virtually unknown by white audiences in their time. But the antislavery script was powerful. As a sign of how intense that civil war of letters had become, University of Virginia professor James P. Holcombe declared in the *Southern Literary Messenger* in 1856 that "the success of 'Uncle Tom's Cabin,' is an evidence of the manner in which our enemies are employing literature for our overthrow."[25] He urged a narrative counterstrategy to this political and existential threat. "Let Southern authors, men who see and know slavery as it is, make it their duty to deluge all the realms of literature with a flood of light on this subject."[26]

Anti-abolitionist and proslavery authors needed no such cues. Some responded by satirizing the earnestness of antislavery sentimentalists and others by elaborating the proslavery argument using *Uncle Tom's Cabin* as a touchstone. J. W. Page's *Uncle Robin in His Cabin in Virginia, and Tom without One in Boston* (1853) borrowed from slave narratives but played their tune in reverse: an abolitionist-reared northerner learns the truth about slavery's goodness in the bosom of a Virginia plantation household. While a seller makes out a bill of sale, the buyer and an observer, a native Virginian, discuss it. The buyer remarks that "the old man, though he is an abolitionist, knows how to sell niggers, I tell you! He has made me pay him more than I have given anyone else."[27] William L. G. Smith's *Life at the South; or, "Uncle Tom's Cabin" as It Is* (1852) romanticized slavery in the Shenandoah Valley of Virginia. Instead of a slave trader appearing at the plantation of Mr. Erskine, a bookseller arrives, and the two haggle over an account. Erskine educates his bondspersons, and the reversal for Smith's Uncle Tom is the duplicity of the schoolteacher who ostensibly shows him the way to freedom, only to victimize him and lead him into a northern perdition. Simms's near-immediate response to *Uncle Tom's Cabin* was *The Sword and the Distaff; or, "Fair," "Fat," and "Forty": A Story of the South at the Close of the Revolution* (1852), republished in 1854 as *Woodcraft; or, The Hawks about Dovecote: A Story of the South at the Close of the Revolution*. It amplified his long-running romance of the American founding, the most recent installment of which was *Katharine Walton; or, The Rebel of Dorchester* (1851).[28] In large measure because of Uncle Tom mania, proslavery novels were commercially successful and supplied the chief cornerstone of secessionist rhetoric. But the resulting Civil War left three quarters of a million dead and millions more displaced, mainly African-descended former slaves.

Faulkner and the Reconciliation Script

Literary contests reemerged during and after Reconstruction, and the reconciliationist script William Faulkner argued against was a convergence of racial politics and historical amnesia. According to David Blight, national reconciliation after Reconstruction hinged on a peculiar memory of the Civil War and its meanings, elevating white manhood and denigrating the emancipation of slaves as an aim of the conflict. Initially, memories of the Lost Cause crafted by historians like Edward A. Pollard updated and defended the proslavery version of the antebellum South. Against such apologetics, formerly enslaved people along with former abolitionists, including historians like William Wells Brown, insisted that the verdict of the war was for black freedom and disputed the racist premises of the Lost Cause.[29]

Toward the end of Reconstruction, literary representations of the pre-war South were softened as New South regionalists promoted a vision of white supremacy under law and conjured a nostalgic version of the slave past that was ostensibly a model for Jim Crow social relations. It was a vision that transcended region. Organized and systematic political violence against African Americans had largely undermined the radical elements of Reconstruction. But in the stories of Thomas Nelson Page and Joel Chandler Harris, African Americans dispensed folk wisdom with no breath to spare for protests. Southern humorists reclaimed a southern slave past for a national audience. New South writers characterized black subjects as apolitical. Uncle Remus was a desexualized counterpoint to a reign of terror focused on eroding black aspirations to economic opportunity and political participation. There was no room in such a vision for a Martin Delany or a Frederick Douglass.[30] Yet white southern writers did not all share the same view.

As in the proslavery script, New South reconciliation had its underbelly, which white authors joined African American writers in exposing. In *The Adventures of Huckleberry Finn* (1884), Mark Twain excoriates slavery's legacy through Huckleberry Finn, a committed white supremacist who imbibes the old proslavery ideology and yet cannot execute its commands, delaying the freedom of putative runaway slave Jim. Twain used the central elements of the antislavery script to pillory white supremacism and the emerging reconciliation, slanting it with Finn's localism. "A couple of nigger-traders come along," Huck Finn narrates, "and the king sold them the niggers reasonable, for three-day drafts as they called it, and away they went, the two sons up the river to Memphis, and their mother down the river to Orleans."[31] An initially unsympathetic Finn is moved at the sight. "I can't ever get it out of my memory, the sight of them poor miserable girls and niggers hanging around each other's necks and crying; and I reckon I couldn't a stood it all," he recalls, tempering the scene with the knowledge that the drafts would be protested and the slave property returned.[32] The scene is one of several featuring Finn's moral hesitation to return Jim to slavery, and while Twain critiques reconciliation he does not endorse an emancipationist script. Jim was free all along, we find out, the reversal again coming at the stroke of Miss Watson's pen. The moral ambiguity is left unresolved.[33] Other white southern regionalists such as Tennessean Charles Edwin Röbert and Louisianan George Washington Cable argued against violence and racial hatred, even articulating a far-reaching vision for a South reconciled to historical progress.[34]

African American historians and writers faced the deadly realities Twain satirized, and black scholars and novelists invigorated the emancipation script as a literary-historical counterpoint to New South reconciliationism and Lost Cause militarism. Veteran abolitionists like Douglass joined African American novelists in accenting white violence and intransigence, arguing for black freedom and male citizenship. George Washington Williams, William Wells Brown, and Joseph T. Wilson wrote against the mythologizing tendencies of Jefferson Davis and other ex-Confederates from whose pens emerged apologias and memoirs. Emancipationist authors such as Francis Ellen Watkins Harper, Octavia Victoria Rogers Albert, Pauline Elizabeth Hopkins, and Kate Chopin delineated the grotesque faces of southern violence, accenting the pretzel-like logic of a society that lynched black men for supposed sexual transgressions while celebrating white gentility.[35]

Faulkner's vision of slavery's legacy was influenced by but did not overlap significantly with that of emancipationists and their legatees, the architects of the Harlem Renaissance. Yet it did contribute to a civil rights script forming in the early twentieth century in the scholarship of African American historians who critiqued New South reconciliationists from the margins. Carter Woodson and W. E. B. Du Bois argued that slavery was a horrific institution that left a terrible legacy. Sociologists like E. Franklin Frazier took ex-slave autobiographies seriously as primary sources pointing to the damage done to black families by slavery's enforced separations. But the tide of popular understanding rose against such analyses. Between the 1890s and the 1930s Joel Chandler Harris's appropriation of slaves as conduits of folk wisdom had blossomed into a national literature, which complemented a long tradition of white-performed blackface minstrelsy and the related commercialization of black figures such as Aunt Jemima. Du Bois and other African-descended American writers like Charles W. Chesnutt and James Weldon Johnson struggled to demystify American slavery and its racial legacies and unmask New South reconciliationism that hid lynching and other Jim Crow violence.[36] As the contest over slavery's narrative unfolded in the Jim Crow era, history professionalized. But the architects of that profession, such as Ulrich B. Phillips, had more sympathy for the reconciliation script than for its alternatives. The Phillips school was considerable and included a number of contemporary historians including Charles S. Davis, Edwin Adams Davis, Ralph B. Flanders, and Weymouth T. Jordan.[37]

By the end of the 1930s American slavery was theorized according to a reconciliationist historiography and dramatized according to a recrudescent Lost Cause mythology. Influenced by the neo-Confederate vision of Thomas Dixon, Margaret Mitchell's *Gone with the Wind* (1936) elaborated a flattering view of the Old South's fall, forgiving its excesses without confessing its sins. Simms's romance of the American founding was bookended with a romance of a lost civilization crushed by a Yankee leviathan. Mitchell's novel epitomized southern white women's support of white supremacist patriarchy that had roots in Caroline Gilman's and Mary Henderson Eastman's novels, along with a memory of the Civil War and Reconstruction that saw these events as sequential tragedies of northern aggression and northern vengeance. *Gone with the Wind* was endorsed by some of the country's leading historians, including Columbia University's Henry Steele Commager and Robert E. Lee biographer Douglas Southall Freeman, giving scholarly authentication to a commercially successful vision of the Old South and slavery.[38] William Faulkner dissented.

Published the same year as Mitchell's novel, Faulkner's *Absalom, Absalom!* unfolds the tragedy of ambition at the center of the slave South. Planter-on-the-make Thomas Sutpen is ambitious, like Rhett

Butler, but his failure is largely of his own making. Sutpen paid the towering cost of racial slavery and his struggles to master his world from one side of a color line he in fact straddles. Faulkner expanded that denunciation of slavery's legacy in *Go Down, Moses*, which was close to Chesnutt's and other social realists' portrayals of the South. Phillips asked what kind of men plantation slavery made. Mitchell's response was Rhett Butler, and Faulkner answered with Lucius Quintus Carothers McCaslin (1772–1837), whose records revealed sexuality and intimacy across divides of race and slavery.

Faulkner's use of archival records to represent the past was a literary device that mimicked the historian's craft and endorsed an abolitionist tradition of using business records to cast slavery as a moral contradiction. In *Go Down, Moses*, Ike McCaslin suffers a reversal as the records of the past intrude on the present. Examining family business records, McCaslin becomes a horrified witness to history when he discovers that his grandfather fathered a child with one of his bondspersons, Eunice, who gave birth to a daughter, Tomey. McCaslin's grandfather eventually had an incestuous relationship with Tomey, who gave birth to a son, Turl or Terrel, in 1833, dying in the process. Records also revealed Eunice's suicide on Christmas Day, 1832, which was a consequence of the horrors of sexual abuse and incest. The abbreviated ledger entries cram the human tragedy into absurd notations of dates, dollars, and death.

3 Nov 1841 By Cash to Thucydus McCaslin $200. dolars Set Up blaksmith in J. Dec 1841 Dide and burid in J. 17 feb 1854
Eunice Bought by Father in New Orleans 1807 $650. dolars. Marrid to Thucydus 1809 Drownd in Crick Cristmas Day 1832.[39]

The legacy of a past preserved in paper and ink is shattering. After Ike McCaslin's discovery he refuses to accept his inheritance and argues that the land was never his and never his ancestors'. It wasn't the Indians' from whom they bought it, either. Faulkner was not alone among white writers, Frances Gaither's *Follow the Drinking Gourd* (1941) being merely one counternarrative to Mitchell's novel using plantation records as counterclaims to the reconciliationist script. Arna Bontemps's *Black Thunder* (1936) dramatized Gabriel's 1800 rebellion in Virginia, anticipating to some extent Joseph Cephas Carroll's *Slave Insurrections in the United States, 1800–1865* (1938) and Herbert Aptheker's *American Negro Slave Revolts* (1943) and contradicting the premises of Mitchell and other New South reconciliationists.[40]

Faulkner had learned the history Phillips wrote and even participated with him in the 1930 Conference on Southern Writers in Charlottesville. But life in Faulkner's Yoknapatawpha County persistently disputes

Phillips and the school of historians who followed him, as Ike's response
to the ledger entries illustrate. "The old frail pages seemed to turn of
their own accord even while he thought *His own daughter His own
daughter*," Faulkner writes (270), imagining Ike McCaslin's response to
his discovery in a florid flood of emotion that contrasts sharply with the
curt account entries.[41] Other authors who departed from the Phillips
School revived an abolitionist script more explicitly. Edmund Fuller's
A Star Pointed North (1946) dramatized the life of Frederick Douglass,
using realism rooted in the perspective of African-descended subjects,
which was recognized as a literary innovation.[42]

The Civil Rights Script and Neoabolitionism

As James C. Cobb argues in this volume, Faulkner's writings made history and were made into history by others. *Absalom, Absalom!* and *Go
Down, Moses* anticipated by a decade or more the critiques of the South's
legacy of slavery by white southern historians like C. Vann Woodward,
who became a signal voice in southern history by rejecting the reconciliation script in his 1951 *Origins of the New South: 1877–1913*.[43] Faulkner
was among the first white southern writers to ask what slavery did *to*
southerners rather than what it did *for* them, and Woodward credited
Faulkner and his contemporaries Thomas Wolfe, Robert Penn Warren,
and Eudora Welty with "[bringing] to realization for the first time the
powerful literary potentials of the South's tragic experience and heritage."[44] In Faulkner's telling, slavery's legacy hurt southerners regardless
of race, yet his gradualist approach to African American civil rights separated him from radical African-descended authors of the era. It took the
civil rights movement to bring perspectives like that of Woodson and Du
Bois into the mainstream of the historical profession.

At the same time, James Baldwin, Ralph Ellison, Richard Wright,
and others articulated a robust civil rights script. Ellison's scene in *Invisible Man* (1952) of an eviction in Harlem includes the discovery of a
manumission certificate, "a fragile paper, coming apart with age, written
in black ink grown yellow," attesting, "*Be it known to all men that my
negro, Primus Provo, has been freed by me this sixth day of August, 1859.
Signed: John Samuels. Macon.*"[45] Slavery's past, to paraphrase Faulkner,
was not dead, the "free papers" reminding the reader that the past is
not even past. Stemming the tide of *Gone with the Wind*, civil rights
literature and especially novels of slavery became cultural transmitters of
ideas about African American self-determination and antiracism, including histories theorizing slave resistance and a slave community.[46]

As the neoabolitionist script developed, black experience rather than white consciousness illuminated the social landscape, and white authors joined African-descended writers in representing slavery from black perspectives. In Margaret Walker's *Jubilee* (1966), Vyry's resistance was one response to sale, humiliation, and torture, framed within a theme of racial ambiguity reminiscent of *Clotel*. "Hysterical now, she had thrown off piece after piece of her clothing," Walker writes, "and now in the moonlight the men stood horrified before the sight of her terribly scarred back. The scars were webbed and her back had ridges like a washboard," physical records of slavery's evils that survived the Civil War.[47] Walker represented a female side of the story decades before historians did so. Abolitionist categories were also part of William Styron's novel of Nat Turner.

The slaveholders narrated in Styron's *Confessions of Nat Turner* (1967) are congenital money-grubbers obsessed with the world of affairs. Turner recalls the theft of a ten-dollar gold coin taken from him by owner Thomas Moore, declaring that "this final act of piracy left me numb and beyond rage."[48] Of Margaret Whitehead, Turner recalled, "she had never once removed herself from the realm of ledgers, accounts, tallies, receipts, balance sheets, purse strings, profits, pelf—as if the being to whom she was talking and around whom she had spun such a cocoon of fantasy had not been a creature with lips and fingernails and eyebrows and tonsils but some miraculous wheelbarrow."[49] Whites could not help but commoditize black bodies, and Turner's uprising showed them the costs. Ernest Gaines, Alex Haley, Daniel Panger, and Ishmael Reed articulated black resistance with black voices, accenting violence and black self-awareness, if not a philosophy of freedom.

Since the 1980s historians' cultural and linguistic turns explored the intersections of race and class, sexuality and gender, family life and labor. Toni Morrison's *Beloved* (1987) reimagined slavery's history and legacy through the consciousness of African-descended characters, mostly female, who do the moral and historical accounting. That accounting comes early in *Beloved*. "Ten minutes for seven letters," Sethe agrees, selling her body for a headstone commemorating her dead baby.[50] Slavery became exceedingly complex, defying the idea of a slave community bounded by common interests and inheritances.

Movement rather than rootedness became central to understanding slavery. Novelists have been exploring the Middle Passage since at least Mary Johnston's *The Slave Ship* (1924), but Charles Johnson's *Middle Passage* (1990) sought to recapture the historicity of what Du Bois called "the most magnificent drama in the last thousand years of human history."[51] As historians and novelists borrowed extensively from one another, reviving abolitionist themes, cross-disciplinary critiques emerged. Perhaps the most stinging rebuke of the historical endeavor emerges in Edward P. Jones's *The Known World* (2003), which paints slavery on a sprawling social canvas even as it indicts historians' methods and sources. Jones's approach mimics and mocks the historian's craft while presenting significant challenges to the idea of racial solidarity or slave community, disrupting historians' authority while affirming the reality of a version of the slave past. Jones's fictional Manchester County, Virginia, also has many parallels to Faulkner's Yoknapatawpha. Fictitious sources support claims and read like footnotes. Jones indicts historians' reliance on written records with his account of a census taker who had a fight with his wife and got his figures wrong. Like *Go Down, Moses* with its McCaslin ledgers, *The Known World* uses the authority of a fake historiography. In one case Jones uses a fake book by a real historian, blurring the lines—as the novel does—between fiction and history.

Novelists and writers have also taken fresh account of the slavery business, reassessing the records and chipping away at the tenacity of the reconciliation script. In Alice Randall's *The Wind Done Gone* (2001), a satire of *Gone with the Wind*, bondspersons sold at auction in Charleston are contrasted with sex workers or prostitutes. "The girls who sell themselves at Beauty's are saved the pain of words on paper; their prices disappear, spoken and forgotten in the air."[52] The contrast points to the neoabolitionist project of seeing slavery in trafficked female subjects, an updating of abolitionist critiques going back to the early nineteenth century. In Peg Kingman's *Original Sins: A Novel of Slavery and Freedom* (2010), ledger entries reveal financial claims on human bodies, chains of property ownership that reverse the fortunes of subjects. The odyssey of Aminata Diallo in Lawrence Hill's *Someone Knows My Name* (2007) involves the "Book of Negroes," a 1783 catalog of African-descended black loyalist refugees from New York City, most of whom sailed to Nova Scotia to escape recapture by Patriot owners. The ledger there acts in the opposite way from the account ledgers in which people were listed as property, though the harsh conditions expatriates faced scarcely make the catalog an emancipation document. Diallo departs Nova Scotia for Freetown, Sierra Leone. Christine Duff uses Toni Morrison's term "rememory" to argue that Diallo's narration of her experience remedies the historical amnesia about the black immigrants recorded in the 1783 book.[53]

Margaret Wrinkle's *Wash* bookends an aesthetic strategy of telling historical truths about slavery by representing moral problems through ledger entries, the dry paper defying the ostensible purposes of its creation by preserving records of human terror, brittle testimony to the results of commoditizing human beings. The legacies of slavery among even those formerly enslaved suggest the limitations of a Faulknerian take on slavery's legacies read between the lines of account books. Wrinkle's *Wash* gives this strategy an ironic twist, as slaveholder James Richardson seeks to profit from coercive sexual relations, redolent of the abolitionist critique of breeding human beings for the market.

The tradition of storytelling about slavery in which Faulkner took part retrieved a venerated component of black autobiography and used it to reverse the fortunes of one of slavery's white legatees, laying bare a horrible history and lingering on Ike McCaslin's anguished response. Abolitionists who condemned what they saw as the crying sin of the age bequeathed to Faulkner and other writers an effective storytelling device that continues to interpret the past and to perform the cultural work of making the history of American slavery accessible by revealing its unmistakably human legacies. Neither Pennington nor any other abolitionist could have intended or imagined the ramifications of conjuring dry paper as a potent agent of enslaved people's reversals and a window onto the tragedy of ambition and moral catastrophe that was the slave South.

NOTES

1. Sally Wolff, *Ledgers of History: William Faulkner, an Almost Forgotten Friendship, and an Antebellum Plantation Diary* (Baton Rouge: Louisiana State University Press, 2010); Glenn Meeter, "Molly's Vision: Lost Cause Ideology and Genesis in Faulkner's *Go Down, Moses*," in *Faulkner and Ideology: Faulkner and Yoknapatawpha, 1992*, ed. Donald M. Kartiganer and Ann J. Abadie (Jackson: University Press of Mississippi, 1995), 277–96; Tim A. Ryan, *Calls and Responses: The American Novel of Slavery since "Gone with the Wind"* (Baton Rouge: Louisiana State University Press, 2008); Joel Williamson, *William Faulkner and Southern History* (New York: Oxford University Press, 1993).

2. David W. Blight, *Race and Reunion: The Civil War in American Memory* (Cambridge, MA: Harvard University Press, 2001); Jeannine Marie Delombard, "Representing the Slave: White Advocacy and Black Testimony in Harriet Beecher Stowe's *Dred*," *New England Quarterly* 75.1 (March 2002): 80–106.

3. Erik Dussere, *Balancing the Books: Faulkner, Morrison, and the Economies of Slavery* (New York: Routledge, 2003); Susan V. Donaldson, "Telling Forgotten Stories of Slavery in the Postmodern South," *Southern Literary Journal* 40.2 (Spring 2008): 267–83.

4. See Matthew J. Pethers, "Talking Books, Selling Selves: Rereading the Politics of Olaudah Equiano's *Interesting Narrative*," *American Studies* 48.1 (Spring 2007): 101–34.

5. Solomon Bayley, *A Narrative of Some Remarkable Incidents in the Life of Solomon Bayley, Formerly a Slave in the State of Delaware, North America; Written by Himself, and Published for His Benefit; to Which Are Prefixed, a Few Remarks by Robert Hurnard* (London: Harvey and Darton, 1825), 28, http://docsouth.unc.edu/neh/bayley/bayley.html (accessed February 9, 2016).

6. James W. C. Pennington quoted in William L. Andrews, *To Tell a Free Story: The First Century of Afro-American Autobiography* (Urbana: University of Illinois Press, 1988), 78.

7. James W. C. Pennington, *The Fugitive Blacksmith; or, Events in the History of James W. C. Pennington, Pastor of a Presbyterian Church, New York, Formerly a Slave in the State of Maryland, United States* (London: Charles Gilpin, 1849), iv, http://docsouth. unc.edu/neh/penning49/penning49.html (accessed October 9, 2014). For additional historical context, see Edward E. Baptist, *The Half Has Never Been Told: Slavery and the Making of America* (New York: Basic, 2014).

8. Solomon Northup, *Twelve Years a Slave: Narrative of Solomon Northup, a Citizen of New-York, Kidnapped in Washington City in 1841, and Rescued in 1853, from a Cotton Plantation near the Red River in Louisiana* (Auburn, NY: Derby and Miller, 1853), 53.

9. Ibid., 32.

10. Ibid., 230.

11. For more on Northup, see David Fiske, Clifford W. Brown, and Rachel Seligman, *Solomon Northup: The Complete Story of the Author of "Twelve Years a Slave"* (Santa Barbara, CA: Praeger, 2013); Trish Loughran, *The Republic in Print: Print Culture in the Age of US Nation Building, 1770–1870* (New York: Columbia University Press, 2007), 303–61.

12. George Tucker, *The Valley of Shenandoah; or, Memoirs of the Graysons*, vol. 3 (New York: C. Wiley, 1825), 128.

13. Ibid., 119.

14. Sarah Josepha Hale, *Northwood; or, Life North And South: Showing the True Character of Both* (New York: H. Long and Brother, 1852), 405.

15. John Pendleton Kennedy, *Swallow Barn; or, A Sojourn in the Old Dominion*, vol. 2 (Philadelphia: Carey & Lea, 1832), 230.

16. Scott Romine, *The Narrative Forms of Southern Community* (Baton Rouge: Louisiana State University Press, 1999), 78.

17. Michael E. Woods, *Emotional and Sectional Conflict in the Antebellum United States* (New York: Cambridge University Press, 2014).

18. William Gilmore Simms, *The Yemassee: A Romance of Carolina*, vol. 1 (New York: Harper and Brothers, 1835); Masahiro Nakamura, *Visions of Order in William Gilmore Simms: Southern Conservatism and the Other American Romance* (Columbia: University of South Carolina Press, 2009); John Caldwell Guilds, *Simms: A Literary Life* (Fayetteville: University of Arkansas Press, 1992).

19. Joseph G. Baldwin, *The Flush Times of Alabama and Mississippi: A Series of Sketches* (New York: D. Appleton and Co., 1853), 301.

20. Ibid., 92. See also Johanna Nicol Shields, *American Freedom in a Slave Society: Stories from the Antebellum South* (New York: Cambridge University Press, 2012); Michael H. Hoffheimer, "Race and Terror in Joseph Baldwin's *Flush Times of Alabama and Mississippi* (1853)," *Seton Hall Law Review* 39.2 (2009): 725–78.

21. Harriet Beecher Stowe, *Uncle Tom's Cabin* (London: John Cassell, 1852), 107.

22. [Emily Clemens Pierson], *Cousin Franck's Household; or, Scenes in the Old Dominion, by Pocahontas* (Boston: Upham, Ford and Olmstead, 1853), 191. See also Robert S. Tilton, *Pocahontas: The Evolution of an American Narrative* (Cambridge, UK: Cambridge University Press, 1994), 154–60.

23. Sterling Brown, *The Negro in American Fiction* (Washington, DC: Associates in Negro Folk Education, 1937), 34.

24. William Wells Brown, *Clotel; or, The President's Daughter*, 62, http://docsouth. unc.edu/southlit/brown/brown.html (accessed November 13, 2014). See also Robert S.

Levine, "Introduction: Cultural and Historical Background," in *Clotel; or, The President's Daughter*, William Wells Brown (Boston: Bedford/St. Martin's, 2000), 3–27.

25. James P. Holcombe, "The Duty of Southern Authors," *Southern Literary Messenger* 23.4 (1856): 243.

26. Ibid., 242. For more on southern responses to *Uncle Tom's Cabin*, see Joy Jordan-Lake, *Whitewashing "Uncle Tom's Cabin": Nineteenth-Century Women Novelists Respond to Stowe* (Nashville, TN: Vanderbilt University Press, 2005), and Michael T. Gilmore, *The War on Words: Slavery, Race, and Free Speech in American Literature* (Chicago: University of Chicago Press, 2010), 1–196.

27. J. W. Page, *Uncle Robin in his Cabin in Virginia, and Tom without One in Boston* (Richmond: J. W. Randolph, 1853), 92.

28. William Gilmore Simms, *The Sword and the Distaff; or, "Fair," "Fat," and "Forty": A Story of the South at the Close of the Revolution* (Charleston, SC: Walker, Richards, 1852; Philadelphia: Lippincott, Grambo, and Company, 1852); Simms, *Woodcraft; or, the Hawks about Dovecote: A Story of the South and the Close of the Revolution* (New York: Redfield, 1854); Simms, *Katharine Walton: or, The Rebel of Dorchester* (Philadelphia: A. Hart, 1851; New York: Redfield, 1854; New York: W. J. Widdleton, 1854). See also Jordan-Lake.

29. Blight, *Race and Reunion*; Caroline E. Janney, *Burying the Dead but Not the Past: Ladies' Memorial Associations and the Lost Cause* (Chapel Hill: University of North Carolina Press, 2008); Grace Elizabeth Hale, "The Lost Cause and the Meaning of History," *OAH Magazine of History* 27.1 (January 2013): 13–17.

30. Douglas A. Blackmon, *Slavery by Another Name: The Re-Enslavement of Black Americans from the Civil War to World War II* (New York: Doubleday, 2008).

31. Mark Twain, *The Adventures of Huckleberry Finn* (1884; New York: Harper Brothers, 1912), 243.

32. Ibid.

33. For more on Twain's portrayal of slavery, see Tuire Valkeakari, "Huck, Twain, and the Freedman's Shackles: Struggling with *Huckleberry Finn* Today," *Atlantis* 28.2 (December 2006): 29–43; and James S. Leonard, Thomas A. Tenney, and Thadious M. Davis, eds., *Satire or Evasion? Black Perspectives on "Huckleberry Finn"* (Durham, NC: Duke University Press, 1992).

34. See James Robert Payne, "George Washington Cable's *John March* and *Gideon's Band*: A (White) Boy Is Being Beaten," *American Literary Realism* 38.3 (Spring 2006): 239–48.

35. Edward L. Ayers, *The Promise of the New South: Life after Reconstruction* (1992; repr., New York: Oxford University Press, 2007); Robert S. Levine, *Martin Delany, Frederick Douglass, and the Politics of Representative Identity* (Chapel Hill: University of North Carolina Press, 1997); Lois Brown, *Pauline Elizabeth Hopkins: Black Daughter of the Revolution* (Chapel Hill: University of North Carolina Press, 2014); Michael Stancliff, *Frances Ellen Watkins Harper: African American Reform Rhetoric and the Rise of a Modern Nation State* (New York: Routledge, 2010); Blight, *Race and Reunion*; Jennifer James, "'Civil' War Wounds: William Wells Brown, Violence, and the Domestic Narrative," *African American Review* 39.1–2 (Spring–Summer 2005): 39–54.

36. Eugene Levy, *James Weldon Johnson: Black Leader, Black Voice* (Chicago: University of Chicago Press, 1973); Eric Lott, *Love and Theft: Blackface Minstrelsy and the American Working Class* (New York: Oxford University Press, 1993); Grace Elizabeth Hale, *Making Whiteness: The Culture of Segregation in the South, 1890–1940* (New York: Pantheon, 1998); M. M. Manring, *Slave in a Box: The Strange Career of Aunt Jemima* (Charlottesville: University Press of Virginia, 1998); W. E. B. Du Bois, *Black Reconstruction in America 1860–1880* (New York: Harcourt, Brace, 1935).

37. Ulrich B. Phillips, *American Negro Slavery: A Survey of the Supply, Employment, and Control of Negro Labor as Determined by the Plantation Regime* (1918; repr., Baton Rouge: Louisiana State University Press, 1966); Charles S. Davis, *The Cotton Kingdom in Alabama* (Montgomery: Alabama Department of Archives and History, 1943); Edwin Adams Davis, *Plantation Life in the Florida Parishes of Louisiana, 1836–1846: As Reflected in the Diary of Bennet H. Barrow* (New York: Columbia University Press, 1943); Ralph B. Flanders, *Plantation Slavery in Georgia* (Chapel Hill: University of North Carolina Press, 1933); Weymouth T. Jordan, *Hugh Davis and His Alabama Plantation* (Tuscaloosa: University of Alabama Press, 1948).

38. Sarah E. Gardner, *Blood and Irony: Southern White Women's Narratives of the Civil War, 1861–1937* (Chapel Hill: University of North Carolina Press, 2004); Chris Ruiz-Velasco, "Order out of Chaos: Whiteness, White Supremacy, and Thomas Dixon Jr.," *College Literature* 34.4 (Fall 2007): 148–65; Lawrence J. Oliver, "Writing from the Right during the 'Red Decade': Thomas Dixon's Attack on W. E. B. Du Bois and James Weldon Johnson in *The Flaming Sword*," *American Literature* 70.1 (March 1998): 131–52.

39. William Faulkner, *Go Down, Moses* (New York: Random House, 1942), 267. Subsequent references to this edition will appear parenthetically in the text. See also Wolff, *Ledgers of History*, 29–38.

40. Mary Kemp Davis, "Arna Bontemps' *Black Thunder*: The Creation of an Authoritative Text of 'Gabriel's Defeat,'" *Black American Literature Forum* 23.1 (Spring 1989): 17–36; Tim A. Ryan, "Designs against Tara: Frances Gaither's *The Red Cock Crows* and Other Counternarratives to *Gone with the Wind*," *Mississippi Quarterly* 59.2 (Spring 2006): 243–69.

41. See also Williamson, *William Faulkner and Southern History*, 232.

42. See Charles H. Nichols, *Many Thousands Gone: Ex-Slaves' Account of Their Bondage and Freedom* (Leiden: Brill, 1963).

43. C. Vann Woodward, *Origins of the New South: 1877–1913* (Baton Rouge: Louisiana State University Press, 1951).

44. C. Vann Woodward, *The Burden of Southern History* (Baton Rouge: Louisiana State University Press, 1960), 24.

45. Ralph Ellison, *Invisible Man* (1952; repr., New York: Vintage, 1995), 272.

46. Jacqueline Miller Carmichael, *Trumpeting a Fiery Sound: History and Folklore in Margaret Walker's "Jubilee"* (Athens: University of Georgia Press, 1998); and Ryan, *Calls and Responses*.

47. Margaret Walker, *Jubilee* (1966; repr., New York: Mariner, 1999), 484.

48. William Styron, *The Confessions of Nat Turner* (1967; repr., New York: Vintage, 1992), 248.

49. Ibid., 327–28.

50. Toni Morrison, *Beloved* (New York: Vintage, 1987), 5. See also Linda Krumholz, "The Ghosts of Slavery: Historical Recovery in Toni Morrison's *Beloved*," *African American Review* 26.3 (Autumn 1992): 395–408; and Joanna Wolfe, "'Ten Minutes for Seven Letters': Song as Key to Narrative Revision in Toni Morrison's *Beloved*," *Narrative* 12.3 (October 2004): 263–80.

51. Du Bois, *Black Reconstruction*, 727. On Charles Johnson, see Barbara Z. Thaden, "Charles Johnson's *Middle Passage* as Historiographic Metafiction," *College English* 59.7 (November 1997): 753–66.

52. Alice Randall, *The Wind Done Gone* (New York: Houghton Mifflin, 2001), 77.

53. Christine Duff, "Where Literature Fills the Gaps: *The Book of Negroes* as a Canadian Work of Rememory," *Studies in Canadian Literature / Études en littérature canadienne* 36.2 (December 2011): 237–54. See also Stephanie Yorke, "The Slave Narrative Tradition in Lawrence Hill's *The Book of Negroes*," *Studies in Canadian Literature / Études en littérature canadienne* 35.2 (June 2010): 129–44.

Monuments, Memory, and Faulkner's Nathan Bedford Forrest

ANDREW B. LEITER

In one of the more recent installments in the ongoing struggle over public space, memory, and southern history, both the statue of Nathan Bedford Forrest and Forrest Park came under fire in Memphis in 2013. A Confederate hero to many southern whites since the Civil War, the "Wizard of the Saddle" is memorialized throughout the South. The public reverence for Forrest—a slave trader, Confederate general, commanding officer at the Fort Pillow massacre of black Union soldiers, and first Grand Wizard of the Ku Klux Klan—is obviously problematic for a multicultural South, and particularly so around such prominent battlegrounds of the civil rights struggle as Memphis and Selma, Alabama, where a similar controversy over a Forrest statue peaked in 2012. Historians disagree about Forrest's culpability for the Fort Pillow massacre, while his neo-Confederate defenders temporize his slave trading as comparatively humane and his participation with the Klan as short lived, but more than any other Confederate hero, Forrest, in both his civilian and military careers, represents the brutal materialism of slave society, the effort to maintain that society through war, and the terroristic effort to ensure white supremacy after the war.[1] In the case of the recent Memphis controversy, the Memphis City Council acted hurriedly to preempt a proposed state law that was introduced to prohibit renaming the park, and it changed the name of Forrest Park to Health Sciences Park. The bronze equestrian statue, however, remains above the graves of Forrest and his wife, emphasizing gallant soldiery and the inherent exculpation of Forrest's egregious racial depredations.

The Forrest statue was unveiled in 1905 amid a flurry of Civil War monuments throughout the South, including those in Oxford, Mississippi. Arguably the height of southern Lost Cause propagandizing, this period was the culmination of successful southern attempts to define the meaning of the Civil War from a white southern perspective. As David

W. Blight has shown in *Race and Reunion: The Civil War in American Memory*, "The white supremacist vision, which took many forms early, including terror and violence, locked arms with [regional] reconciliationists of many kinds, and by the turn of the century delivered the country a segregated memory of its Civil War on Southern terms."[2] Blight demonstrates that such segregated memory marginalized but could not eradicate black memory or experience. Similarly, in a study more specific to public spaces and southern memory, W. Fitzhugh Brundage has shown how blacks were excluded from places of public memory in the synthesis of southern white identity but contested such exclusion by maintaining their own rites of memory.[3] Coming of age immersed in Lost Cause glorification and living in the segregated South for the majority of his life, William Faulkner both witnessed and engaged the civil rights movement in the last decade of his life; however, he did not live to see the robust reclamation of southern history and public memory that African Americans have orchestrated over the last fifty years. This essay considers some of Faulkner's romanticized fictions as Lost Cause literary monuments that establish southern history as the domain of patriarchal white memory but that cannot fully erase dissenting voices or memory. Specifically, I engage Faulkner's interest in public monuments relative to his depictions of Nathan Bedford Forrest in *Go Down, Moses*, "Dull Tale," and "My Grandmother Millard and General Bedford Forrest and the Battle of Harrykin Creek." These works highlight Faulkner's alternately romantic and condemnatory treatments of southern history, as well as his obsession with the troubled contemporary construction of that history. Faulkner's interest in monuments of distorted southern history can be considered analogous to his thoughts on his literary memorials to the Civil War South, and such concerns anticipate subsequent contention over Confederate monuments in the (recently acknowledged) hybrid culture of the post–civil rights South.

In the decades following the Civil War, Forrest occupied a prominent place in north Mississippi memory, as he had fought there and many men of the region had served under him. Faulkner family legend maintained that Faulkner's great-grandfather William C. Falkner fought under Forrest after the "Old Colonel" had been voted out of his command in Virginia, and while biographers question these accounts— suggesting that Falkner more likely spent the last two years of the war smuggling cotton and other goods into and out of Memphis or other Union-held territory—William Faulkner repeated them.[4] According to family lore, Falkner was riding with Forrest when Falkner's body servant Nate became separated from Falkner and was captured, interrogated, and released by Union troops. Based on their encounter with Nate, the

Union forces "returned quickly to Memphis believing a rebel force to be near," and their retreat supposedly precipitated Forrest's famous raid on Memphis earlier than intended in August 1864.[5] It is perhaps not surprising that Forrest's presence permeates Faulkner's work more thoroughly than that of any other historical figure of the Civil War, and while Forrest is hardly ubiquitous, the men who fought with him are sprinkled liberally throughout Faulkner's fiction, issuing their occasional rebel yells with varying gradations of valor and ridiculousness. Forrest's presence usually reflects the standard Lost Cause perspective of the Civil War as a gallant failure, and readers of *Go Down, Moses* or *The Reivers* will likely remember descriptions of Forrest's raid on Memphis and specifically the assault on the Gayoso Hotel in which Theophilus McCaslin "had ridden into Memphis as a member of Colonel Sartoris' horse in Forrest's command, up Main street and (the tale told) into the lobby of the Gayoso Hotel where the Yankee officers sat in the leather chairs spitting into the tall bright cuspidors and then out again, scot-free—"[6]

Faulkner was enamored with the familial and regional tales of Civil War daring and gallantry such as the Memphis raid, but he was equally interested in the perils and limitations of such memory for later generations. Richard H. King, John Lowe, and Barbara Ladd have noted the similarities that Faulkner's fiction bears to Nietzsche's modes of historical consciousness.[7] Various Faulkner characters and works correlate readily with Nietzsche's three modes of historical memory: the *monumental*, which entails looking to the great moments or achievements of the past for models of inspiration; the *antiquarian*, in which the individual looks backward with a reverential desire "to preserve what survives from ancient days, and [to] reproduce the conditions of his own upbringing for those who come after him"; and the *critical*, which subsumes the historical to the purposes of the living and which "must bring the past to the bar of judgment, interrogate it remorselessly, and finally condemn it."[8] Clearly, Faulkner's engagement of something akin to Nietzsche's critical mode contributed to his brilliant studies of historical consciousness in *Go Down, Moses* and *Absalom, Absalom!*, but I am interested here in Faulkner's romantic vision and his treatment of the cultural icons that he, his family, and his community identified with from Faulkner's earliest years, a treatment that reflects at best the monumental desire for models and at worst empty antiquarianism. In his discussion of *The Unvanquished*, Lowe argues, "The problem for the artist, who must transform history—and in Faulkner's case, family history—into art, is to preserve the figurative ground, while simultaneously stripping away its illusions."[9] I would like to suggest that the figure of Forrest in Faulkner's fiction offers particularly rich ground for studying the precarious balance

of history and illusion because Forrest, as arguably the primary regional
model for monumental inspiration, specifically invites the suspension
of the critical mode, a suspension of which Faulkner, even at his most
romantic, was not entirely capable.

"Dull Tale," together with the interrelated "The Big Shot," and "A
Return" (also known as "Rose of Lebanon"), forms a cycle of Memphis-
based stories that Faulkner wrote in the late twenties. Focusing on the
interplay between Civil War experience, including the culture of public
and private memory, and a crass modern society, these stories may have
been intended as parts of a novel, but Faulkner cannibalized much of
the material to develop other works and such characters as Popeye, Gail
Hightower, Thomas Sutpen, and Flem Snopes. "Dull Tale" personifies
the culture of memorialization in Memphis in the character of Dr. Gavin
Blount, a Hightower precursor, who is fixated on the Civil War and
serves as the chairman of the Nonconnah Guards, an elite social group
descended from the genteel Civil War soldiers among Memphis's first
families. Presiding indifferently over an evaporating medical practice
and of limited means, Blount soothes his disillusionment with his contemporary world by finding solace in the public memorialization of Civil
War heroes,

> calling the streets before he reached them: the names evocative of old lost
> battles, of men in—he liked to believe, to think of them—some valhalla of the
> undefeated, galloping with long tossing hair and brandished sabres forever on
> tireless horses: Beauregard, Maltby, Van Dorn; Forrest Park with a stone man
> gallant on a gallant stone horse; Forrest: a man without education, a soldier
> as Goethe was a poet, whose tactics for winning battles was to git thar fustest
> with the morest men, and in whose command Blount's grandfather had been
> killed.[10]

Juxtaposed to Blount's acute case of Lost Cause-ism is the parvenu Dal
Martin. A Snopes/Sutpen prototype, Martin has ascended from tenant farming to Memphis boss through corrupt construction and pave-
ment contracts, the shoddy results of which Blount refers to ironically
as Martin's "monuments."[11] Martin attempts to bribe Blount to allow
his daughter onto the elite social roster of the Nonconnah Guards ball,
and when money does not work, Martin successfully corrupts Blount by
offering to build an art gallery named for Blount's Civil War grandfather.
Unable to bear having betrayed the honor he associates with Forrest
Park, Van Dorn Avenue, and the Nonconnah Guards, Blount commits
suicide while the art gallery is being built.

The limited criticism of "Dull Tale" details the story's relationships to later works and stresses the materialistic, grasping New South corruption as antagonistic to the vanishing Old South honor that is exemplified in the Civil War monuments.[12] Such a juxtaposition certainly exists, particularly in Blount's mind, but within this interpretive framework, the criticism overlooks the manner in which the text undermines the sanctity of the monuments and the history that they represent. Blount's inefficacy in the modern world and his eventual suicide suggest the sterility of his antiquarian dreaming and vague monumentalist notions of honor, but Faulkner brings the critical mode to bear through Martin's unwitting and boorish pragmatism when he pitches his exchange to Blount:

> "You have a street named for your grandpaw. [. . .] You wont want that. Some of them have got parks named for them; ones that aint no more worthy of it, but that happen to have more money. I could do that. [. . .] I'd do more than that. I'd do for you what them that deserve you and your grandpappy haven't done. The one that was killed with Forrest, I mean. My grandpappy was killed too. We never knowed what army he was in nor where he went. He just went off one day and never come back; maybe he was just tired of staying at home. But my sort dont count. There was plenty of us; always was, always will be. It's your sort, the ones that's got the names the streets and the parks would want."[13]

Bereft of honor and significance by his poor-white status, Martin's dismissed grandfather serves as a scathing reminder that public memorialization is the prerogative of wealth and power, time and circumstance, not honor. As we know both historically and in Faulkner's fiction, wealth and power in the antebellum world had far more to do with human bondage and ruthless brutality than with honor.

Faulkner evinced persistent concerns about the nature of war monuments and preferred the inclusive memorialization of soldiers and their sacrifices to individualized monuments. In 1947 he wrote the inscription for Lafayette County's monument for the World War II dead and argued for the inclusion on the monument of the names of the local African American soldiers killed overseas.[14] A Fable, which Faulkner worked on for over a decade, culminates in the entombment of a Christ-figure in the French Tomb of the Unknown Soldier, a character whose sacrifice starkly contrasts with the public funeral and memorialization of the satanic old general at the conclusion of the novel. "Dull Tale" addresses the same problems in terms of Confederate memorialization. In this sense, the monuments and public spaces of the story do not have the same symbolic resonance as the Confederate soldier monument at the conclusion of The Sound and the Fury, which my students variously (and reasonably) interpret as the burden of southern history, the past in the present, a failing New South, a site of nostalgia, and so on. Rather, Faulkner questions the impetus behind the public construction of Confederate memory and challenges the individualized memorialization of romanticized heroes. What then are we to make of Faulkner's own romanticized fiction of the Civil War, particularly when he so clearly thought of his fiction as his own monument, his "scratch on that wall—Kilroy was here—that somebody a hundred, a thousand years later will see"?[15] "Dull Tale," as a story about the flawed construction of Civil War memory, connects to what I contend are moments on Faulkner's part of self-conscious reservations about his romantic writings and specifically about his construction of Forrest in the highly romanticized "My Grandmother Millard and General Bedford Forrest and the Battle of Harrykin Creek," published in 1943.

Very much in character with the series of short stories that Faulkner published several years earlier in the *Saturday Evening Post* before revising them for his 1938 novel, *The Unvanquished*, "My Grandmother Millard" is structured around the repeated drill of burying and unburying a trunk full of Sartoris family silver to protect it from raiding Yankees. The story features young Bayard Sartoris as narrator, Ab Snopes, Ringo, Granny, and various Sartoris slaves including Lucius, whose "misguided" notions of freedom are cured by Granny's no-nonsense correctives. In the same vein, Granny summarily declares the family slaves as "free folks" and the whites as "the rest of us that aint free," suggesting in true plantation tradition that white slave owners bear the burden of responsibility for the well-being of the extended family.[16] In addition to such racial tripe and the buried silver motif, Faulkner highlights a comedic moonlight-and-magnolias love affair between Cousin Melisandre, who has joined the family from Memphis, and Lieutenant Philip St-Just Backhouse. The love affair begins when Backhouse (or Cousin Philip, as Bayard anachronistically refers to him) saves Melisandre from raiding Yankees who have swept onto Sartoris plantation without sufficient warning for the family to bury the silver. Granny has Melisandre hide in the privy with the silver and hopes that the soldiers will not invade her privacy. The Yankees, however, shatter the outhouse, revealing Melisandre inside, just as Backhouse gallops onto the scene and drives them off the plantation. Cousin Philip falls instantly in love with "that beautiful girl,"[17] but when Bayard formally introduces him, the last name of Backhouse presents Melisandre with an apparently insurmountable obstacle to their relationship because of its association with the indelicate circumstances of her rescue. The knight saving the damsel in distress is thus succeeded by the trials and motifs of courtly love, with Philip recklessly charging and routing Yankee troops because he no longer cares whether he lives or dies and Melisandre torturing the family as she pines away on Granny's dulcimer. Granny sends Lucius to summon Forrest to Sartoris so they can settle the matter, but Forrest, busy battling Yankees at Tallahatchie Crossing, respectfully declines at first. When Philip's recklessness endangers Forrest's plans, however, the latter arrives at Sartoris where Granny concocts a scheme to have Backhouse declared dead at the mythical battle of Harrykin (Hurricane) Creek and Forrest makes it so with his signature. The newly named Philip St-Just Backus marries Cousin Melisandre at Sartoris, and the story concludes with the family reburying the silver at Granny's directive.

Variously described as "a fantasy, as improbable in a workaday world as a scene from a Scott romance," as a "comedy of manners," as "deliberately intended to invoke laughter" and "void of any deeper significance," as "a romantic farce in costume," and as a "spoof of the romanticism so dear to the South's self-image and myth," the story is, admittedly, light fodder on the surface, and this likely accounts for how very little critical attention it has received by Faulknerian standards.[18] Critics have discussed "My Grandmother Millard" as an exemplum of courage and unity that spoke to the wartime context in which it was published, an approach that resonates with Faulkner's own comment, "I think it's a good funny story, and I think it has its message for the day too: of gallant indomitability, of a willingness to pull up the pants and carry on, no matter with whom, let alone what."[19] Others have noted discrepancies between the historical details of the story and the actual dates of Forrest's Mississippi fighting, but within this body of criticism little work if any has been done to flesh out the details beneath the surface of the comedy and romance for their relevance to Faulkner's historical vision.[20]

The story is characterized by similar but subtler challenges to the class, gender, and racial inflections of southern patriarchal power than those evident in *The Unvanquished*, where Ab Snopes is an upstart poor white, Drusilla is a cross-dressing southern belle soldier, and Lucius (Loosh) betrays the happy slave stereotype. Ab occupies the same marginalized space in both works as an uncouth poor white who must be watched around the house to prevent theft, who is unfit to approach the front door of the big house, and who is better suited to horse-stealing than to soldiery. In a scene from the story reminiscent of *The Unvanquished*, Granny disputes Ab's claims to captured horses and seizes the abandoned Yankee mounts in the wake of the skirmish at the outhouse, whereupon Ab exclaims, "I just hope for the sake of the Confedricy that Bed Forrest don't never tangle with you with all the horses he's got."[21] Unlike in *The Unvanquished*, Ab's discontent here is easily contained and dismissed within the class hierarchy, although the scene is similar to

Ab's later betrayal of Rosa Millard, which leads to her death in the novel. More significantly in the context of the short story, the confrontation with Ab adumbrates the later scene when Granny does "tangle" with Bedford Forrest, whose very presence in the story speaks to the permeable class lines that Faulkner's presentation of Ab seems to deny.

Born into a poor family in rural Tennessee and receiving little formal education, the historical Forrest was a self-made product of the rough-and-tumble frontier South. A shrewd businessman, Forrest accumulated his substantial wealth as a plantation owner and slave trader before the Civil War, but with his poor and rural origins he would have had as much in common with Ab Snopes or Dal Martin's inconsequential grandfather as with the more genteel southerners to whom his wealth provided access. In "My Grandmother Millard," Forrest is described as "a big, dusty man with a big beard so black it looked almost blue and eyes like a sleepy owl,"[22] but he is characterized primarily through his rustic and uneducated language. He calls Granny Miss Rosie instead of Rosa, much to her annoyance, and as Bayard explains, "He said 'fit' for fought just as he said 'druv' for drove and 'drug' for dragged. But maybe when you fought battles like he did, even Granny didn't mind how you talked."[23] Faulkner stresses the linguistic indicators of Forrest's lower-class status to emphasize how the exigencies of the war effort obviate class lines. The suggestion that valor trumps class can be read in a positive light and likely emanates from the World War II context in which Faulkner wrote; however, Faulkner seems to recognize Forrest as a more problematic figure in relation to the romanticized categories of gender and race in the antebellum South.

The gender issues of the story center on the dreadfully embarrassed Melisandre. She has very little in common with Drusilla, who so delightfully challenges gender norms as a cross-dressing soldier; rather, Melisandre is a comic southern belle caricature who is happily hoop-skirted, ridiculously histrionic, and seemingly unfit for anything except a role in one of the bad romances she reads. The details of her rescue and that of the Sartoris valuables—a screaming southern belle with a trunk of silver in the remnants of a shattered outhouse—contribute to the farcical quality of the story, and they allow for the possibility that Faulkner intentionally associates the romanticized plantation tradition with excrement. I would contend further, however, that the indelicate rescue scene represents one element of a more robust assault on notions of sanctified virginal southern femininity. The silver and the virgin in the outhouse, in short, take on sexual connotations as the outhouse and the hole for the silver become thematically paired holes. The repeated penetrations of the earth and the deposits of the silver bracket the story as well as alternate internally with the emphasis on outhouse/backhouse. Likewise, the sexually suggestive motif of trampled flowers runs through the story, beginning with Ab Snopes's arrival at Sartoris in front of the Yankee soldiers who intrude upon Melisandre, continuing when Philip Backhouse and his cavalry troop pay a midnight suitor's visit to the plantation, and concluding with Granny cutting all of the flowers at Sartoris for the wedding. The combined reiterations of holes and flowers transform Melisandre's position in the outhouse from embarrassingly unladylike to sexual in nature. Such imagery leads one to wonder just what the Yankees might have intended had Philip not arrived on the scene, and moreover what exactly interests Philip, who falls so ardently in love despite never having spoken with the lovely Melisandre.

To an extent we might read the sexual innuendo as reflective of the southern tendency to conflate southern femininity with regional identity. Faulkner's contemporary W. J. Cash labeled this conflation "gyneolatry" and contended, with his particular hyperbolic flair, "I verily believe, the ranks of the Confederacy went rolling into battle in the misty conviction that it was wholly for [the southern lady] that they fought."[24] In such a reading of "My Grandmother Millard," the violation of the southern homefront by Yankee invaders has its correlative in the violation of Melisandre's decency, which it is not a stretch to describe as a metaphoric deflowering, as becomes increasingly clear. Philip eagerly desires to restore her honor, but he is unable to erase her shame by giving her his unfortunate patronymic. General Forrest declines to take an interest in the debacle at Sartoris when first summoned by Granny, but when it effects his war effort he arrives looking for a quick solution. Forrest's negotiations with Granny play out as a contest between the military and the cultural defense of the antebellum South. Forrest intends the quick subordination of feminine honor to military necessity. "Just put your foot down," he suggests to Granny. "Make her. Mr. Millard would have already done that if he had been here. And I know when. It would have been two days ago by now."[25] Likewise, as the wedding nears, Bayard expects that perhaps "General Forrest would let Father bring him, with Cousin Philip maybe handcuffed to Father and the soldier with the bayonet following, or maybe still just handcuffed to the soldier until he and Cousin Melisandre were married and Father unlocked him."[26] Such patriarchal coercion smacks more of a shotgun wedding in response to a pregnant or violated daughter than it does of a fully clothed woman revealed among the remnants of a privy. Forrest, however, cannot coerce Granny to insist on the wedding and must defer instead to the proprieties of feminine honor as determined by Granny and Melisandre. Forrest must literally rewrite history by fabricating a battle and a casualty that restore Melisandre's violated honor, and in so doing he establishes the sanctity of southern womanhood as central to the defense of the South. We can reasonably understand this as Faulkner's self-conscious commentary on the problematic aspects of the romantic tradition and its rewritings of southern history, and it might best be read in conjunction with a similarly self-conscious indictment of the romanticized depictions of slavery in the story.

At one point Forrest reprimands the love-struck Philip Backhouse for his reckless endangerment of troops, saying, "maybe you don't consider me a shrewd enough trader in human meat?"[27] Ostensibly a reference to battle tactics, the comment is also a sly and troubling allusion to Forrest's history as a slave trader that resonates intertextually with *Go Down, Moses*. Forrest figures into that novel not only as a general but also as the uneducated slave trader who sells the inept Percival Brownlee to Uncle Buck (Theophilus McCaslin), "as if the four years during which [Buck] had followed the sword of the only man ever breathing [i.e., Forrest] who ever sold him a negro, let alone beat him in a trade, had convinced him not only of the vanity of faith and hope but of orthography too" (261–62). Faulkner had completed *Go Down, Moses* only three months before submitting "My Grandmother Millard" to his agent, and given such timing, Faulkner could only have intended "trader in human meat" as a wry reminder of the racial atrocities and brutal materialism underlying the veneer of the plantation tradition that he explores so powerfully in *Go Down, Moses*, where Forrest's slave dealings are recorded in the McCaslin ledgers. The intrusion of this harsh reality—that Forrest, icon of the Confederacy, built his wealth, as did the antebellum South as a whole, on the sweat and sale of black bodies—recasts Granny's imperious redefinition of Lucius's notion of freedom earlier in the story. While Granny may have cowed Lucius into denying his desire for freedom by so authoritatively redefining freedom as the absence of responsibility, Forrest's presence and his comment on "human meat" reintroduce the concrete relationship between enslaved and free that Granny would like to refute. "Definitions" in master-slave relations may have "belonged to the definers—not the defined," as Toni Morrison writes in *Beloved*, but the perspectives of the defined are more easily masked than fully erased once they have been voiced.[28] Readers of *The Unvanquished* would be aware that Lucius later reveals the location of the silver to the Yankees and makes a bid for freedom, but not before articulating his disgust with the supposedly benign plantation family that has inhumanely coerced his labor: "Let God ax John Sartoris who the man name that give me to him. Let the man that buried me in the black dark ax that of the man what dug me free."[29]

I do not want to suggest that such moments redeem Faulkner's romantic Civil War stories from the "moonlight and magnolias" school of southern historical fiction; however, the occasional rents in the romantic façade reveal Faulkner's clear awareness of the inadequacies of his literary monuments to the Lost Cause. These stories bear out Blight's and Brundage's assessments of how codified southern white memory marginalized but could not erase black memory and experience, and their odd, incongruous moments and subtexts not only acknowledge what is being masked but originate from the same Faulknerian impulse that creates a character like Lucas Beauchamp. It is no coincidence that, in portraying Lucas's resistance to white subjugation, both *Go Down, Moses* and *Intruder in the Dust* indicate a correlation between Confederate memorialization and racial injustice. In the titular story of *Go Down, Moses*, for example, the body of Lucas's executed grandson, Samuel Worsham Beauchamp, circles "the Confederate monument and the courthouse" on its way to burial (364). Likewise, the Confederate monument appears multiple times in *Intruder in the Dust*, perhaps most notably as a "slender white pencil . . . against the mass of the courthouse" in a scene that also includes Gavin Stevens explaining that whites expect blacks to "act like niggers" and a man issuing a latter-day rebel yell, "a squall significant and meaningless," from a car circling the square.[30] The conjunction of memorialization with racial subordination in these passages represents more than simply the burden of racial history; it suggests Faulkner's acknowledgment of the problematic nature of southern memorialization as part and parcel of the contemporaneous racial hierarchy. Any author as interested as Faulkner in monuments, the flaws of memorialization, and the corresponding racial implications in a southern context would certainly have felt the pull of the counternarratives and counter-voices that resist erasure even in his most romanticized literary memorials to the Lost Cause.

Faulkner's Civil War short stories are not necessarily underappreciated, but they are understudied. These stories—and we might include "A Return," "Mountain Victory," and the "Unvanquished" cycle (though not necessarily the novel)—have been largely dismissed as aesthetically uncomplicated, written for money, or thematically uncomfortable from a post–civil rights perspective. When we ignore these stories as not representative or not "real" Faulkner, we prioritize—to return to Nietzschean terms—the historical vision evident in *Absalom, Absalom!* and *Go Down, Moses*, where Faulkner's critical perspective overshadows his romanticism. This prioritization even allows us to assign an inaccurate trajectory to Faulkner's career that posits growth away from the romanticism of his earliest Yoknapatawpha material in *Flags in the Dust*. The Civil War stories, however, force us to recognize that, as late as the 1940s, Faulkner maintained imaginative ties to the romantic tradition and thus that his art does not evince development away from romanticism, with its antiquarian and monumentalizing elements, so much as a simultaneous and sustained interest in all three Nietzschean modes of historical memory. Reading the stories against the novels puts us in a better position to see not only the critical deviations from pure romanticism that emerge in the stories but the romantic deviations from the critical mode that emerge in the novels—complexities that suggest a much closer affiliation between the historical vision of accepted Faulkner classics and that of his supposedly "second-class" stories.

NOTES

1. See Jack Hurst, *Nathan Bedford Forrest: A Biography* (1993; repr., New York: Vintage, 1994); Paul Ashdown and Edward Caudill, *The Myth of Nathan Bedford Forrest* (Lanham, MD: Rowman & Littlefield, 2005); and Robert Selph Henry, *"First with the Most": Forrest* (Indianapolis: Bobbs-Merrill, 1944). Faulkner owned a copy of Henry's biography of Forrest, and it is indicative of Forrest's reputation in the 1940s.

2. David W. Blight, *Race and Reunion: The Civil War in American Memory* (Cambridge, MA: Harvard University Press, 2001), 2.

3. W. Fitzhugh Brundage, *The Southern Past: A Clash of Race and Memory* (Cambridge, MA: Harvard University Press, 2005).

4. Joel Williamson, *William Faulkner and Southern History* (New York: Oxford University Press, 1993), 44–45; and Joseph Blotner, *Faulkner: A Biography* (New York: Random House, 1974), 31–32. Faulkner publicly asserted that his great-grandfather served with Forrest, but whether he believed this or was finessing public perception is less clear. See *Faulkner at West Point*, ed. Joseph L. Fant and Robert Ashley (1964; repr., Jackson: University Press of Mississippi, 2002), 99.

5. Blotner, *Faulkner*, 30.

6. William Faulkner, *Go Down, Moses* (1942; repr., New York: Vintage International, 1990), 224. Subsequent references to this edition will appear parenthetically in the text.

7. Richard H. King, "Memory and Tradition," in *Faulkner and the Southern Renaissance: Faulkner and Yoknapatawpha, 1981*, ed. Doreen Fowler and Ann J. Abadie (Jackson: University Press of Mississippi, 1982), 138–57; John Lowe, *"The Unvanquished*: Faulkner's Nietzschean Skirmish with the Civil War," *Mississippi Quarterly* 46 (Summer 1993): 407–36; Barbara Ladd, *Resisting History: Gender, Modernity, and Authorship in William Faulkner, Zora Neale Hurston, and Eudora Welty* (Baton Rouge: Louisiana State University Press, 2007), 79–107.

8. Friedrich Nietzsche, *The Use and Abuse of History* (1874), trans. Adrian Collins (Indianapolis: Bobbs-Merrill, 1957), 18, 21.

9. Lowe, *"The Unvanquished,"* 423–24. Similarly, Ashdown and Caudill argue in their study of the Forrest mythology in literature and popular imagination that "Faulkner's Forrest, a part of the novelist's own family history, is a man of the South, helping define and, paradoxically, mystify the region. Cleverly, Faulkner uses the character to impose himself even more intimately on the history of the South and into his family's blood" (134).

10. William Faulkner, "Dull Tale," in *Uncollected Stories of William Faulkner*, ed. Joseph Blotner (1979; repr., New York: Vintage, 1981), 534.

11. Ibid., 528.

12. Max Putzel, "Faulkner's Memphis Stories," *Virginia Quarterly Review* 59 (Spring 1983): 254–70; Robert Woods Sayre, "Artistic Self-Theft as Obsession and Creative Transformation: The 'Memphis' Stories and Beyond," *Faulkner Journal* 13 (Fall 1997): 37–55; Edmond L. Volpe, *A Reader's Guide to William Faulkner: The Short Stories* (Syracuse, NY: Syracuse University Press, 2004).

13. Faulkner, "Dull Tale," 540–41.

14. Blotner, *Faulkner,* 1226.

15. *Faulkner in the University: Class Conferences at the University of Virginia, 1957–1958*, ed. Frederick L. Gwynn and Joseph L. Blotner (1959; repr., Charlottesville: University Press of Virginia, 1995), 61.

16. William Faulkner, "My Grandmother Millard and General Bedford Forrest and the Battle of Harrykin Creek," in *Collected Stories of William Faulkner* (1950; repr., New York: Vintage, 1977), 669.

17. Faulkner, "My Grandmother Millard," 678.

18. Elmo Howell, "William Faulkner's General Forrest and the Uses of History," *Tennessee Historical Quarterly* 29 (1970): 290; John Lewis Longley, *The Tragic Mask: A Study of Faulkner's Heroes* (Chapel Hill: University of North Carolina Press, 1963), 113; Hans H. Skei, *William Faulkner: The Novelist as Short Story Writer: A Study of William Faulkner's Short Fiction* (Oslo: Universitetsforlaget, 1985), 273; Theresa M. Towner and James B. Carothers, *Reading Faulkner: Collected Stories* (Jackson: University Press of Mississippi, 2006), 362; Ashdown and Caudell, *The Myth of Nathan Bedford Forrest,* 135.

19. Joseph Blotner, ed., *Selected Letters of William Faulkner* (New York: Random House, 1977), 150. On the story's relationship to its World War II context, see M. E. Bradford, "A Coda to *Sartoris*: Faulkner's 'My Grandmother Millard and General Nathan Bedford Forrest and the Battle of Harrykin Creek,'" in *Critical Essays on William Faulkner: The Sartoris Family*, ed. Arthur F. Kinney (Boston: G. K. Hall, 1985), 318–23, and Volpe, *A Reader's Guide to William Faulkner,* 265–67.

20. Charles S. Aiken, *William Faulkner and the Southern Landscape* (Athens: University of Georgia Press, 2009), 107; Ashdown and Caudell, *The Myth of Nathan Bedford Forrest,* 135.

21. Faulkner, "My Grandmother Millard," 686.

22. Ibid., 691.

23. Ibid., 692.

24. W. J. Cash, *The Mind of the South* (1941; repr., New York: Vintage, 1991), 86.

25. Faulkner, "My Grandmother Millard," 694.

26. Ibid., 698.

27. Ibid., 693.

28. Toni Morrsion, *Beloved* (1987; repr., New York: Vintage, 2004), 225.

29. William Faulkner, *The Unvanquished*, rev. ed. (1934; repr., New York: Vintage International, 1991), 75.

30. William Faulkner, *Intruder in the Dust* (1948; repr., New York: Vintage, 1972), 49, 48, 49.

"A Well-Traveled Mudhole": Nostalgia, Labor, and Laughter in *The Reivers*

Rebecca Bennett Clark

"Two dollars?" Ned said. "This sho beats cotton. He can farm right
here setting in the shade without even moving. What I wants Boss
to get me is a well-traveled mudhole."

Critics have called William Faulkner's final novel, *The Reivers*, alternately "the least ironic of his novels,"[1] an "engagingly happy"[2] "fairy
tale,"[3] and "a surrender to sententious banality."[4] In short, the book
has been understood as "sentimental, nostalgic, optimistic, and limited
in both reach and grasp."[5] Faulkner himself called the book simply "A
Reminiscence," its subtitle. This paper will push against these established readings of the novel to argue—through a focus on nostalgia,
labor, and laughter in the text—for its value, instead, as an often uncomfortable study in Jim Crow-era engagements with the equally uncomfortable idea of southern history.

The Reivers was published in 1962, eight years after *Brown v. Board
of Education* and six years after Faulkner received a challenge from
W. E. B. Du Bois, in a telegram sent to *Time* magazine, "to debate on
the steps of Court House, Sumner, Mississippi where Emmett Till case
was tried, on subject of your 'go slow now' advice to Negroes," which
Faulkner turned down with little more than a curt "I do not believe
there is a debatable point between us."[6] It is not, on its surface, a novel
that tackles either the racial and political questions that Du Bois was
eager to debate, or the nexus of memory, trauma, and historical haunting that makes heavy hitters like *Absalom, Absalom!* and *The Sound and
the Fury* so haunting themselves. *The Reivers* has, instead, been understood—and dismissed—as a comic and more-than-occasionally embarrassing exercise in that lowbrow historical affect we call nostalgia.

Nostalgic parable in the novel, however, is aerated with moments of
cutting social criticism that reveal a keen, if conflicted, historiographic

imagination at work. Nowhere is this stippling more stark, perhaps, than in the novel's mudhole scene, which dares readers both to get bogged down in mythic allegory and to skip across the surface of real and distressing subtexts of racial violence. By examining how Faulkner defines marginalized modes of labor—both physical and linguistic—within this scene, this essay proposes that the hazardous physical and interpretive morass of the mudhole can also be read as Faulkner's self-conscious figure for the novel's (and its imagined readers') own flirtations with nostalgia.

"Nostalgia" is not an ancient Greek word, but it sounds like it should be. Its Greek roots belie and temporally misplace its origins in a way that is particularly evocative for an analysis of Faulkner's rollicking road-trip Slip 'N Slide. As Svetlana Boym puts it so well, "'Nostalgia' is only pseudo-Greek, or nostalgically Greek."[7] A Swiss medical student named Johannes Hofer coined the term, a confederation of *nostos* ("return home") and *algia* ("longing") for his 1688 dissertation. Seventeenth-century medical science promptly embraced the term, promising that nostalgia, the pathologized longing for a home that no longer exists or never has, was a curable disease, treatable with "opium, leeches, and a journey to the Swiss Alps."[8]

It was only in later centuries that nostalgia migrated from the halls of medicine to the pages of novels. Nicholas Dames, writing about nostalgia in nineteenth-century British fiction, argues that it "is as much self-definition as memory."[9] This self-definition is a dance of both greedy incorporation and equally eager omission, not only different from but in fact at violent odds with what he calls "pure memory." "It consists of the stories about one's past that explain and consolidate memory rather than dispersing it into a series of vivid, relinquished moments, and it can only survive by eradicating the 'pure memory,' that enormous field of vanished detail, that threatens it."

Nostalgia quests for coherence as it tilts at windmills of both facts and forgetting. It is both exorcism—banishing the ghosts of details past (if only Quentin Compson, that "barracks filled with stubborn back-looking ghosts,"[10] had just settled for a good dose of nostalgia with an Alpine rest cure chaser)—and (con)quest. Dames's evocative spatial metaphor for what nostalgia tries to tame and transform, "that enormous field of vanishing detail," is telling in more ways than just its vulnerability to being turned quickly by overeager critics. Landscape is deeply implicated in the battle that nostalgia pitches. Nostalgia is, in Susannah Radstone's words, a "transitional phenomenon," blurring distinctions especially between time and space.[11] "As both cultural materiality and affect and desire, it troubles the boundary between 'inside' and 'outside.' As both a sociological perspective and an object of study it muddles the borders between subject and object, and in its most straightforward sense as homesickness and longing for times past, it melds time with space."[12]

New contrivances with the aura of old truths, longings for pasts that never were, dissolving details, and blurred boundaries are the milieu not only of nostalgia in all of its valences but of Faulkner's mudhole in all of its muddiness.

Framed as a grandfather's reminiscence of his 1905 youth, *The Reivers* follows twelve-year-old Lucius Priest (our narrator's younger self), Boon Hogganbeck, one of the Priest family's white employees, and Ned McCaslin, the family's black stableman turned stowaway, as they travel by stolen car from Jefferson, Mississippi, to Memphis, Tennessee. Hijinks, horse races, and whorehouses ensue. But before innocent young Lucius finds himself racing stolen horses, brawling (and bawling) over reformed prostitutes, or evading agents of the law with names like Butch Lovemaiden, he and his traveling companions have to face the challenge of Hell Creek bottom.

Only a few miles before Memphis, Lucius, Boon, and Ned find themselves—and their stolen car—stuck in a vast man-made mudhole. This trap is created, maintained, and overseen by a man who spends his days waiting, in the shade, with his mule team to do his self-appointed "work" of rescuing stuck automobiles, for the not-insignificant fee of two dollars a head. The episode redefines "farming," pits mule again machine, and renders mud-caked men of both races equally indistinguishable and ineffectual in their futile labor. As the novel's protagonists become coated in muck, indistinguishable either from each other or the boggy terrain that traps both them and their—well, not really *their*—automobile, Faulkner reveals the complex inner and interworkings of labor, land, and language in a South that is at once rapidly changing and, like the mud, stubbornly intractable.

Though this scene first dares an allegorical interpretation, a pitting of nature against machine in which mule-power proves the lie of the automobile's vaunted horsepower, nostalgia thumbs its nose at modernization, and "go slow now" wins the day, the real and far messier web of comparisons Faulkner is making is among traditional agriculture, the mudhole proprietor's mock-farming, and Ned's own unacknowledged social and linguistic labor. Through two socially and economically marginalized men—one poor-white, the other black—the mudhole scene presents two models of survival-mode labor, of subsistence farming that yields no physical crop. In the latter half of the novel, Lucius defines intelligence, using the mule as his model, as "the ability to cope with environment: which means to accept environment yet still retain at least something of personal liberty" (119). The mud farmer and Ned share and exemplify the mule's intelligence. They both labor to turn a hostile land, somehow, to their advantage.

Lucius's journey is, as John Bassett writes, "symbolically suggestive: the wilderness, the descent into Hell (Hell Creek Bottom), the struggle between nature and machine, the entry into 'Civilization.'"[13] The temptation of this "suggestively" easy symbolism has seduced many a reader and critic, and perhaps with good reason. In what has been called "the most simply written of all Faulkner's novels,"[14] the narration beckons us into this "Hell" with a temporary return to the serpentine syntax and evocative piling-on of language that mark Faulkner's earlier tragic works, seeming to invite us into a realm of lush allegory and backward-looking or -bending symbol. In this first glimpse of the mudhole, the road becomes for Lucius a peaceful, primitive morass, in which automobile, men, boy, mule, and time alike are suspended, becoming all ponderous, particulate, poetic matter.

> There was something dreamlike about it. Not nightmarish: just dreamlike— the peaceful, quiet, remote, sylvan, almost primeval setting of ooze and slime and jungle growth and heat in which the very mules themselves, peacefully swishing and stamping at the teeming infinitesimal invisible myriad life which was the actual air we moved and breathed in, were not only unalien but in fact curiously appropriate, being themselves biological dead-ends and hence already obsolete before they were born . . . (85)

And with this pause, readers have only made it to the first semicolon of a page-long sentence—an unusual excess for this simple, "limited" book. The road is figured as a prehistoric landscape and the mules as living dinosaurs within it, completely at home in the mudhole before time. Faulkner *seems* to be setting up the opposition between mechanical progress and natural endurance as the scene's central binary. His description of the mules is about suspended time and near-mythic immortality.[15] They are "biological dead-ends and hence already obsolete before they were born," and as such are "in fact curiously appropriate" for the primordial sludge. They work against the "expensive useless mechanical toy" (85) and everything that it portends: mules and mud against machines and the men who love them.

But "this primeval setting" of enduring nature is not only newly and artificially arrived on the geologic scene; it exists exclusively for profit. The dreamlike mythopoetics of suspension, suction, and swampy equilibrium are just that—dreamed up. Though the mudhole dares us with

an essentially and contentedly regressive interpretation, a nostalgic, ooz-
ing, almost prelapsarian vision of southern life and land and harmony—
in which everything but the awkward, helpless automobile belongs as
if since time immemorial—these readings are, like the mules, "already
obsolete before they were born." They do not fit this book, this story,
this mudhole, or, most significantly, this man who works it, and who, as
soon as he speaks, brings the luxurious, lofty prose back down to soggy
earth. What the mudhole becomes then is not a regressive dream but
a progressive (or at least prospective, and almost certainly cynically so)
model of land and labor—in short, of history—in the American South.

The Reivers is set at a hinge moment, 1905, in the history of technology in the South. The automobile is novel, romantic, perhaps porten-
tous, but so far inessential. It can still be bested by a mud patch and a
mule team. One year later, in 1906, the city of Jackson set its first automobile speed limit at 12 mph for straightaways and 7 mph for turns.[16]
Though the floundering car is key to this early scene and to launching
the ragtag trio on their adventure, it in fact quickly drops out of the
narrative altogether, traded for a racehorse of questionable provenance
and only regained at the novel's end. The entire exercise of for-profit
mudhole extraction, the game for which this toy is not yet suited, is also a
very new one. And its inventor, the mud farmer, whom Theresa Towner
describes as "Donald Trump's prototype,"[17] is engaged in a new type of
"agricultural" labor. He works the land with time-honored tools like mid-
dlebusters and mules, but raises no crop except cash. As he says to Ned,
"Dont hold that against us. . . . Mud's one of our best crops up thisaway"
(87). Brannon Costello argues that the mud farmer "symbolizes a transition between an agrarian past and a business-oriented future."[18] His
"work" makes a mockery of the word "farming" while making profits
that put traditional agricultural practices to shame. Mules, the staple
and symbol of sharecropping (another valence, perhaps, of their being
"already obsolete"), enact a sort of smug, and what we and Faulkner's
readers in 1962 all know can only be temporary, vengeance against the
mechanization that will eventually supplant them. But for the moment
their poor-white owner has finally managed to make the land work for
him in a way that actual sharecropping never had and never would. His
intelligent scheme takes aim at a system of agriculture in which cultivating the land is always already obsolete, less profitable than miring
unsuspecting passersby in it. As Ned says, "Two dollars? . . . This sho
beats cotton. He can farm right here setting in the shade without even
moving. What I wants Boss to get me is a well-traveled mudhole" (84).

Working the land, then, is one kind of economy the mudhole mud-
dies. Though the apparent victory of the hole seems to be that of mule

over machine, the real battle is cynically and tenaciously pitched by the poor-white "entrepreneurial individualist,"[19] or mercenary capitalist, against the entrenched obsolescence and futility of traditionally inequitable models of working the land—and the poverty in which they have, up until now, mired him. Opportunistically profiting off of the vehicle of the future, the mud farmer prefigures the prevalence of cropless labor that the machine is inexorably heralding. Were we to follow him, he might very well be another of Faulkner's ascendant poor-white sharecroppers, like the Snopeses.

But the mud farmer is not the scene's only laborer. The punch line he gives to the episode draws attention to the other work—arguably far from ascendant—of the scene. In defeat, Boon tries to bargain down the farmer's per-head price by pointing out that Ned "aint even white!" The man responds, "Son . . . both these mules is color-blind" (89). The farmer, however, and the times and the novel in which he finds himself, are anything but.

The Reivers begins with a definition of labor. At the age of twelve, Lucius explains, he has already entered the workforce by delivering receipts on Fridays for his father's livery business: "the idea (not mine: your great-grandfather's) being that even at eleven a man should already have behind him one year of paying for, assuming responsibility for, the space he occupied, the room he took up, in the world's (Jefferson, Mississippi's, anyway) economy" (3). Here, Lucius introduces the nexus of assumptions about manhood, money, responsibility, and place that Faulkner will subtly—perhaps too subtly—test, complicate, and crack open over the course of the novel. It is a nexus that is particularly vexed in the context of the Jim Crow South that the text both inhabits and evades, and as Lucius is initiated into the world outside of Jefferson and beyond boyhood, his grandfather's easy definition of labor is uncomfortably shadowed and undermined by assumptions about and performances of race. Lucius begins to realize that the work of "assuming responsibility" for the space one occupies does not earn the same wages, or even trade in the same currency, across the color line. Indeed, in Hell Creek bottom, as easily as the grime of the mudhole and the suction of its tempting allegorical nostalgia temporarily efface racial differences, a "misunderstanding" averted, as we will see, brings them tumbling back.

Faulkner describes the floundering car as "held helpless and impotent in the almost infantile clutch of a few inches of the temporary confederation of two mild and pacific elements—earth and water" (85). Temporary confederations of two entities of different hues were anything but "mild and pacific" in the American South of either 1905 or 1962. Ned is proud to remind everyone that he is the result of one such union. "He was our family skeleton; we inherited him in turn, with his legend (which had no firmer supporter than Ned himself) that his mother had been the natural daughter of old Lucius Quintus Carothers himself and a Negro slave" (31). Both confederations—of earth and water and of black and white—prove treacherous in the microcosmic South of the mudhole.

Historian Barbara J. Fields and sociologist Karen E. Fields suggest that "the landscape of Jim Crow can . . . be envisioned as a minefield" in which "the actions of those involved in any given encounter determine the placement of the mine, as well as when or whether it goes off."[20] The muddy, confederated landscape of Hell Creek bottom is more Jim Crow minefield than road-trip mudhole, and its volatile terrain, they go on to assert, writing specifically about *The Reivers*, "illustrates the role of laughter in the complex etiquette of racist subordination."[21]

When the mud farmer explains that he has a new "reserve patch" on the other side of the bridge through which he will graciously haul the intrepid trio's car for no added fee, Ned pipes up, and it becomes clear that the transmogrified landscape is still rigged. He compares the farmer's second mudhole to an antebellum plantation's "Christmas middle" crop, cultivated and reserved for slaves to have a Christmas share of come winter.

> "It's how we done at McCaslin back before the Surrender when old L.Q.C. [Lucius Quintus Carothers, the McCaslin patriarch and Ned's reputed grandfather] was alive, and how the Edmonds boy still does. Every spring a middle is streaked off in the best ground on the place, and every stalk of cotton betwixt that middle and the edge of the field belongs to the Christmas fund, not for the boss but for every McCaslin nigger to have a Christmas share of it. That's what a Christmas middle is." (88)

After this patronizing lesson in southern aristocratic paternalism, Ned continues, driving home his mockery of the mud farmer's ignorance, poverty, and crass parasitism—essentially calling him a redneck.

> "Likely you mud-farming folks up here never heard of it." The man looked at Ned awhile. After a while Ned said, "Hee hee hee."
> "That's better," the man said. "I thought for a minute me and you was about to misunderstand one another."

In this complicated exchange, Ned, called by one critic "the epitome of the masking joker,"[22] first evokes his own intimacy (in more than one sense) with the aristocratic class of the Old South and its gentlemanly code of *noblesse oblige*, then weaponizes it, accusing the mud farmer of being a poor, ignorant, lazy white who will never be a true gentleman and cannot even muster being an honest farmer. An exchange of looks between the two men contains the violence that Faulkner never speaks in the novel—and that he perhaps dares his nostalgia-bogged readers to ignore. When Ned rescinds with a "hee hee hee," it signifies that his insult has hit home and the unspoken threat has been equally effective.

The labor of Ned's "hee hee hee" is the most complex in the book. Those three syllables are doing just as much "work"—assuming responsibility for the space one occupies, the room one takes up—in the economy of the South as the mud farmer and his mules, Miss Reba and her girls, or Boss Priest and his *noblesse oblige*. In many ways, Ned's laughter has the highest stakes of any labor in the novel. As Fields and Fields point out, "this incident ends with a giggle; but it might easily have ended with fire and a rope."[23] Ned's quick laughter keeps the circles he talks from weaving into a noose around his own neck. His "yield" or "profit" is his bodily safety—which he only attains by yielding to the masking joker role expected of him, bogging back down in the mud of violently nostalgic white expectations of jocular black obedience. This very real violent possibility is barely hinted at and never fully articulated in *The Reivers*, an uncomfortable and problematic omission for which many critics have rightly taken Faulkner to task.

While acknowledging the uneasy way in which *The Reivers* "mostly makes light of [many] painful realities" of racial violence, John T. Matthews points out that "what's at the core of Lucius Priest's memory is . . . an unwanted and extremely troubling initiation into the desperate measures forced on the disadvantaged."[24] This setting, these men, this laugh, form a network of historically contingent (and trapped) subsistence labor that undercuts the novel's jaunty comic cutting-up. The mud farmer and Ned both take advantage of situations that have very little inherently advantageous about them—ground that is fallow or potentially explosive. They could even be thought of as the real work-mules of the mudhole scene, each possessing the Faulknerian intelligence of coping with environment. That the former gets six dollars and the latter merely retains his bodily safety at the end of the transaction shows Faulkner's awareness, if not necessarily Lucius's, that the mud is deeper on the other side of the color line.

Faulkner, too, with this scene, dramatizes just how potent the appeal of nostalgia—itself an artificially confederated term—is. He enacts the weight of this longing for a past and place that never existed by putting his own heavy rhetorical finger on the scales as he descriptively draws his readers into the mudhole. The historically real danger Ned faces is contained in a glance and a giggle, while the romantically back-facing vision of the mudhole as boggy preindustrial, race-evacuated Eden is described at lush linguistic length. Nostalgia, Faulkner seems to be acknowledging (even as he appears to indulge it), doesn't play fair. Just like Ned and company, though, readers of *The Reivers* have to work and pay their way out of that warm embrace if they want to get anywhere.

NOTES

William Faulkner, *The Reivers: A Reminiscence*, rev. ed. (1962; repr., New York: Vintage International, 2011), 84. Subsequent references to this edition will be cited parenthetically in the text.

1. John E. Bassett, "*The Reivers*: Revision and Closure in Faulkner's Career," *Southern Literary Journal* 18.2 (1986): 54.

2. Michael Millgate, *The Achievement of William Faulkner* (New York: Random House, 1966), 258.

3. Kevin Railey, *Natural Aristocracy: History, Ideology, and the Production of William Faulkner* (Tuscaloosa: University of Alabama Press, 1999), xiv.

4. James B. Carothers, "The Road to *The Reivers*," in *"A Cosmos of My Own": Faulkner and Yoknapatawpha, 1980*, ed. Doreen Fowler and Ann J. Abadie (Jackson: University Press of Mississippi, 1981), 96.

5. Theresa M. Towner, *Faulkner on the Color Line: The Later Novels* (Jackson: University Press of Mississippi, 2000), 38.

6. Louis Daniel Brodsky, "Faulkner and the Racial Crisis, 1956," *Southern Review* 24.4 (Autumn 1988): 801.

7. Svetlana Boym, "Nostalgia and Its Discontents," *Hedgehog Review* 9.2 (2007): 7.

8. Ibid.

9. Nicholas Dames, *Amnesiac Selves: Nostalgia, Forgetting, and British Fiction, 1810–1870* (New York: Oxford University Press, 2001), 4.

10. William Faulkner, *Absalom, Absalom!*, rev. ed. (1936; repr., New York: Vintage International, 1990), 7.

11. Susannah Radstone, "Nostalgia: Home-comings and Departures," *Memory Studies* 3 (2010): 187.

12. Ibid., 187–88.

13. Bassett, "*The Reivers*," 60.

14. John T. Matthews, *William Faulkner: Seeing through the South* (New York: Wiley-Blackwell, 2012), 284.

15. "In a word, free of the obligations of ancestry and the responsibilities of posterity, he has conquered not only life but death too and hence is immortal" (Faulkner, *The Reivers*, 120).

16. "Mississippi History Timeline," Mississippi Department of Archives and History, http://mdah.state.ms.us/timeline/zone/1906/.

17. Towner, *Faulkner on the Color Line*, 78.

18. Brannon Costello, *Plantation Airs: Racial Paternalism and the Transformations of Class in Southern Fiction, 1945–1971* (Baton Rouge: Louisiana State University Press, 2007), 87.

19. Ibid., 97.

20. Karen E. Fields and Barbara J. Fields, *Racecraft: The Soul of Inequality in American Life* (New York: Verso, 2012), 90.

21. Ibid.

22. Walter Taylor, "Faulkner's *Reivers:* How to Change the Joke without Slipping the Yoke," in *Faulkner and Race: Faulkner and Yoknapatawpha, 1986,* ed. Doreen Fowler and Ann J. Abadie (Jackson: University Press of Mississippi, 1987), 118.

23. Fields and Fields, *Racecraft,* 91.

24. Matthews, *William Faulkner,* 280.

Interrogation, Torture, and Confession in William Faulkner's *Light in August*

W. FITZHUGH BRUNDAGE

Buried in *Light in August* is an easily overlooked account of police torture. The scene, to which Faulkner devotes six pages, unfolds roughly midway in the novel. In it, the burning Burden mansion on the outskirts of Jefferson attracts a crowd, including the sheriff and his deputies. Both appalled and titillated by the discovery of the nearly decapitated corpse of Joanna Burden, the throng speculates about the perpetrator and his crime. Everyone immediately presumes that the murder was "an anonymous negro crime."[1] With the crime scene destroyed by fire, the sheriff begins his investigation with the predictable command, "Get me a nigger" (613). A random black man is detained and dragged into a nearby cabin, where, away from the curious gaze of the crowd, he is given the third degree. As a belt is lashed across his back, the sheriff asks him who lived in the recently occupied cabin behind the Burden mansion. The black man claims ignorance, protesting that he doesn't "live nowhere near here" (615). The beating persists, punctuated by the question, "You remember yet?" Eventually, the torture victim divulges: "It's two white men. . . . You can whup the blood outen me. But that's all I know." An unidentified observer of the beating concurs, interjecting, "It's that fellow Christmas. . . . You could have picked out any man in Jefferson that his breath smelled right and he could have told you that much." "I reckon that's right," the sheriff concedes, and the interrogation concludes.

Other instances of confession, interrogation, and coercion are scattered throughout the novel. Byron Bunch repeatedly seeks out Gail Hightower to serve as his informal confessor. In chapter 7, we learn that Mr. McEachern, Joe Christmas's foster father, relentlessly interrogated and periodically beat the young boy in an effort to compel him to memorize his catechism. Several years later, McEachern again questioned and beat Joe with the aim of forcing him to confess the surreptitious sale of his calf. Then, after Joe and Joanna Burden begin their furtive sexual relationship, Joe is ordered, at gunpoint, by Joanna to pray with her. Finally, in the novel's closing pages, when the men clamoring to murder Christmas burst into Gail Hightower's home, the disgraced minister responds by offering an urgent, almost incoherent and unconvincing (false) alibi for Joe.

In a novel marked by complex narrative structure and murders, a threatened lynching, and castration, these instances of confession—both coerced and freely given—fade into the background. Contemporary reviewers of the novel made no mention of this thread. Instead, their attention was drawn to the "usual quota of half-crazed individuals, driven by uncontrollable impulses" and "all the repulsive qualities the public has learned to love."[2] Nevertheless, the recurrence of confession, interrogation, and torture is directly relevant to Faulkner's larger creative ambition. And the inclusion of the application of the third degree in the cabin in the novel coincided with the cresting of a strenuous national debate about police brutality. Although Americans had argued about police brutality for several decades before the publication of *Light in August*, not until the 1920s did Faulkner and other American commentators prod Americans to ponder the deepest wellsprings of police torture.

Admittedly, the police torture in *Light in August* was of a piece with the recurring violence in Faulkner's oeuvre that chafed some early reviewers. Well before Faulkner's contributions to the genre, violence, along with chain gangs, racial strife, and social pathologies writ large, was a well-established southern trope. Beginning in the 1830s (and arguably even earlier), the region was purported to incubate a distinctive culture of violence. Humorists rendered it as comical, foreign visitors as exotic, and opponents of slavery as barbarous. For some, Madame Lalaurie embodied the region's pathological violence. She was the infamous New Orleans slaveholder whose alleged torture of her slaves in 1834 made her internationally notorious and a figure of interest to commentators ranging from Harriet Martineau to George Washington Cable. Faulkner, thus, traversed well-traveled ground.[3]

He, however, did much more than rework familiar tropes. His incorporation of and attention to violence, including police violence, is a constituent element of his modernist aesthetics. Faulkner leaves ambiguous many of the salient "facts" in the novel, most especially whether Joe Christmas is white or black. Faulkner explores the subjectivity of "truth" and of "knowing," exposing how experience, reason, faith, and memory determine what the characters in the novel "know." Violence, both threatened and enacted, contributes to the recurring challenges that characters in the novel confront: the difficulty of knowing, the indeterminacy of truth, and the ambiguity of identity. Seen in this light, the account of the brutal questioning of the black man is neither an inconsequential gesture to southern gothic conventions nor a minor plot embellishment.

∘ ∘ ∘

Historical context helps to clarify the significance of interrogation and confession in Faulkner's novel. Otherwise, it is easy to assume that the abuse of the black man in the cabin is just another manifestation of senseless southern violence. Tradition and white privilege may seem adequate to explain why the sheriff resorted to the third degree when the knowledge he gleaned was easily accessible without it. After all, as the interrogation proceeds, we learn that the black man has no special knowledge about the cabin's occupants and is selected for torture solely on the basis of his race. Faulkner seemingly sought to remind us of the violent pathology of white racism, which Joel Williamson has summarized as "in violence veritas."[4] The interrogation, then, is a mere pretext for a staged and ritualized performance of domination that affirms the power of whites to humiliate blacks and maim their bodies virtually at will. The beating in the cabin was, as it were, a twentieth-century replication of a slave whipping. As Caleb Smith suggests, "The white agents of power, disturbed by the crime and the incineration of one of their proudest symbols, the antebellum mansion, resort to the old violence of slave discipline and reconstitute their own supremacy."[5]

Faulkner, however, had more in mind than to emphasize the persistence of the rituals of white power and the prerogatives of white violence. Notably, he does not render the sheriff as a pathologically violent law officer but instead as an upholder of reason and order amid a gathering mob. Even while the sheriff reflexively seizes a black for interrogation, his violence is purposeful and measured. Moreover, his use of violence to advance a criminal investigation was unremarkable for the era. It is worth recalling that southern law officers were no more predisposed to harsh interrogation techniques than lawmen elsewhere in the nation.[6] The methods the sheriff employs in the cabin on the Burden plantation would not have offended the sensibilities of policemen in New York City, Chicago, El Paso, or Seattle.

Not until after World War I did interrogation techniques like those employed by the sheriff arouse sustained public debate. Other forms of violence by legal authorities had stirred concern among Americans. Americans, for instance, engaged in strenuous debate about the justice of harsh prison treatment and capital punishment. But the public granted authorities wide latitude to employ harsh measures on behalf of law and order. Little controversy arose, for instance, if authorities subjected slaves to extreme violence when rumors of slave uprisings circulated. Many urban Americans also tolerated the propensity of early police forces to rely on their brawn and billy clubs to assert authority and impose order. This behavior did fuel ongoing skirmishes with lower-class residents and, on occasion, provoked lawsuits from middle-class citizens who experienced it firsthand. But for the first quarter century after the founding of police forces during the 1850s, the charges typically leveled against police were that they were too quick and heavy-handed with their billy clubs while on the beat, not that they employed torture to extract confessions or humiliate suspects in custody.[7]

As a consequence of headlong urbanization and immigration and of the perceived disorder in the nation's cities, metropolitan police forces after the Civil War assumed responsibilities and acquired powers that were unprecedented and without clear legal authority. The increasing use of one new power—custodial interrogation—transformed the role of police in the gathering of evidence used in criminal prosecutions. Previously, interrogations of alleged criminals had been conducted by officers of the court in the context of trials. Now police, who lacked relevant professional training and were recruited largely on the basis of their partisan allegiance, relied more and more on coerced information and confessions to perform their jobs.[8]

By the 1880s the practice of harsh interrogation had become sufficiently common and varied to generate a new lexicon and elicit public comment. In an 1887 memoir, George Washington Walling, police superintendent of New York, introduced to a wide audience the police slang of "getting the third degree" as a euphemism for aggressive questioning.[9] Subsequent newspaper reports dubbed New York police inspector Thomas Byrnes the "inventor" of the third degree, but it seems more likely that he garnered his nickname only because he employed the technique more vigorously, systematically, and flamboyantly than his peers. Newspapers made famous his mastery of "dramatic ordeals" and "mysterious arts" that he applied "without mercy" and, allegedly, with unfailing success.[10] With each passing year, crime reporters from coast to coast made more and more frequent references to police "sweating" alleged criminals and applying the third degree. News accounts after the arrest of suspects routinely predicted that police would apply the third degree. Subsequent reports would tally how long, strenuous, and productive had been the bouts of interrogation. Many accounts even judged the strength of character displayed by the accused while under duress.[11] By the turn of the nineteenth century, the practice was sufficiently familiar to justify a lengthy column tracing its history in the *New York Times*.[12]

As the procedure simultaneously became more commonplace and drew increasing scrutiny, police sought to shield it from the public gaze.[13] Police commissioners grumbled that yellow journalists, misinformed do-gooders, and shyster lawyers in the pay of career criminals grossly exaggerated its frequency and intensity. They dissembled about the third-degree techniques that they used by insisting that the third degree entailed a battle of wills and a test of intelligence rather than of stamina or tolerance of pain. In response to the increasing notoriety of the third degree, Richard Sylvester, superintendent of police in the nation's capital and president of the International Association of Police Chiefs, protested that the third degree produced "volunteer confessions" as a result of "diligent inquiry of a prisoner for explanation of facts and circumstances."[14] Like other apologists then and later, he acknowledged that "some years ago a rough usage was resorted to in some cities in order to secure confessions" but assured readers that "such procedure does not obtain at large nowadays." For decades to come, police spokesmen would parrot the bromide that the third degree was an archaic practice that had been superseded by modern scientific police methods.

Crime reporters dissembled as well, perhaps because they sympathized with or were beholden to the police. Rather than detailing the police interrogation methods that they had often witnessed, reporters instead described them in evocative but enigmatic terms. Of Inspector Byrnes's methods, for instance, one newspaper divulged that "many mysterious tales have been told" about them; another revealed they "are devious and vary with each candidate."[15] Such cryptic depictions were almost certainly intended to tantalize readers by heightening the mystery and terror associated with the practice and in turn to provoke a "wholesome fear among the criminal classes."[16]

Substantive accounts of police interrogation techniques, nevertheless, surfaced in court appeals, civil suits brought against police departments, or the occasional explicit news reports. By 1910 a composite portrait of the third degree could be sketched. It typically occurred while in custody of the police, before charges were brought against the suspect, and in the absence of counsel. It might consist of being compelled to stand in exhausting positions for hours on end, being deprived of sleep and food for days, being threatened with lynching, electrocution, or death, being beaten with rubber hoses, fists, and clubs, being confined in a dark cell for days, or being subjected to simulated drowning (also known as the "water cure"). In at least one case police held a criminal by his feet and dangled him out a window high above the street. Police in another instance used a dental drill to coerce a confession from a suspect, and in yet another police drenched a fifteen-year-old with gasoline and held a lit match close to his dripping clothes until he confessed.[17] In San Francisco police employed a battery of macabre techniques to coerce a Sicilian immigrant to implicate her husband in a murder. First, they took her infant child from her, then they interrogated her for hours, and they concluded by showing her the mangled remains of the murder victim in the autopsy room and forcing her to handle the blood-encrusted cleaver used in the murder and the blood-drenched blanket in which the victim had been concealed. Rather than eliciting a confession, the trauma induced an extended fit of hysteria.[18]

These and similar techniques were so notorious that the American soldiers prosecuted in 1902 for war crimes during the Philippine Insurrection defended themselves by contrasting their actions with those of American police. Speaking of his use of the "water cure" against Filipino insurgents, one officer maintained that "it did not compare in cruelty with methods resorted to by American police officials to extort confessions."[19] A newspaper editorial conceded that "there was more truth than poetry" in his defense.[20]

As the third degree gained notoriety, writers, especially those intent on rendering the milieu of the nation's tumultuous cities, seized on its dramatic possibilities. Charles Klein, an English-born playwright and actor who emigrated to America in 1883, made the practice the dramatic center of *The Third Degree*, published in 1908. Now forgotten, Klein enjoyed great success until his death on the *Lusitania*, writing stage melodramas that focused on contemporary themes.[21] The inspiration for his 1908 play was the case of Richard Ivens, a simple-minded youth tried and convicted for the rape and murder of a Chicago woman in 1906. Despite no physical evidence linking Ivens to the crime and considerable testimony that provided him with an alibi, he was prosecuted on the basis of a confession that police wrung out of him.[22] Criminologist J. Sanderson Christison and Ivens's defense lawyers objected that the police had effectively hypnotized the highly suggestible youth to extract his confession. After the youth's execution, Harvard University psychologist Hugo Munsterberg concurred, censuring the state for killing an innocent man on the basis of a coerced confession.[23] While taking license with the specifics of the Ivens case, Klein's play centers on the plight of a weak man who succumbs during his interrogation and admits to a murder he did not commit. The play encouraged audiences who might otherwise uncritically endorse police methods to ponder the ambiguity of confessions and to sympathize with the suspect broken by the third degree. Because of Klein's mastery of the melodramatic conventions of the day and the timeliness of its subject, the play was performed widely during the next two decades. It also was turned into a novel and inspired the screenplays for films in 1913, 1919, and 1926—the last an acclaimed adaptation directed by Michael Curtiz of *Casablanca* fame.[24]

By the late 1920s the third degree was a staple in American popular culture. References to it peppered Hollywood films. Roland West's *Alibi*, released in 1929, employed a Broadway cast and a visual style derived from German Expressionism to provide an early rendering of the third degree in a "talkie." Contemporary radio dramas such as *Calling All Cars* also acknowledged the third degree even while they sought to appease defenders of law and order (and appease parents concerned about young children being exposed to accounts of police lawlessness) by focusing on "modern" scientific police methods.

The interest filmmakers and playwrights displayed in the third degree was complemented by intensifying public debate about the practice. Police across the nation responded to the crime wave associated with Prohibition by employing the third degree indiscriminately. They adopted the same techniques to suppress radicals and union organizers. In response, local citizens' groups rallied to scrutinize and publicize police excesses while the National Association for the Advancement of Colored People and the newly founded American Civil Liberties Union launched campaigns to expose and eradicate police brutality.[25] Oswald Garrison Villard, a prominent reformer and grandson of the abolitionist William Lloyd Garrison, wrote the widely discussed exposé "Official Lawlessness," published in *Harper's* in 1927.[26] And in January 1931 the presidential Commission on Law Observance and Enforcement, more commonly known as the Wickersham Commission, released its expansive investigation of police methods used to enforce Prohibition. The report provided the most comprehensive official acknowledgment of the third degree and its widespread use. Popular writers quickly translated the report's findings into searing indictments of police and their methods of interrogation.[27] By 1932, when readers first cracked open *Light in August*, police brutality, specifically the third degree, was widely discussed as one of the most pressing issues of the day.

∘ ∘ ∘

Let us revisit the scene of police torture in *Light in August*. Caleb Smith has suggested that Faulkner uses the episode to demonstrate the "temporality of ritual violence." For Smith, the violence in the cabin has little to do with the production of truth and instead is one moment in an ongoing exercise of violent power that preceded it and will follow it. One interrogation begets another and another and another, and in this manner "questioning transforms torture from a repetition into a threshold, leading indefinitely into the future."[28] Smith, like many other contemporary analysts of torture, discounts the idea that torture is aimed at producing truth. From Edward Peters to Elaine Scarry, scholars have concluded that torture is exclusively a tool to suppress and silence. As Peters explains, "It is not primarily the victim's information, but the victim, that torture seeks to win—or reduce to powerlessness."[29]

The flogging in *Light in August* complicates this assumption about torture by revealing the enduring logic of torturers that binds together the body, pain, interrogation, and the pursuit of truth. When placed in a larger historical context, the interrogation of the black man is consonant with the long-established if no longer state-sanctioned belief that coercion, and especially physical pain, can render truth visible and audible. Ancient Greeks bequeathed to Western tradition the belief that truth is not the outcome of public negotiation and tedious accumulation of evidence but is rather an often-hidden secret that exists independent of reason. Truth is a mystical and unitary artifact that can be recovered whole. (Recall the truth that the philosopher discerns in Plato's Allegory of the Cave in *The Republic*.) Classicist Page duBois has explained how the Greek word for "touchstone" evolved into the word for a test for purity and eventually became the name for physical torture. She concludes that for ancient Greeks, torture was a physical testing that exposed authentic truth just as a chemist's test revealed an ore's purity. This conceptualization of truth resolved the challenge of locating truth in a society where human chattel were commonplace. Because slaves purportedly lacked the capacity to reason, they could not give evidence—speak truth—in the same manner as a citizen, who by definition possessed rationality. Through the application of torture, the slave body could be compelled to offer up truth that would otherwise be inaccessible. Indeed, the ancient Greeks were more confident in the authenticity of the truth extracted from slave bodies than from the testimony of citizen slave masters. Truth extorted by torture was free of the distortions produced by guile and artifice. Consequently, Greeks looked to the truth extracted from the bodies of slaves to corroborate or discredit the evidence of free men.[30]

The classical concept of truth proved to be both influential and durable. It subsequently informed Roman law and, after the thirteenth century, Western thought more broadly. The classical understanding of torture and truth exerted renewed influence beginning during the thirteenth century, when first religious and then secular authorities shifted from relying upon God's intervention to discern guilt (whether of heresy or criminality) to accumulating evidence and applying reason to determine culpability. To divulge responsibility, whether in a church confessional or before a court of law, was to create truth. This elevation of confession to the highest level of religious and secular proof was, to a degree, a practical necessity. If culpability could no longer be ascertained by God's overt intervention, how could reason be applied and guilt determined in those instances when physical evidence or witnesses were absent? And in the period after the thirteenth-century reforms but before the advent of forensic science, what evidence other than confessions were accessible to civil authorities? Furthermore, at a time when the capacity of European states to coerce the compliance of their subjects was limited, the practice of confession enlisted individuals to assent to and thereby assume responsibility for their own subjugation. Predictably, perhaps even inevitably, confessions became the "queen of evidence" in the Western legal tradition.[31]

Practical considerations alone, however, are inadequate to explain the cultural importance attached to confessions from the thirteenth century on. With ample justification, historian Jean Delumeau has observed, "The history of modern western reason passes by way of the confession."[32] Perhaps best epitomized by Jean-Jacques Rousseau's *Confessions*, the self-exegesis of confession became the preeminent mode of self-knowledge and was understood to be the most authentic expression of selfhood possible.[33]

Because of the extraordinary cultural and judicial weight assigned to confessions in both ecclesiastical and lay justice, it may seem altogether predictable that authorities applied physical coercion to elicit confessions. Yet the rationale for physical coercion, including torture, in the early modern West had less to do with expediency than with ideas about the will, the body, and truth. The Christian theology of original sin encouraged the belief that the human will is inherently corrupt and that all willed acts are polluted by that corruption. As historian Lisa Silverman has observed, "In this context, to tell the truth voluntarily is a near impossibility, precisely because human will is suspect."[34] Given the likelihood of deceit in any act of will, such as the testimony of a suspect, medieval jurists employed torture as the preferred method to secure testimony that was uncorrupted by human guile. Through inflicting pain on an accused, the torturer destroyed the willful obfuscation that otherwise diminished or confused testimony. The expression of truth was a spontaneous ejaculation rather than a deliberate recital. Truth could be gleaned from the human body no less than from the verbal testimony of a suspect. Torture, in short, was the means by which the body revealed authentic truth.

This ideal of corporeal truth came under attack from Enlightenment-era critics who contested inherited ideas about human suffering and whether violence to the body could produce truth independent of the mind. Voltaire, Montesquieu, Beccaria, and other eighteenth-century philosophes dismissed many of the justifications that had sustained and legitimated judicial torture. At the heart of their reevaluation was the conviction that pain corrupted and prevented the full exercise of free will. Whereas medieval jurists presumed that pain was needed to overcome the will and reveal truth, Enlightenment critics identified pain as a barrier to both personal agency and any articulation of pure truth. Whereas pain had once been seen as useful to tame willfulness and thereby reveal truth, it now was understood to be destructive of the self, to extinguish human identity, and to mute the capacity to voice truth.[35]

This critique inspired reevaluations of torture, public execution, prison practices, and many forms of corporal punishment, such as flogging and branding. By the early nineteenth century statutory torture had largely disappeared from the West, where the growing power of emerging modern states to disarm civilians, control violence, and enforce law and order went hand in hand with the abolition of torture. The founding documents of the American republic, which explicitly outlaw the use of coercive methods of interrogation and cruel punishments, demonstrate the influence of Enlightenment ideas about how and for what purpose a state should employ physical violence to coerce suspects and to punish wrongdoers.[36]

Extralegal state torture, however, persisted in the shadow of constitutional and statutory prohibitions of torture. As discussed previously, during the second half of the nineteenth century American law officers routinely employed methods of interrogation that contemporaries compared to those of medieval inquisitors. Although judicial torture no longer enjoyed legal sanction, the belief that calibrated pain and coercion could elicit truth endured. My point here is not to suggest that the third degree, as practiced across the United States and in the cabin behind the Burden mansion, was evidence of a timeless, transhistorical belief. The pervasiveness of torture throughout history may persuade us that, as Argentine torturer Julio Simon has contended, "Torture is eternal." He explains, "It has always existed and it always will. It is an essential part of the human being."[37] But to adopt Simon's perspective risks downplaying the importance of the development of modern state institutions, racial ideologies, and class hierarchies to the proliferation and institutionalization of the third degree. It was the combination of these developments with the persisting conviction that the cumulative application of pain could overwhelm otherwise intractable human will and elicit truth that mitigated the Enlightenment critique of state violence.

Let us return again to the bout of police brutality in *Light in August*. If the sheriff interrogated the black man without resort to violence, how could he be certain that the man would not dissemble? Faulkner draws our attention to the black man's expressionless face: "the negro did not look back; there came only into his face when the strap fell across the back a wince, sudden, sharp, fleet, jerking up the corners of his mouth and exposing his momentary teeth like smiling. Then his face smoothed again, inscrutable" (614). The searing pain of the lash enables the sheriff to peer through the veil of inscrutability behind which the black man seeks shelter. By tormenting the body of the black man, the sheriff elicits information that corroborates the knowledge that he and the unidentified spectator already possess. The black man's avowal that "[y]ou can whup the blood outen me" establishes that his confession is the authentic truth. In a novel in which so much is opaque, here is a moment when confessional speech provides a glimpse of authenticity, of transparency, of "truth."

❋ ❋ ❋

In March 1934, two years after the publication of *Light in August*, Raymond Stuart, a white planter in Kemper County, Mississippi, was murdered. Within days Arthur Ellington, Ed Brown, and Henry Shields, three black tenant farmers, were arrested for the crime. At their trial, the prosecution's principal evidence was their confessions given while in police custody. Prosecution witnesses freely admitted that the defendants confessed only after being brutally whipped by police, and, in one instance, being strung up by the neck from a tree. Nevertheless, the presiding judge admitted the confessions into evidence and they were the basis for the defendants' convictions and death sentences. The men appealed their convictions to the Mississippi Supreme Court, which affirmed their sentences. Eventually their appeals reached the US Supreme Court, which in a unanimous decision in 1936, reversed their convictions. The court held that a defendant's confession that is extracted by police violence cannot be entered as evidence and violates the due process clause of the Fourteenth Amendment. (I cannot fail to note that the prosecutor at the trial level, John Stennis, went on to represent Mississippi in the US Senate for forty-two years.)[38]

The *Brown v. Mississippi* decision was a milestone in the judicial restriction of coercive interrogation in the United States. Over the next three decades, culminating in the 1966 *Miranda v. Arizona* decision, the court labored to prevent the kind of police procedures that Faulkner depicted in his novel. Among the legal innovations of the second half of the twentieth century, the regulation of criminal investigation procedures ranks among the most important and transformative.

Even so, in recent years exposés of systematic and ongoing torture by the Chicago and Los Angeles police as well as the Bush administration's embrace of "enhanced interrogation" have underscored how widely and often these protections against coerced confessions are abrogated. These episodes are reminders that contemporary notions of truth, justice, and the efficacy of coercion continue to give license to public officials to employ torture. Faulkner's deceptively straightforward depiction of torture in the service of "law and order" is as timely now as it was eighty years ago.

NOTES

1. William Faulkner, *Light in August*, in *Novels 1930–1935*, ed. Joseph Blotner and Noel Polk (New York: Library of America, 1985), 611. Subsequent references to this edition will be cited parenthetically in the text.

2. *Forum and Century* 88 (December 1932): 6; Herbert Agar, *English Review* 56 (February 1933): 226.

3. For a larger discussion of the southern culture of violence, see Dickson D. Bruce, *Violence and Culture in the Antebellum South* (Austin: University of Texas Press, 1979); Bertram Wyatt-Brown, *Southern Honor: Ethics and Behavior in the Old South* (New York: Oxford University Press, 1982); W. Fitzhugh Brundage, "The Long Shadow of Torture in the American South," in *Oxford Handbook to the Literatures of the US South*, ed. Fred Hobson and Barbara Ladd (New York: Oxford University Press, 2016).

4. Joel Williamson, *The Crucible of Race: Black-White Relations in the American South since Emancipation* (New York: Oxford University Press, 1984), 180.

5. Caleb Smith, "Torture, Interrogation, and American Modernist Literature," *Northern Illinois University Law Review* 29 (2009): 438.

6. The so-called Wickersham Report provides extensive examples of interrogation techniques used across the nation, especially in the nation's largest cities. See Zechariah Chafee Jr., Walter H. Pollak, and Carl S. Stern, *The Third Degree: Report to the National Commission on Law Observance and Enforcement* (Washington, DC: United States Government Printing Office, 1931), 52–151.

7. For a larger discussion of nineteenth- and early twentieth-century police brutality, see Jeffrey S. Adler, "Shoot to Kill: The Use of Deadly Force by the Chicago Police, 1875–1920," *Journal of Interdisciplinary History* 38 (Autumn 2007); Adler, "'The Killer behind the Badge': Race and Police Homicide in New Orleans, 1925–1945," *Law and History Review* 30 (May 2012); Marilynn S. Johnson, *Street Justice: A History of Police Violence in New York City* (Boston: Beacon Press, 2003); Dennis C. Rousey, *Policing the Southern City: New Orleans, 1805–1889* (Baton Rouge: Louisiana State University Press, 1996); Marcy S. Sacks, "'To Show Who Was in Charge': Police Repression of New York City's Black Population at the Turn of the Twentieth Century," *Journal of Urban History* 31 (September 2005); Allen Steinberg, *The Transformation of Criminal Justice: Philadelphia* (Chapel Hill: University of North Carolina Press, 1989); Christopher Thale, "The Informal World of Police Patrol: New York City in the Early Twentieth Century," *Journal of Urban History* 33 (January 2007).

8. Adler, "Shoot to Kill," 251; Lawrence Friedman, *Crime and Punishment in American History* (New York: Basic Books, 1993), 108; Steven Penney, "Theories of Confession Admissibility: A Historical View," *American Journal of Criminal Law* 25

(1998): 323–25; Samuel Walker, *Popular Justice: A History of American Criminal Justice* (New York: Oxford University Press, 1980); Richard A. Leo, *Police Interrogation and American Justice* (Cambridge, MA: Harvard University Press, 2008), 66–69.

9. George Walling, *Recollections of a New York Chief of Police* (New York: Caxton Book Concern, 1887), 189–90.

10. *Louisville Courier-Journal*, October 6, 1889; *Atlanta Constitution*, September 29, 1894.

11. For examples, see *Chicago Daily Tribune*, August 15, 1902; *Louisville Courier-Journal*, October 22, 1905; *Washington Post*, March 12, 1906.

12. *New York Times*, October 6, 1901; British readers received a historical survey of the American practice of the third degree in the *London Spectator*, July 10, 1909.

13. *Louisville Courier Journal*, October 22, 1905; *Washington Post*, March 12, 1906.

14. Richard Sylvester, "A History of the 'Sweat Box' and 'the Third Degree,'" Proceedings of the International Association of Chiefs of Police. Reprinted in John Henry Wigmore, *The Principles of Judicial Proof* (Boston: Little, Brown, 1913), 551; see also *New York Times*, April 9, 1910.

15. *Atlanta Constitution*, September 29, 1894.

16. *Louisville Courier Journal*, October 6, 1889.

17. Chafee et al., *The Third Degree*, 164–69, 206.

18. *San Francisco Call*, April 7, 1905; April 8, 1905; April 9, 1905; April 11, 1905; April 12, 1905.

19. *Chicago Daily Tribune*, August 15, 1902.

20. *Washington Post*, February 5, 1901.

21. *New York Times*, December 2, 1906.

22. The Ivens case can be followed in the *Chicago Daily Tribune*, January 15, 1906; January 20, 1906; January 31, 1906; February 13, 1906; February 23, 1906; March 6, 1906; March 7, 1906; March 8, 1906; March 9, 1906; March 10, 1906; March 11, 1906; March 13, 1906; March 17, 1906; March 20, 1906; March 21, 1906; March 22, 1906; March 23, 1906; March 24, 1906; March 25, 1906; March 27, 1906; March 28, 1906; April 22, 1906; June 21, 1906; June 22, 1906; June 23, 1906.

23. J. Sanderson Christison, *The Tragedy of Chicago: A Study in Hypnotism, How an Innocent Young Man Was Hypnotized to the Gallows, Denouncements by Savants* (Chicago: n. p., 1906); *Washington Post*, December 27, 1906.

24. Charles Klein, *The Third Degree: A Play in Four Acts* (New York: S. French, 1908); Charles Klein and Arthur Hornblow, *The Third Degree, A Narrative of Metropolitan Life* (New York: Grosset & Dunlap, 1909).

25. For one of the few accounts of the NAACP's campaign against police brutality before World War II, see Silvan Niedermeir, "Torture and 'Modern Civilization': The NAACP's Fight against Forced Confessions in the American South (1935–1945)," in *Fractured Modernity: America Confronts Modern Times, 1890s to 1940s*, ed. Thomas Welskopp and Alan Lessof (Munich: Oldenbourg Verlag, 2012), 169–89. On the early activities of the ACLU, see Robert C. Cottrell, *Roger Nash Baldwin and the Civil Liberties Union* (New York: Columbia University Press, 2000), 218; Samuel Walker, *In Defense of American Liberties: A History of the ACLU*, 2nd ed. (Carbondale: Southern Illinois University Press, 1999), 87–88; and Donald Johnson, "American Civil Liberties Union: Origins, 1914–1924" (PhD diss., Columbia University, 1960).

26. Oswald Garrison Villard, "Official Lawlessness," *Harper's Monthly* (October 1927): 605–14.

27. Chafee et al., *The Third Degree*; Emanuel Henry Lavine, *The Third Degree: A Detailed and Appalling Exposée of Police Brutality* (New York: Vanguard Press, 1930).

28. Smith, "Torture, Interrogation, and American Modernist Literature," 439.

29. Edward Peters, *Torture* (Philadelphia: University of Pennsylvania Press, 1996), 164; Elaine Scarry, *The Body in Pain: The Making and Unmaking of the World* (New York: Oxford University Press, 1985), 27–59.

30. Page duBois, *Torture and Truth* (New York: Routledge, 1991), especially 9–68.

31. James Q. Whitman, *The Origins of Reasonable Doubt: Theological Roots of the Criminal Trial* (New Haven, CT: Yale University Press, 2008). As Peter Brooks has pointed out, "Only when the culpable avow themselves as culpable, verbally assume their guilt, can there be purgation." See Brooks, *Troubling Confessions: Speaking Guilt in Law and Literature* (Chicago: University of Chicago Press, 2000), 155.

32. Jean Delumeau, *L'aveau et le Pardon: Les Difficultés de la Confession XIII–XVIII Siècle* (Paris: Fayard, 1990), 9. For Michel Foucault's discussions of confession, see Foucault, *The Hermeneutics of the Subject: Lectures at the College de France, 1981–82*, ed. Frederic Gros, trans. Graham Burchell (New York: Palgrave, 2005); and Jean-Michel Landry, "Confession, Obedience, and Subjectivity: Michel Foucault's Unpublished Lectures 'On the Government of the Living,'" *Telos* 146 (Spring 2009): 111–23.

33. Brooks, *Troubling Confessions*, 8–34.

34. Lisa Silverman, *Tortured Subjects: Pain, Truth, and the Body in Early Modern France* (Chicago: University of Chicago Press, 2001), 9.

35. Lynn Hunt, *Inventing Human Rights* (New York: Norton, 2007), 70–112; Peters, *Torture,* 74–141; Silverman, *Tortured Subjects*, 153–78.

36. Louis P. Masur, *Rites of Execution: Capital Punishment and the Transformation of American Culture, 1776–1865* (New York: Oxford University Press, 1989); Michael Meranze, *Laboratories of Virtue: Punishment, Revolution, and Authority in Philadelphia, 1760–1835* (Chapel Hill: University of North Carolina Press, 1996), 173–216.

37. Quoted in Marguerite Feitlowitz, *A Lexicon of Terror: Argentina and the Legacies of Torture* (New York: Oxford University Press, 1998), 212.

38. Richard C. Cortner, *A "Scottsboro" Case in Mississippi: The Supreme Court and "Brown v. Mississippi"* (Jackson: University Press of Mississippi, 1986).

"Who Are You?": Modernism, Childhood, and Historical Consciousness in Faulkner's *The Wishing Tree*

HANNAH GODWIN

The idea for this essay was born out of research performed for a larger project that interrogates how American modernist writers engage the gothic in fictional representations of children and childhood. In this project, I read competing theories of child development and sexuality from the late nineteenth and early twentieth centuries alongside modernist literary texts to reveal the gothic child as a rich interpretive locus for negotiating cultural anxieties about futurity, sexuality, and physical and cultural reproduction. The intersection of American modernism and childhood studies proves a dynamic confluence, ripe with possibilities for attaining new understandings of childhood's centrality to the modernist enterprise. Faulkner's work, perhaps unsurprisingly, plays a vital role in this undertaking, and while researching for chapters on *The Sound and the Fury* and *Absalom, Absalom!*, I encountered in the scholarship, often in the footnotes or indexes, reference to a Faulkner text new to me: *The Wishing Tree*. My curiosity piqued. Faulkner wrote a children's book? With great determination and not a small amount of effort, I tracked this text down. That procuring this book—and even learning of its existence—took quite some digging and perseverance on my part, testifies to *The Wishing Tree*'s exclusion, its existence on the periphery of Faulkner's corpus. I recount this personal narrative by way of posing my essay's aim: to gesture toward an understanding of why this strange and intriguing text receives such scant scholarly attention and to make a case for its critical reevaluation. *The Wishing Tree* emerges as a compelling site for those interested in the relationship between modernism and children's literature and modernism and childhood studies, and for those struck by Faulkner's investments in children and childhood, both fictional and real.

As Karin Westman helpfully articulates, the predominant conceptualization of children's literature in terms of genre (fables, fairy tales, picture books, etc.) renders it "particularly susceptible to losing its historical grounding."[1] Westman identifies a problem with using genre as an "organizing principle" when intended audience is the primary measure of classification, as is the case with children's literature.[2] Genre, then, can potentially obstruct the generation and apprehension of meaning, which prompts the question: what is gained when we read children's literature into literary history? The case of modernism and children's literature is a particularly complicated one, as Kimberley Reynolds asserts: "The relationship between children's literature and modernism is convoluted and contradictory . . . given modernism's indebtedness to the idea of the child and early play of language, on the one hand, and, on the other, the (mis)perception that modernism's formal play and complex themes could not find a home in texts written for children."[3] Thus, modernism and children's literature persist in uneasy yet potentially fruitful confluence, perceived as at odds with each other due to modernist valorizations of opacity, though modernist experimentations in narrative and poetics remain indebted to explorations of language formation in childhood and to the child's presumed freshness of perspective. However, as Westman notes, for scholars working at the intersection of modernism and children's literature, the "new modernisms" model of periodization and expansion of canon parameters has bestowed upon children's literature a little more critical influence: "Here, children's literature benefits primarily from the 'vertical' expansion of modernism's defining boundaries: 'low' texts for children, produced for a mass audience on a range of themes, are resituated within or help reconfigure a modernist frame."[4] By examining works written for children by modernist authors, scholars, particularly those invested in childhood as a field of inquiry, will have a more extensive and complex range for contextualization. Given that modernist experimentation flourished in a period that saw the blossoming of children's literature, I am interested in how childhood was perceived as a keen source for exploring different modes of consciousness and perception, and also in how modernist children's literature reveals how the child was conceived of in this historical moment. After all, claims literary scholar Karen Sánchez-Eppler, "Books written for children remain one of the best gauges we have for a particular society's views of childhood."[5]

Emblematic of physical and cultural reproduction, the child functions as a dynamic symbolic locus with irrevocable ties both to the past and to the future. The child operates as a powerful cipher, able to absorb and accrue meaning ascribed by adults. Intensely malleable yet incredibly potent, the child becomes a complex interpretive site for depositing and negotiating a culture's fears and anxieties. The child has long been a vessel for the projection of a contradictory assemblage of thoughts, but insofar as the child is historically and socially constructed, the child at the modernist moment bears its own particular set of cultural resonances and concomitant burdens. Through competing discourses in emerging and developing fields such as psychoanalysis, evolutionary psychology, and child development and education, the early twentieth century initiates widespread alterations to the child's cultural import, which modernist writers and visual artists aptly engage. The child retains its conceptual force because it remains so open to competing claims, and at the turn of the twentieth century, as a product of these tensions and discordances, a more sophisticated treatment of the child emerges. Although modernist artists draw on the Romantic reverence for the child as transcendent and inspirational, the cultural landscape has been irrevocably altered by the psychoanalytic assault on childhood innocence. Thus, modernist artists tap into the Romantics' celebration of the child but change its emphasis.[6] Covering a vast array of fields of artistic production ranging from the Italian Futurists' explosive technocentric infantilist rhetoric to visual artists popularizing conceptions of the artist as child to a fascination with primitivism as an outlet for accessing authentic experience, the twentieth century heralds the century of the child.[7] As the child becomes a model for avant-garde art, an interest in representing child consciousness develops as a central innovation. Indicative of the shift in narrative emphasis from attention to external phenomena to an interest in inner experience, the child becomes a vessel of consciousness to be plumbed in depth. Fascinated with the instinctual, intense perceptions of childhood, modernist artists turn to the child in order to free themselves from past ways of surveying, experiencing, and representing the world.

Yet despite this vibrant nexus of childhood that modernists themselves were fervent to engage, modernism and childhood remains a peculiarly undertheorized field, particularly given the breadth of scholarship on the Victorian child. Although this curious dearth persists in broad-gauge studies on modernism and the child, Faulkner scholars often note the significance of the child in his body of work, homing in on his southern clans as they reckon with their troubled familial pasts and move, often falteringly, into uncertain futures. Noel Polk investigates the "emotional and psychic baggage" that Faulkner's dark houses create for his fictional "children to carry with them for the rest of their lives."[8] And of course *The Sound and the Fury*, emerging out of the short story "Twilight," begins "as the opening of a narrative space for the voices of children."⁹ Childhood in Faulkner's texts is often figured as trauma, as powerlessness, rendered so in labyrinthine narratives that explore the child's fragility, its vulnerability to forces beyond its control.¹⁰ I'm thinking of Joe Christmas, of Vardaman, of Quentin and Caddy, and of Bon. Given Faulkner's established interest in the child as a source of artistic inspiration in his experimental modernist masterworks, what changes or becomes illuminated when he not only represents fictional children but also addresses children as a readership? *The Wishing Tree* offers us the opportunity to engage this question.

Previous scholarship on *The Wishing Tree* traces its complex and fascinating textual history,¹¹ identifies its potential merits and utility in the contemporary classroom,¹² and acknowledges its significance as a testing ground for thematic preoccupations that Faulkner later explores in his radically innovative modernist works.¹³ *The Wishing Tree*'s textual history is itself an engrossing subject, the accuracy of which remains open to debate. Louis Brodsky's explication in *Studies in Bibliography* remains the most sustained and detailed explanation to date. Brodsky notes that the text was originally given to Estelle Franklin's daughter, Victoria, on the occasion of her eighth birthday, February 5, 1927, and then a different version of the text was gifted to a dear friend's terminally ill child, Margaret Brown, just six days later.¹⁴ Writing against most critical opinions concerning *The Wishing Tree*'s convoluted textual history, Brodsky claims that the Brown version was constructed first and that the Victoria version serves as a refinement of the Brown text. To support his argument, he proposes that the Victoria version remains consistent with Faulkner's revision practices. Brodsky painstakingly notes the differences and discrepancies between the Victoria version and the Brown version, and details the salient revision techniques he argues Faulkner employed to improve the Victoria version—paring away of dialect, decreasing the number of "figurative and literary allusions," diminishing the roles of lesser characters, "reducing the quantity of dialogue and improving the quality of the dialect" of the black nurse, Alice, and her husband, Exodus.¹⁵ These alterations, for Brodsky, remain indicative of Faulkner's desire to improve upon the Brown version, yet Faulkner himself does nothing to clear up the confusion over which text came first. Victoria's copy bears the dedication that he wrote it specifically for her birthday, but when opposing Mrs. Brown's wish to publish Margaret's copy, Faulkner claims that he wrote it explicitly for her, "as a gesture of pity and compassion for a doomed child."¹⁶

Regardless, however, of which version came first—and this is likely to remain unresolved—each remains distinct.¹⁷ *The Wishing Tree* remained unknown to the general public, as Brodsky explains, until its appearance in the April 8, 1967, issue of the *Saturday Evening Post*, which was then followed three days later by the Random House first trade printing as a novella. (Random House first published five hundred copies of a numbered limited edition in 1964.) Brodsky contends that the Random House trade edition is a distinct version of the "Victoria" text, with which the anonymous editor takes too many editorial liberties.[18] For the purposes of this essay, however, I have chosen to employ the Random House edition, as this still remains the version most accessible to the reading public.[19]

The Wishing Tree's plot has a dream-vision framework: in brief, a strange boy with golden eyes visits a young girl, Dulcie, on her birthday and leads her on a fantastic journey to find the mythical wishing tree. Initially consisting of her little brother, Dicky, her neighbor George, and Alice, Dulcie's traveling cohort expands to include an old man, Egbert, and Alice's long-lost husband, Exodus, who had never returned home from fighting in the Great War. Along the way the group is able to make individual wishes on the leaves of a mellomax tree, and though some of these wishes prove delightful, others harbor potentially dangerous consequences. Presumably composed quite soon before the inception of *The Sound and the Fury*, although it is impossible to ascertain an exact time frame for the text's incubation and revisionary process, *The Wishing Tree* shares some thematic preoccupations with Faulkner's revered modernist tour de force. John Ditsky claims that Faulkner rediscovers the fictional potential of his native soil in *The Wishing Tree* and that this text helps release the creative energies that precipitate the astounding innovation of *The Sound and the Fury*.[20] Parallels between the two narratives include significant affinities between Dulcie and Caddy: both climb out of windows, both are brave, and both look after their younger brothers. Indeed, Dulcie may well function as what James Ferguson calls "a kind of first draft of Faulkner's 'heart's darling.'"[21] Though this text serves, to an extent, as a site that resonates with conceptualizations of childhood explored more explosively in *The Sound and the Fury*, *The Wishing Tree* reveals how, in writing for a child, Faulkner taps into his creative potential at a pivotal point in his career. As Reynolds suggests, "Writing for children releases visionary potential during periods of upheaval and uncertainty."[22] The estranging experience that results from writing for children and from a childish perspective, from thinking about childhood and the desires of the child reader, gives children's literature a transformative power that fosters the exploration of defamiliarizing perspectives and encourages radical experimentation in art.

Indeed, *The Wishing Tree*'s experiments with childish perspective make the text a worthy locus for investigating a burgeoning modernist's indebtedness to childhood as a source of artistic inspiration. *The*

Wishing Tree functions as a textual hotbed of fantasy, dreams, innovation, and the imaginary that helps Faulkner develop his modernist craft, and he demonstrates an astute understanding of what will appeal to the child's imagination.[23] Faulkner employs the dream motif, a common one in children's literature, which, according to Reynolds, "reflects the modernist concern with the inner world of the self and the operations of the psyche, at the same time gesturing toward such typical interests of literary modernism as the potential of narrative to convey the subjective and shifting experience of time passing."[24] In addition to employing the dream-vision framework, *The Wishing Tree* revolves around wish-fulfillment. The text, then, seemingly owes a debt of inspiration to Lewis Carroll's *Alice's Adventures in Wonderland*. Juliet Dusinberre explains that writers at the forefront of literary modernism were from the generation that grew up reading *Alice's Adventures in Wonderland* and that their concerns with "mastery over language, structure, vision, morals, characters and readers" are based in part upon that childhood reading.[25] Although Dusinberre does not explicitly reference *The Wishing Tree* in her book-length study of how children's literature prepares the way for modernism, Faulkner's text bolsters her argument.[26] The central alignment between these two texts revolves around wish-fulfillment and questions of desire. Alice, like Dulcie, witnesses her wishes actualized and discovers their implications. This fulfillment sometimes proves disconcerting, dangerous even, which disrupts predominant assumptions about the simplicity, security, and pleasure of childhood. *The Wishing Tree*, a fecund site for developing the author's imaginative capabilities, demonstrates that childhood is not so facile or safe as it seems on the surface. There are hints of a darkness to come, a heaviness that will shroud most of Faulkner's work that engages childhood.

Indeed, there persists a weight, "an air of fatality," as Ditsky puts it, about this text that incites the reader to wonder: is this children's literature?[27] Philip Weinstein, in evaluating Faulkner's interest in narrating childhood as the genesis of *The Sound and the Fury*, writes in his biography *Becoming Faulkner* that "childhood wrought upon [Faulkner] feelings of incapacity, of being among others who were big" and that "to narrate [the] experience of childhood would require an unconventional sense of how things occurred," an awareness that "what namelessly assaults the child, in the moment of now, has its nameable roots in what occurred earlier, before the child was born."[28] Though the Compson children succumb in precisely this way to the weight of historical and familial forces beyond their control, and though Faulkner brilliantly reveals their awareness of their disempowered status, in *The Wishing Tree*, he seemingly creates a narrative space where children retain a sense of power, where wishes are fulfilled in equal fashion for children and for adults. Yet though Faulkner develops a narrative space in which imaginative fantasy allows for a temporary invalidation of adult power over children, he tempers this fantasy with history's heft, exerting the pressure of adult choices that impact children's lives, forces beyond the child's control. Like the Compson children to come, the children of *The Wishing Tree* must confront the consequences of adult mistakes. Even in a text written for a child audience, Faulkner does not depart from the dense historical awareness that saturates his literary output. Despite *The Wishing Tree*'s powerful sense of fantasy, replete with imaginary creatures like the gillypus and human bodies shrinking and growing depending on what they wish for—a clear nod to *Alice's Adventures in Wonderland*—Faulkner punctuates the narrative's imaginative dream structure with key invocations of the historical crises of the Civil War and World War I, events that retain poignant psychic resonance for his characters.

The text's specific references to the Great War and the Civil War offer a point of connection between two male characters who exist on the social margins of 1920s southern society. In a profound exchange, Egbert, the old man whom Alice repeatedly deems white trash, and Alice's newly returned husband, Exodus, reflect on their shared war experiences. As the two men compare war stories, they concur that "they're all about alike" (46) but acknowledge that they must have fought in different wars. Egbert claims, "They came right down in my pappy's pasture and fought the war I went to. . . . And there was another war I went to. It was at a place named Seven Pines" (47). Exodus fights his war "across the big up and down water. . . . I don't know how in the world folks ever dammed up a pond that big. Nor what they can do with it. That water 'ud hol' all the excursion boats in the rentire world" (46–47). When Dulcie asks Egbert, "Who won the war you were in?" (47), he replies, "I don't know, ma'am. . . . I didn't" (48), whereupon Exodus rejoins, "That's right, too. . . . I never seed a soldier yet that ever won anything in a war." Ultimately, Egbert and Exodus conclude that all wars are the same and commiserate over a mutual sense of powerlessness that becomes resonant in light of the fact that *The Wishing Tree*'s entire cast of adult characters retains only marginal social power based on their race and class positions. Alice, Egbert, and Exodus, like the children, Dulcie, Dicky, and George, find common ground in their experience of power-lessness. In this way, they are all positioned to level a critique at those in power who have controlled history's course and made violent and often selfish choices that impact the future. Despite this war critique, though, Exodus and Egbert engage in exaggerated reminiscences about their heroic exploits. Egbert exclaims, "I bet I wouldn't be scared of a hundred enemies. . . . I bet I'd just ride right into 'em and slice 'em in two with a sword like this" (52). Egbert's verbal bravado, however, possesses dangerous consequences, as his posturing inspires Dicky, the youngest of the crew, to wish for a weapon of his own, which he then employs to slice Egbert's gillypus in two. Dicky's violent actions cause him to shrink down to a size "no bigger than a lead soldier" (59), and his traveling companions shrink as well in a gesture of solidarity and to offer him protection. Egbert's temporary glorification of masculinist fantasies thus endangers the entire group by influencing a child not yet old enough to understand the implications of his actions.

By infusing his text with war criticism, Faulkner perhaps meant his child readers to see through the heroic illusion of war, offering them a place of presumed simplicity from which to critique adult relations and impart a lesson about abuses of power. If so, *The Wishing Tree* confounds assumptions about good children's literature as ahistorical; the text instead demands attention to its historicity, to its intense involvement in the moment of its cultural production. Why this blend of fantasy and historical reality? Why this invocation of war and violence in a book written for a child? Faulkner's text works to imbue the child reader with a sense of historical consciousness, to acknowledge the child's vulnerability to historical machinations precipitated by adults but also to recognize that the child bears the promise and the weight of a more hopeful future.

Faulkner remains acutely attuned to how the child exists implicated in a complex web of historical forces. In *The Wishing Tree*, he refuses to generate children's literature that serves as an escape from the pressures of modernity, instead immersing the child subject in history's import. This text, crafted for specific southern child subjects, engages the region's historical burden, its psychic inheritance, through references to war. Not even the child—or perhaps, especially not the child—can elude the infringements of this burden, its intrusions upon the present. Faulkner seems particularly mindful of the child's susceptibility to forces beyond its control, yet he simultaneously accords children awareness of how the past continues to reverberate. Interestingly, Faulkner imparts this sense of historical consciousness to the child to demonstrate that the child is not a pure, clean slate, symbolic of unhindered futurity, but rather a subject impacted by the choices of those who came before it. In this way, Faulkner participates in shattering the myth of childhood innocence, a myth being addressed across multiple registers in the early twentieth century. He recognizes all too keenly the child's social and symbolic burden—the ascription of innocence—and its fraught position suspended between past, present, future.

Though Faulkner demonstrates an unusual sensitivity to the child's position as harbinger of utopian futurity, this awareness doesn't alter the fact that his text possesses a future orientation, one with personal implications. Faulkner clearly links a sense of historical consciousness to the transmission of values; in short, the text is meant to instruct. *The Wishing Tree* is not simply a wish-fulfillment fantasy in which characters realize their desires; rather, Faulkner constructs a fable wherein the consequences of the characters' wishes shape a path for future behavior in readers. This distinction becomes crucial when considering the ultimate message this slim book imparts: "People who care for and protect helpless things cannot have selfish wishes" (77). The question Dulcie poses to the golden-eyed Maurice at the outset of the tale—"Who are you?" (6)—is one that the author seems to be simultaneously posing to the child reader. Despite gesturing toward the inescapable unevenness in power dynamics between children and adults, Faulkner's fable encourages the child reader to fashion herself into the person she wishes to be by learning from adult corruption.

Significantly, this message is directed toward a specific child, one whom the author hopes to include in his family, to make his stepdaughter, to become implicated in his own future. *The Wishing Tree* thus emerges as a fascinating site of desire—one rich not only with national and regional implications but with ramifications familial and personal. The text reveals further multiplicities, depths, and resonances when it's imagined as addressed to two audiences: the child herself, Victoria, and Estelle, whom Faulkner was again courting at the time of the text's composition.[29] Seen in this dual light, the text takes on another layer of complexity, as it may have been meant to aid in securing a desired future for the author.[30] *The Wishing Tree*, then, produces a powerful example of cross-writing, a crucial concept in childhood studies theorized by U. C. Knoepflmacher and Mitzi Myers as "any text that activates a traffic between phases of life we persist in regarding as opposites."[31] Cross-written texts contain "a dialogic mix of older and younger voices" and often address both children and adults.[32] Addressing both audiences, *The Wishing Tree* additionally offers a polyphony of adult and child voices. What message, then, might the fable impart to Estelle, if she persists as the shadow audience, the covert adult behind the text? Posing this question, though, only raises the related issue of Faulkner's motive in writing for a child: if power dynamics are always at the crux of relations between children and adults, is this text a seduction of sorts, captivating both the child and her mother?

As *The Wishing Tree* draws to a close, Dulcie awakens safe in her bed to her mother's caress, full of anticipation for her birthday spoils and the promise of another year. The mother in the text appears shadowy and ethereal, carefully waking her child: "Dulcie's mother was beautiful, so slim and tall, with her grave unhappy eyes changeable as seawater and her slender hands that came so softly about you when you were sick" (81). This representation aligns with Estelle's physical appearance and mannerisms; Dulcie's mother, clearly preoccupied with worrisome thoughts, evokes the personal circumstances that attended Estelle's upcoming divorce from Cornell Franklin. Notable, too, is that the text makes no reference to a father. Despite her "grave unhappy eyes," however, Dulcie's mother offers a nurturing and comforting presence. Through its reference to maternal hands "that came so softly about you when you were sick," the fable reflects Victoria's experience of being sick on her birthday.[33] If Estelle was meant to see herself in Dulcie's mother, she would find a favorable comparison. Through feeling her mother's presence, the child departs the dreamworld and reenters reality securely ensconced in her bed. *The Wishing Tree*, like many other narratives written for children, thus follows the pattern of home, and indeed (bed)room, as point of origin and return. Ultimately, home is portrayed as a safe space, a place of comfort and respite, a place the author himself seeks to occupy.

Reconsidering *The Wishing Tree*'s unique contributions to both modernist writing and children's literature ultimately allows for a more capacious understanding of the potentially generative space between them. By reshaping how we think about Faulkner's investments in children and childhood, the text—his only tale written explicitly for a child audience—becomes crucial not just for Faulkner scholars but for scholars of childhood studies, too. What can we learn from neglected children's books by modernist authors? What can we surmise about childhood in the early twentieth century? Or childhood in the South at that historical moment? One of our greatest American writers shed important light on these questions in a text that breaks down universalist attitudes toward childhood by engaging a specific biological and historical child—not an imagined one—as its audience, a child with whom the author retains personal ties. What sets *The Wishing Tree* apart is not only that it critiques adult power dynamics (through its references to war) but also that it proposes to the child reader that children are not simply powerless and prey to an adult world. Rather, they are active agents and participants in culture-making—a position not often gleaned from the works that Faulkner directed toward an adult audience. *The Wishing Tree* deserves our critical attention for its remarkable potential to foster cross-disciplinary dialogue between modernist studies, childhood and children's literature studies, and Faulkner studies alike.

NOTES

I would like to thank the Oregon Humanities Center at the University of Oregon for granting me a Graduate Research Support Fellowship to attend the 2014 Faulkner and Yoknapatawpha Conference. I also wish to express my gratitude to Mark Whalan for comments on an earlier version of this essay.

    1. Karin Westman, "Children's Literature and Modernism: The Space Between," *Children's Literature Association Quarterly* 32.4 (Winter 2007): 284.

    2. Karin Westman, "Beyond Periodization: Children's Literature, Genre, and Remediating Literary History," *Children's Literature Association Quarterly* 38.4 (Winter 2013): 465.

    3. Quoted in Westman, "Beyond Periodization," 466–67.

    4. Westman, "Beyond Periodization," 467.

    5. Karen Sánchez-Eppler, "Childhood," in *Keywords for Children's Literature*, ed. Philip Nel and Lissa Paul (New York: New York University Press, 2011), 37.

    6. Some of the most thorough and excellent resources on the topic of modernism and childhood include Sally Shuttleworth, *The Mind of the Child: Child Development in Literature, Science, and Medicine, 1840–1900* (Oxford, UK: Oxford University Press, 2010) and Carolyn Steedman, *Strange Dislocations: Childhood and the Idea of Human Interiority, 1780–1930* (Cambridge, MA: Harvard University Press, 1995). For work centered on childhood in America, see Caroline Levander and Carol Singley, eds., *The American Child: A Cultural Studies Reader* (New Brunswick, NJ: Rutgers University Press, 2003); Steven Mintz, *Huck's Raft: A History of American Childhood* (Cambridge, MA: Harvard University Press, 2004); and David Macleod, *The Age of the Child: Children in America, 1890–1920* (New York: Twayne, 1998). For work on childhood, memory, and modernism, see Lorna Martens, *The Promise of Memory: Childhood Recollection and Its Objects in Literary Modernism* (Cambridge, MA: Harvard University Press, 2011).

    7. See Jonathan Fineberg, ed., *Discovering Child Art: Essays on Childhood, Primitivism, and Modernism* (Princeton, NJ: Princeton University Press, 1998) for helpful discussions of the modernist employment of childish perspective in the visual arts. John Carlin's essay "From Wonder to Blunder: The Child Is Mother to the Man" is particularly useful for its exploration of how the "modernists took the romantics' use of the child as a metaphor of pure vision to its logical conclusion by using it to undermine the form of traditional art and not just the content" (245).

    8. Noel Polk, *Children of the Dark House: Text and Context in Faulkner* (Jackson: University Press of Mississippi, 1996), 31.

    9. Wesley Morris and Barbara Alverson Morris, "A Writing Lesson: The Recovery of Antigone," in *William Faulkner,* The Sound and the Fury: *An Authoritative Text, Backgrounds and Contexts, Criticism*, ed. David Minter, rev. ed. (1987; repr., New York: W. W. Norton & Company, 1994), 404.

    10. Faulkner scholars have noted his preoccupation with childhood experienced as trauma, as his fictional children labor under the weight of troubled familial, national, and racial pasts. In addition to Polk, see David Vanderwerken, *Faulkner's Literary Children: Patterns of Development* (New York: Peter Lang, 1997), for a reading of Faulkner as a "poet of crippled childhood" (20).

    11. Louis Brodsky, "A Textual History of William Faulkner's 'The Wishing-tree' and 'The Wishing Tree,'" *Studies in Bibliography* 38 (1985): 330–74.

    12. Nancy Hargrove, "Faulkner's *The Wishing Tree* as Children's Literature," *Children's Literature Association Quarterly* (1991): 132–40.

    13. John Ditsky, "William Faulkner's *The Wishing Tree*: Maturity's First Draft," *The Lion and the Unicorn* 2.1 (1978): 56–64.

14. Brodsky, "A Textual History," 330–31.

15. Ibid., 339–41.

16. Joseph Blotner, ed., *Selected Letters of William Faulkner* (New York: Random House, 1977), 421.

17. The two versions possess distinct titles. The text presented to Margaret Brown is called *The Wishing-Tree*, and the Victoria version, with one exception, is referred to as *The Wishing Tree*. One of the most striking differences between the texts is that the young female protagonist has different names: in the Brown version, she is called Daphne; in the Victoria version she is referred to as Dulcie (Brodsky, 338). In addition, the Brown version contains 11,100 words and the Victoria version consists of 9,858 words (Brodsky, 339). As discussed earlier in-text, Brodsky attributes this variation in length to Faulkner's revision efforts to distill and refine his prose style.

18. Ibid., 335–36.

19. William Faulkner, *The Wishing Tree* (New York: Random House, 1967). All further references to this edition will be cited parenthetically in the text by page number. Brodsky does make a compelling case for the potential problems with the Random House edition, claiming that it presents an adulterated text edited with a 1960s audience in mind, one acutely susceptible to the derogatory racial language common in the 1920s South (342). Regrettably, it is not within the scope of my essay to engage fully with the differences between the Brown and Victoria versions, though I can imagine an alternative project that thinks through how these changes reflect the author's awareness of the particular child subject for whom he was writing.

20. Ditsky, "William Faulkner's *The Wishing Tree*," 59.

21. James Ferguson, *Faulkner's Short Fiction* (Knoxville: University of Tennessee Press, 1991), 27. Ferguson, like Ditsky, notes the interesting relationship between *The Wishing Tree* and works dealing with the Compsons, particularly *The Sound and the Fury* and "That Evening Sun."

22. Kimberley Reynolds, *Radical Children's Literature: Future Visions and Aesthetic Transformations in Juvenile Fiction* (New York: Palgrave Macmillan, 2007), 14.

23. Faulkner's biographers have often noted his affection for children. Philip Weinstein, in *Becoming Faulkner: The Art and Life of William Faulkner* (New York: Oxford University Press, 2010), observes that Faulkner's "tenderness toward children was notable his entire life" (44), and references Faulkner's service as scoutmaster for a local Boy Scout troop. See also Dean Faulkner Wells, *The Ghosts of Rowan Oak: William Faulkner's Ghost Stories for Children* (Oxford, MS: Yoknapatawpha Press, 1980), for a delightful recounting of the ghost tales that Faulkner shared with the children of Oxford.

24. Reynolds, *Radical Children's Literature*, 25–26.

25. Qtd. in Kimberley Reynolds, "Modernism," in *Keywords for Children's Literature*, ed. Philip Nel and Lissa Paul (New York: New York University Press, 2011), 153. It is also fascinating to note here that Faulkner was given Thomas Dixon's *The Clansman: An Historical Romance of the Ku Klux Klan* (1905) by his first-grade teacher, Miss Annie Chandler. As Weinstein suggests, "to offer this book—as pedagogical encouragement—to one of her most promising students speaks volumes about racial norms in the early twentieth-century South" (46), and perhaps, too, speaks to Faulkner's awareness of the southern child's historical burden.

26. Juliet Dusinberre, *Alice to the Lighthouse: Children's Books and Radical Experiments in Art* (London: Macmillan Press, 1987).

27. Ditsky, "William Faulkner's *The Wishing Tree*," 60.

28. Weinstein, *Becoming Faulkner*, 48.

29. I would like to thank Jay Watson for bringing this point of interest to my attention at the Faulkner and History Conference.

30. See Judith Sensibar's *Faulkner and Love: The Women Who Shaped His Art* (New Haven, CT: Yale University Press, 2009) for an expansive and illuminating biographical portrait of Estelle Faulkner.

31. U. C. Knoepflmacher and Mitzi Myers, "From the Editors: 'Cross-Writing' and the Reconceptualizing of Children's Literary Studies," *Children's Literature* 25 (1997): viii.

32. Ibid., vii.

33. Sensibar, *Faulkner and Love*, 460.

The Noble Experiment?
Faulkner's Two Prohibitions

CONOR PICKEN

William Faulkner's *Sanctuary* and its "sequel" *Requiem for a Nun* use the historical bookends of Prohibition and the Sobriety Movement to interrogate the South's static reaction to social change. The novels feature Temple Drake and Gowan Stevens, whose alcoholic drinking in *Sanctuary* reflects the failures of what was called "the Noble Experiment," while their abstention from booze in *Requiem for a Nun* defines one of Prohibition's legacies in the form of recovery. Prohibition was considered politically progressive in its aim to "cure" the American alcoholic republic and restore domestic order. Typified by the rise to prominence of Alcoholics Anonymous by midcentury, the Sobriety Movement successfully retooled the temperance paradigm by conceiving of alcoholism as a physiological disease rather than a disease of the will. By historicizing Temple's and Gowan's experiences through alcoholism and recovery in a specifically southern context, Faulkner challenges the progressive intents of what I call his two Prohibitions.

The Eighteenth Amendment to the Constitution, also known as Prohibition or the Volstead Act, changed the way that people imbibed and the way that the act of drinking was perceived. For the social economy of *Sanctuary*, these changes in patterns of consumption expose the hypocrisy of Faulkner's South: alcohol was demonized as morally wrong by some (think Narcissa and the meddling Baptists) yet recklessly consumed by many. Faulkner's brutal depiction of alcohol and drinking exposes Prohibition as a failure in its progressive aims to rid America of the Demon Rum that affected both public health and domestic stability.[1] Temperance reformers conceived of the domestic problem as drunken men squandering their money on liquor before returning home, bleary-eyed and abusive. Prohibition's aim was to protect women from men and men from themselves, a noble cause to be sure, though one that assumed naively that Prohibition meant *prohibition*.

In viewing Prohibition as the legislative disaster that it was, then, Temple Drake is collateral damage. Within and beyond the town limits of *Sanctuary*'s Oxford, Mississippi, drunken threats to her being are so ubiquitous that they become invisible, and there is little reason to suspect that Gowan Stevens might pose her danger. But this is Prohibition, a time when drinking "likely increased among young and educated city dwellers, in whose sophisticated circles heavy drinking was not merely tolerated, but actively encouraged."[2] Gowan's "education" at the University of Virginia is notable as a place where they "teach you how to drink," a practice to which he remains fully committed.[3] On the morning after a bender, Gowan first meets Temple for a planned trip to a baseball game in Starkville. His disheveled appearance elicits Temple's horrified reaction: "'You're drunk. . . . You filthy pig'" (36). And drunk he is, for Gowan's imbibing reaches frightening proportions, obliterating the line between chivalric southern drinker and reckless alcoholic. His foolish pursuit of liquor lands the couple in the company of Lee Goodwin's roughneck moonshining crew, Popeye among them. Here at the Old Frenchman Place, any inherited social currency Gowan possesses is rendered valueless when he naïvely enters the complex network of underground booze. Gowan's alcoholic consumption makes his pursuit of the liquid prop meant to affirm his identity as southern gentleman all the more dangerous, and he finally "abandons Drake with no second thought—an inverted white knight."[4]

Temple's alcoholic transformation is precipitated by an environment that drew women to booze, something historian Daniel Okrent calls "one of the astonishments of Prohibition, a shock both severe and enduring."[5] Her newfound attraction to gin and cigarettes might merely signal a new drinking demographic emerging at this time were it not for the circumstances—the trauma of rape and kidnapping—that have led her to it. How progressive can Prohibition be, the novel asks, if Temple ends up like *this*? Noble though the cause might have been, Prohibition fails to protect her, an irony compounded by the fact that her gentlemanly "white knight" is partially responsible for her situation. That the novel ends on "a gray day, a gray summer, a gray year" (316) serves Faulkner's critique of Prohibition as a harbinger of social progress in the South, as outdated modes of propriety circumscribed by class and gender leave Temple and Gowan susceptible to the Popeyes of the world. Volstead's enduring legacy for them is despair and alcoholism, the very conditions meant to be controlled by legislated prohibition.

Where *Sanctuary* shows the Noble Experiment's progressive failures through the fallout from Temple and Gowan's drinking, *Requiem for a Nun* considers alcoholism at midcentury as it relates to recovery. The disparity between *Requiem's* temporal action (eight years after the events of *Sanctuary*) and its actual publication (twenty years after the earlier novel) informs the most shocking aspect of the novel: Temple and Gowan are now married and neither drinks a single drop.[6] Much of *Requiem's* action, like *Sanctuary's*, centers on drinking, though Faulkner's characterization of it does not critique the southern tradition of aristocratic consumption but rather the ironic pitfalls associated with sobriety. Faulkner casts the Stevenses' struggles through an emerging preoccupation with alcoholism, making Gowan's admission of being "eight years on the wagon" akin to an Alcoholics Annoymous (AA) repentance (Faulkner, *Requiem*, 61). Temple, too, abstains from drink, though her sobriety remains precarious in a way distinct from her husband's.

After Repeal, a conceptual shift concerning the nature of alcoholism began to take place. In 1949, sociologist Herbert A. Bloch noted, "No longer does John Barleycorn constitute a moral problem, a reprehensible degenerate and an object of scorn or pity to the good ladies of the Temperance Union. *Instead he is now a sick man.* The celebrated target of the pulpits now becomes a matter of . . . the medical profession."[7] Indeed, a seismic paradigm shift radically changed how drinking was perceived in the national consciousness. The political fallout from Prohibition had exhausted a nation with more pressing concerns to address, and the strict moral polemics fueling wet-dry discourse no longer held sway. The Great Depression and World War II (among other factors) facilitated a post-Repeal sentiment wherein scientists of all fields "quite deliberately sought ways to depoliticize the alcohol problem, thus wresting it from the country's dry-wet tug of war."[8] One offshoot to this change was the birth of AA in 1935 and its rise to prominence in the 1940s and 1950s. Buzzwords emanating from the Sobriety Movement became ensconced in the cultural lexicon, as alcohol*ism* was now conceived of as a disease that necessitated recovery. And tentacles from the Sobriety Movement found their way into Faulkner's own life. Joseph Blotner notes that by 1953, Faulkner was officially diagnosed as "an acute and chronic alcoholic" who "could no longer taper off on beer and will power," and the deep unhappiness in his marriage only encouraged heavier consumption by him and Estelle.[9] This dynamic changed in the summer of 1955, however, when Estelle joined AA.[10] Her sobriety ushered in her acceptance not only of her alcoholism but also of the reality of her failing marriage.

Faulkner's marriage perhaps offers precedent for how he conveys Temple's and Gowan's situation by using the discourse of an evolved,

midcentury view of alcoholism and recovery. The novel's conclusion—
what Noel Polk calls "perhaps the darkest and least hopeful of all of
Faulkner's work"—might be reexamined in light of Temple and Gowan's
sobriety.[11] Faulkner's use of recovery as a metaphor for social change in
Requiem's South casts alcoholic consumption as the disease it is while
rendering sobriety as a perilous position for a husband and wife seeking to rectify how actions eight years prior have resulted in the murder
of their infant daughter by the "dope-fiend nigger whore" (Faulkner,
Requiem, 61), Nancy Manningoe. Temple's and Gowan's inability to rec-
oncile their present selves with their shameful pasts contributes to this
marital purgatory. What would help them navigate this malaise—what
they crave—is alcohol. Susan Zieger explains how persons like Gowan
and Temple come to represent "a mid-twentieth century US literary . . .
tradition of depicting white alcoholism and addiction as forms of mel-
ancholy self-medication to assuage guilt for past transgressions touching the core of elite white southern identity."[12] The cruel irony here is
that, being the alcoholics they clearly are, Temple and Gowan simply
cannot turn to the bottle for relief. Thus, their "recovered" drinking
selves remain unable to be "cured" of their role in the fallout presented
in this novel. Just as no measure of pleading to the Governor will pardon Nancy, Faulkner's use of recovery language merely proves ironic.
As alcoholic southerners navigating the backwaters of a region that
remained entrenched in racist hierarchy, they are incurable.

In act 1, scene 2 of *Requiem*, Temple, Gowan, and Gavin convene
in the Stevenses' living room after hearing the verdict against Nancy.
Gowan volunteers to fix drinks, noting that "I'm going to have one
myself. For a change. After eight years. Why not?" (51). The weight
of this admission is substantial: Gowan's actions in *Sanctuary* have, it
seems, shamed him into sobriety. He continues, "Nary a drink in eight
years; count 'em. So maybe this will be a good time to start again. At
least it won't be too soon." Almost as soon as he declares the end to his
self-mandated sobriety, however, he does something curious: "As though
not aware that he had done so, he sets his untasted glass back on the tray,
splashes water from the pitcher into a tumbler and hands the tumbler
to [Gavin] Stevens. . . . Temple has not touched hers either." The entire
scene is fraught with references to alcohol. What becomes immediately
noticeable in the exchange between Gowan and Gavin (whom I will
refer to as the text does, as "Stevens"), is Gowan's tug-of-war between
temptation and self-denial. His push and pull evokes the image of a man
reformed, though still seduced by the idea of a cocktail to take the edge
off. After Temple exits, the men speak:

GOWAN

Drink up. After all, I've got to eat supper and do some packing too. How about it?

STEVENS

About what? The packing, or the drink? What about you? I thought you were going to have one.

GOWAN

Oh, sure, sure. . . . Maybe you had better go on and leave us to our revenge.

STEVENS

I wish it could comfort you.

GOWAN

I wish to God it could. I wish to God that what I wanted was only revenge. (59)

What is left unsaid in this exchange comprises the gravity of the situation, as drinking and revenge become conflated as a metaphorical anodyne to Gowan's hopeless situation. Gowan gives no indication that he seriously considers consuming the drink, as his "Oh, sure, sure" comment implies. However, his suggestion that Stevens "leave us to our revenge" casts the significance of Gowan's potential imbibing in a darker light, marking the cocktail as another, more nefarious actor in the drama. Stevens's wish that "it" could comfort his nephew is freighted with the idea that Gowan's alcoholism makes such "revenge" impossible, since sobriety exempts "it" as a healthy coping mechanism. Though he resists the temptation, Gowan nevertheless acknowledges the physiological pull toward the bottle, going so far as equating his want for revenge with his desire for a sip. What follows this exchange is one source of Gowan's angst: other than the grief he feels for his murdered daughter, he has never forgiven Temple for her transgressions in *Sanctuary*, a fact that deepens his despair since their marriage is atonement for his previous actions.

Gowan's sobriety magnifies his masculine insecurities during a time of shifting gender roles related to drinking. Just as (problem) drinking was once equated with masculine virility, in these therapeutic times it is seen as an obstacle to prosperity:

Domestic ideology dovetailed with consumer capitalism to perpetuate the ideals of the independent male breadwinner and the subordinate female caretaker. . . . For both temperance advocates in the 1910s and therapeutic experts in the 1950s, a husband's alcohol consumption could signify the family's ability—or conversely, its inability—to partake of national plenty, to thrive during hard times, and to convert men's income into sustenance for women and children. (Rotskoff, 15)

Requiem takes place sometime in the late 1930s, a time when "Americans were quick to embrace reassuring images that buttressed men's self-identity as men. Therefore, they may have been less likely to support an ideology that dismissed drinking, a conventional sign of masculine prerogative" (46). The novel's publication date (1951) cannot be ignored when examining Gowan's compromised masculinity, especially since the relationship between drinking and gender underwent considerable conceptual revision after the Great Depression. By the 1940s masculine virility had been emptied of some of its significance among men who drank heavily, as the disease paradigm of alcoholism became widely accepted (Rotskoff, 79).

Where does this leave Gowan? His aversion to actual consumption consistently trumps his craving, suggesting that he has presently mastered the physiological hold of alcoholism. His sobriety still complicates his participation in the modern economy, however. Andrew Barr states that "the martini suited the demands of those people who climbed into the upper-classes in the 1940s and 1950s. The man who had 'arrived' needed a drink that was appropriate to his new position, and found it in the new martini."[13] Professional ascent became tied symbolically to the strength of the drink signifying such success. Although the narrative hardly trumpets Gowan's professional successes, it suggests that his greatest shortcomings are tied to his domestic situation and not to the workplace. Gowan intertwines these things—domestic despair and sobriety—in what amounts to an AA-style monologue explicitly incorporating "recovery" language:

> Eight years on the wagon—and this is what I got for it: my child murdered by a dope-fiend nigger whore. . . . You see? Eight years without the drink, and so I got whatever it was I was buying by not drinking, and now I've got whatever it was I was paying for and it's paid for and so I can drink again. And now I dont want the drink. . . . I had two children. I had to pay only one of them to find out it wasn't really costing me anything—Half price: a child, and a dope-fiend nigger whore on a public gallows: that's all I had to pay for immunity. (Faulkner, *Requiem*, 61)

Gowan repents through sobriety for his part in Temple's victimization, a figurative cost meant to "buy" forgiveness. This investment in sobriety pays no dividends, however, and his penance only begets more grief and suffering. Now that he feels his sacrifice should be recognized, he cannot bring himself to drink. A "recovered" Gowan, however, remains suspended in the ambiguity of the midcentury drinking culture where sobriety—despite legitimate, AA-modeled treatment gaining ground—restricts access in the professional sphere. Regardless, there is still the source of his social purgatory to consider, the person whose actions seemingly prevent him from forgiving himself: Temple.

As Gowan's confession unfolds, he admits that "marrying [Temple] was purest Old Virginia" (63). The problem, he comes to realize, was that *this* time and place is not Old Virginia, and thus that Temple's sexual indiscretion is not something that anachronistic chivalry can undo. As the stage darkens, Gowan pleads to no one in particular, "So help me, Christ. . . . . . So help me Christ" (65). His cries parallel how "doomed" his situation appears to be, and the "help" he needs speaks to the precarious state of his sobriety. Unfulfilled by Nancy's verdict and unable to drink, Gowan is left to appeal to a Higher Power, perhaps the same one responsible for his sobriety.[14] Gowan might be sober, but he is hardly recovered. Bound by his physiological disease and his metaphorical one—exclusion from Jefferson's drinking elite and indifference toward the social implications of Nancy's crime (a point I highlight later)—Gowan will likely never be "cured," rendering sobriety little more than another means by which Faulkner depicts "progress" ironically, particularly for a man who refers to Nancy Manningoe repeatedly as a "dope-fiend nigger whore."

Where the novel reflects the emerging Sobriety Movement through the language of recovery, it also illustrates a shifting perception of women drinkers at this time. After Repeal, drinking became dissociated from the idea of social disintegration, instead cleaving to a midcentury ethos incorporating psychiatry into the Recovery Movement.[15] Psychiatry strongly influenced the culture of sobriety, particularly as it related to the perception of women drinkers, a demographic that underwent conceptual revision after Repeal. Michelle McClellan notes that "nineteenth-century associations of alcohol and female sexuality had often focused on the image of the prostitute," while "mid-twentieth-century discourse held that any woman could be linked with a host of social problems, often defined in medical terms, including frigidity, promiscuity, and homosexuality" (287). Long ignored (or unseen) as problem drinkers, middle-class female consumers did not fall so easily into such categories after Repeal. The link between sexuality and drinking still resonated, though, and the culture of psychiatry often ascribed alcoholism in women to past sexual encounters. With women drinkers now an acknowledged category, they assumed the destructive place in the realm of middle-class domesticity formerly occupied by the men. Now that Gowan is a sober man, in other words, the location of the Stevenses' drunken threat shifts to Temple.

Collapsing categories of race and class, the woman alcoholic became a singular entity, "itself read as a sign of social disintegration" (269). Moreover, such social disintegration issued not only from within the domestic sphere but from the public sphere, where women had greater access to professional opportunity. The improvement in women's professional prospects begat the same sort of problem drinking that once plagued men and abject women only, suggesting that "women's alcohol use was symptomatic of . . . unwelcome social changes" (275). Progress for women was double-edged in that it provided professional opportunity, but in so doing it brought the same alcoholic temptations once reserved for men. Perceptions of alcoholism were still inflected by gender, as woman alcoholics were thought to be more diseased than their male counterparts: "Even as [many psychiatrists of the 1940s] maintained that alcoholism was less common among women than among men because of regulatory gender norms, many doctors concluded that those women who did become alcoholic were therefore, by definition, sicker than their male counterparts" (277). This discrepancy has profound consequences in *Requiem*, as the "sickness" associated with alcoholism assumes a specifically female form in Temple and ushers in deeper, more permanent fallout for the stability of the Stevens family.

"Mrs Gowan Stevens" (Faulkner, *Requiem*, 80) is haunted by actions eight years prior. Mourning the death of her daughter and racked with guilt, she self-medicates yet like her husband cannot bring herself to drink. Temple is not characterized as an alcoholic in the same way as Gowan, however. When Temple, Gowan, and Gavin enter in act 1, scene 2, she immediately orders Gowan, "Will you for God's sake please get me a drink?" (48). Later, after setting her glass down, Temple instructs Gowan to "put ice in it this time, and maybe even a little water" (52). Then, however, without tasting the cocktail, she decides, "I dont want it. I want some milk" (54). The dialogue and stage notes share Temple's detailed preoccupation with the ritual of drinking, though Faulkner omits the same recovery jargon he uses to characterize Gowan. Temple's aversion to the drink defines her disease in a way informed by class and gender categories in the South: where Gowan's alcoholism compromises his masculine professional standing, Temple's disease threatens the feminized realm of domesticity.

Gowan and Temple's marital union must be understood as a contributing factor in their diseases. As psychiatrists sought to define and diagnose the physiological dynamics of alcoholism, they conceived of the entire domestic situation—specifically the roles played by (alcoholic) husband and (sober) wife—as creating a diseased family. Early conceptions of alcoholism centered on men, and wives became necessary figures in the treatment of their husbands. Such women became known as *alcoholic's wives* (Rotskoff, 150). By the middle of the century, psychiatrists and nonmedical caseworkers alike agreed on the concept of the alcoholic marriage, wherein the alcoholic husband's disease is complemented— encouraged even—by his supposedly supportive wife.[16] The alcoholic marriage thus implicated husband and wife in the symbiosis of disease: "In the context of gender prescriptions for manly men and womanly women, experts viewed alcoholic husbands as failed men and their wives as deficient women. . . . Their drama of alcoholism played out when women, as well as men, failed to follow the proper psychological script" (156). Temple's notorious past suggests that her present misery can be traced to Gowan's previous actions and vice versa. Gowan's commitment to sobriety and his precarious place as a sober man in the modernizing social economy mean that Temple plays an integral role in his failure or success. According to the medical-historical understanding of the alcoholic marriage, however, Temple's symbolic location as supportive wife requires further examination, since her own past is not a sober one.

With the exception of the whiskey-for-milk moment in act 1, scene 2, Temple's anxiety about drinking is muted compared to Gowan's, effectively reconfiguring the contours of her alcoholism. During her confession to Stevens and the Governor, her role in the alcoholic marriage comes into focus, notably in her marital infidelity. Note her choice of words, referring to her "Virginia gentleman" (Faulkner, *Requiem*, 113) husband who went to university "trained . . . in gentility" (113–14) but "*relapsed* . . . into one of them at least because at least he married me as soon as he could" (114; emphasis added). The contrast between how Gowan and Temple conceive of the marriage circumstances is striking. Whether or not Gowan really believes that marrying Temple was "purest Old Virginia," the act (seemingly) validates him as an honorable southern man. Temple merely views the act as a "relapse," implying that Gowan's chivalry did no more good than another drink would have. Her tone shifts moments later, however, when she recounts the morning of the car accident at the Old Frenchman Place, confessing how "Gow—*we* ran it into the tree" (121; emphasis added). This admission belies the caustic tone moments earlier, as she now indicts herself as conspirator with Gowan eight years prior. Why? For Temple, literal sobriety provides no "cure" for what truly ails her. Her complicity in Gowan's disease stems from her affliction with a different kind of condition endemic to her gendered role in the alcoholic marriage, a condition Lori Rotskoff

calls *metaphorical alcoholism*. Of this condition, Rotskoff states, "If literal sobriety is the goal for people who have overconsumed alcohol to
dangerous extremes, the phrase 'emotional sobriety' suggests a person
who has 'overindulged' in unsound, excessive emotions. . . . [Instead of
uncontrollable drinking], the metaphorical alcoholic's neurosis presumably stems from unhealthy, uncontrolled *feeling*" (Rotskoff, 174). Temple
notes the absurdity in her husband's sober act of marital chivalry, but she
has a more difficult time reconciling her continuing role in the alcoholic
marriage, one that remains rooted in her actions from *Sanctuary*.

Temple's emotional sobriety has been tested throughout the marriage, most notably in her sexual liaisons with Pete (the brother of Red,
her lover from *Sanctuary*). Her infidelities symbolize what Kelly Lynch
Reames calls Temple's most damaging secret, "her open expression of
insatiable sexual desire for Red," eliciting society's "pervasive cultural
fear of unrestrained female sexuality."[17] Temple's sexuality contributes
to her own emotional excess and to Gowan's emasculation as both
cuckolded husband and sober professional. Her sexual dalliances also
undercut her (once) privileged status as a white southern woman by
linking her to Nancy Mannigoe. Michelle McClellan notes the relationship between alcoholic women and sex at midcentury: "Because of
longstanding stereotypes about women's sexual behavior, many experts
probably expected to find evidence of promiscuity among some alcoholic
women—those whose race, class, or upbringing made them . . . more
likely to engage in deviant sexual behavior, such as prostitutes and . . .
African American women" (286). Because Temple is not explicitly registered "sober" or "alcoholic," her deviant sexuality then supplants drinking as her pathological contribution to the alcoholic marriage. No less
damaging to her social or domestic status than Gowan's self-mandated
sobriety is to his personal or professional reputation, Temple's disease
proves to be emotional and not physiological.

Temple's emotional drunkenness and Gowan's dry drunkenness prevent them from meaningful engagement with the racial and class crisis
symbolized in the murder of their daughter by an African American
domestic servant. Where *Sanctuary* ironically casts the failures of Prohibition's "noble" intent, *Requiem*'s "prohibition," progress-as-sobriety,
meets its critique in Nancy Mannigoe. Temple mockingly identifies "the
Gowan Stevenses" as "so young and modern that all the other young
country-club set applauded when they took an ex-dope-fiend nigger
whore out of the gutter to nurse their children" (Faulkner, *Requiem*,
136). The true motive for employing Nancy, Temple reveals, is that
an "ex-dope-fiend nigger whore was the only animal in Jefferson that
spoke Temple Drake's language." Leigh Anne Duck clusters Temple and

Gowan alongside other Yoknapatawphans who, as "Old South partisans," demonstrate "no efforts toward or even interest in social change."[18] Their employing Nancy, for example, does not distract from their complicity in "maintaining the current role of the town jail as a way of constraining African Americans."[19] Temple and Gowan "seek, in cultivating a certain [Old South] notion of southern culture, to shape local social structures without ever having to engage in an argument about [racist, socially regressive] contemporary institutions." Indeed, Temple's relationship with Nancy smacks of racial paternalism, a worldview that Brannon Costello claims "commits white southerners to an attitude of sycophancy, a permanent performance that keeps them from meaningful engagement with the world and with each other."[20] Temple and Gowan's social justice remains inherently limited in that it was never more than charity in the first place. Their paternalistic gesture toward Nancy, then, further insulates them from addressing the realities of a racially unequal South. Temple identifies with Nancy as someone similar to her sexually, since, as an addict and "whore," Nancy differs from Temple in skin color only. Employing Nancy, then, stands exposed as the self-indulgent product of Temple's emotional drunkenness, Gowan's compromised form of sobriety, and the couple's racial paternalism.

The use of addiction and recovery in *Requiem* complicates Temple's pronouncement that all are "doomed" in the end (Faulkner, *Requiem*, 245). For Gowan, at least, sobriety signifies genuine progress made in the treatment of a physiological disease. Furthermore, as narratives of addiction and recovery evolved to reflect the midcentury medical-scientific model of alcoholism, sober emasculation in the workplace became less of an issue. While this development certainly makes Gowan's sobriety less of a gender and class handicap, it hardly pardons him for his complicity in the drama. Regardless of his sobriety, Gowan remains fundamentally incapable of recognizing how the South's backward cultural ethos has contributed to the tragedy befalling his family. Temple's addiction proves more elusive, as does any prescription for her personal redemption. At the very least, the tragedy and its fallout provide a measure of therapy for her personal ills. By the novel's end, however, any emotional "cure" seems undercut by her inevitable reimmersion in the alcoholic marriage as, after pronouncing doom for all, she robotically answers to Gowan's offstage beckoning.

NOTES

1. See Daniel Okrent, *Last Call: The Rise and Fall of Prohibition* (New York: Scribner, 2010) for a detailed social history of Volstead-era America.

2. John W. Crowley, *The White Logic: Alcoholism and Gender in American Modernist Fiction* (Amherst: University of Massachusetts Press, 1994), 40.

3. William Faulkner, *Sanctuary*, rev. ed. (1931; repr., New York: Vintage International, 1993), 32. Subsequent references to this edition will appear parenthetically in the text.

4. Louis Palmer, "Bourgeois Blues: Class, Whiteness, and Southern Gothic in Early Faulkner and Caldwell," *Faulkner Journal* 22, no. 1–2 (Fall 2006–Spring 2007): 128.

5. Okrent, *Last Call*, 211.

6. The use of terminology germane to the Recovery Movement situates the novel beyond its intended chronological setting. Faulkner chooses to set *Requiem* "between the two great wars," though this clearly does not exempt him from incorporating societal characteristics that postdate this period. See William Faulkner, *Requiem for a Nun* (1951; New York: Vintage, 1975), 46. Subsequent references to this edition will appear parenthetically in the text.

7. Quoted in Lori Rotskoff, *Love on the Rocks: Men, Women, and Alcohol in Post–World War II America* (Chapel Hill: University of North Carolina Press, 2002), 64; emphasis added by Rotskoff. Subsequent references to this edition will appear parenthetically in the text.

8. Ron Roizen, "How Does the Nation's 'Alcohol Problem' Change from Era to Era? Stalking the Social Logic of Problem-Definition Transformation since Repeal," in *Altering American Consciousness: The History of Alcohol and Drug Abuse in the United States, 1800–2000*, ed. Sarah W. Tracy and Caroline Jean Acker (Amherst: University of Massachusetts Press, 2004), 63–64.

9. Joseph Blotner, *Faulkner: A Biography* (1984; rpt., Jackson: University Press of Mississippi, 2005), 574.

10. Ibid., 612.

11. Noel Polk, *Faulkner's "Requiem for a Nun": A Critical Study* (Bloomington: Indiana University Press, 1981), xiii.

12. Susan Zieger, *Inventing the Addict: Drugs, Race, and Sexuality in Nineteenth-Century British and American Literature* (Amherst: University of Massachusetts Press, 2008), 101.

13. Andrew Barr, *Drink: A Social History of America* (New York: Carroll & Graf, 1999), 49–50.

14. The alcoholic's success through the Twelve Steps relies on a concept of God. Alcoholics Anonymous's *Twelve Steps and Twelve Traditions* (New York: Alcoholics Anonymous World Services, Inc., 1952) refers to God conceptually as a Higher Power. For example, Step Two states that recovering alcoholics "came to believe that a Power greater than ourselves could restore us to sanity" (25). Likewise, Step Eleven states, "Sought through prayer and meditations to improve our conscious contact with God *as we understood Him*, praying only for knowledge of His will for us and the power to carry that out" (96).

15. Michelle McClellan, "'Lady Tipplers': Gendering the Modern Alcoholism Paradigm, 1933–1960," in *Altering American Consciousness: The History of Alcohol and Drug Use in the United States, 1800–2000*, ed. Sarah H. Tracy and Caroline Jean Acker (Amherst: University of Massachusetts Press, 2004), 286. Subsequent references to this essay will appear parenthetically in the text.

16. One caseworker, Thelma Whalen, identified four "types" of alcoholic wives, each of whom transposed her own gendered insecurities onto her husband. Suffering Susan, Controlling Catherine, Wavering Winnifred, and Punitive Polly each "chose" their alcoholic spouses in order to meet distinct psychological needs (Rotskoff, 154). Susan and Winnifred played more passive roles in the marriage, where Catherine and Polly asserted their domestic authority more overtly. Temple eschews easy categorization under any of the four labels, due in part to her own struggles with alcohol and sex and in part to the fact that Gowan seems to have controlled his drinking. Had Whalen read *Requiem for a Nun*, she might have identified a fifth member of this notorious sorority: Tempted Temple. Susan, though, might come closest to Temple's role in the alcoholic marriage: Susan's "dominant characteristic was the need to punish herself," so she selected a husband whose own emotional baggage satisfied her own need to be miserable (154).

17. Kelly Lynch Reames, "'All That Matters Is That I Wrote the Letters': Discourse, Discipline, and Difference in *Requiem for a Nun*," *Faulkner Journal* 14, no. 1 (Fall 1998): 35.

18. Leigh Anne Duck, *The Nation's Region: Southern Modernism, Segregation, and US Nationalism* (Athens: University of Georgia Press, 2006), 224, 225.

19. Ibid., 226.

20. Brannon Costello, *Plantation Airs: Racial Paternalism and the Transformations of Class in Southern Fiction, 1945–1971* (Baton Rouge: Louisiana State University Press, 2007), 17.

Mr. Cowley's Southern Saga

Sarah E. Gardner

The story is familiar. Outraged by Faulkner's fading reputation, Malcolm Cowley—former literary editor at the *New Republic* and a consultant with Viking—set out to resuscitate the Mississippi author's career, offering to Americans a Faulkner who spoke to the confusions and anxieties of a nation coming out of depression and war. Other readers had understood Faulkner's relevance, Cowley maintained. "In France," he told anyone who would listen, "Faulkner is a god."[1] Cowley wanted to make Faulkner relevant in his own land; his *Portable Faulkner*, published in 1946 to wide acclaim by influential critics, was the culmination of his effort. In Cowley's hands, Faulkner was not the accumulator of "pointless horrors" as others had made him out to be. Rather, he was "the epic or bardic poet, a creator of myths that he weaves together into a legend of the South."[2]

In *The Portable Faulkner* Cowley tried to make sense of the "living pattern" that he saw running through Faulkner's work.[3] "Each novel, each long or short story," he explained, "seems to reveal more than it states explicitly and to have a subject bigger than itself."[4] As Edmund Wilson noted in his review, Cowley had "unscrambled" a complicated and elusive chronicle, thus providing order to the chaos.[5] In arranging Faulkner's works chronologically by order of the main action—and not by publication date—Cowley grounded the Yoknapatawpha saga in history and provided a narrative arc that, at least Wilson surmised, might have escaped the casual or uninformed reader. Indeed, the thread that ran through the selections connected each story to the others, thus relieving the reader of the demanding task of figuring out how the part—a single story or excerpt—related to the whole. Equally important, Cowley presented a Faulkner who addressed questions of abiding concern that transcended his "little postage stamp of native soil."[6] Faulkner might have written about provincials, Cowley contended, but he wrote for modern readers who, by the time *The Portable Faulkner* appeared, faced an uncertain future in the dawning nuclear age.

Robert Penn Warren said as much in his *New Republic* review: "Cowley's book, for its intelligence, sensitivity, and sobriety in the introduction, and for the ingenuity and judgment exhibited in the selections would be valuable at any time. But it is especially valuable at this time. Perhaps it can mark a turning point in Faulkner's reputation. That will be of slight service to Faulkner, who, as much as any writer of our place and time, can rest in confidence. He can afford to wait. But can we?"[7] Postwar readers needed Faulkner, Warren implied, and Cowley's timely anthology, by emphasizing continuance and endurance, offered an antidote to postwar pessimism and malaise.

Perhaps this story appeals because it looks forward, anticipating that which we know comes later: the Nobel Prize. We can almost hear Faulkner's acceptance speech in Warren's concluding paragraph. For here, Warren seemed to reference obliquely what Faulkner tackled head on, namely the crippling fear born out of the threat of nuclear conflagration: "The basest of all things is to be afraid," Faulkner reminded the next generation of writers. Forget the fear, he advised, "forget it forever." Leave no room in the "workshop for anything but the old verities and truths of the heart, the old universal truths lacking which any story is ephemeral and doomed—love and honor and pity and pride and compassion and sacrifice."[8] That is the Faulkner Cowley presented to postwar American readers. So the story goes.

To be sure, *The Portable Faulkner* was published to a postwar reading audience. Yet Cowley proposed the volume and compiled its readings during the war, when its outcome was still unknown. Scholarly attention to Faulkner's relevance in the atomic age has obscured the ways in which the anthology's table of contents and selections were artifacts of World War II. If the threat of apocalyptic annihilation influenced Cowley's drafting of the anthology's introduction, written toward the end of the book's production, wartime concerns and realities informed Cowley's editorial decisions.

This essay reexamines Cowley's efforts to resuscitate Faulkner's reputation by moving our attention away from the Faulkner who earned the esteem of influential critics, a familiar story that needs no rehearsing here. Instead, it looks at the ways in which Cowley used Faulkner to write a version of southern history that met the demands of a wartime book industry. The Faulkner that emerges from Cowley's *Portable* was not the purveyor of the grotesque of the 1930s; nor was it the Faulkner of the late 1940s and 1950s who represented "the complexities and paradoxes of Cold War existential *angst*, artistic freedom, and unrelenting struggle."[9] Rather, it was the Faulkner who was needed in the national effort defined

by the Second World War and its aftermath, the autochthonous Faulkner
who loved the land and the people who inhabited it.

This last part was critical to Cowley's presentation of Faulkner. "I can
think of no other living American author," Cowley determined, "who
writes with the same intensity or who carries us so completely into a
world of his own."[10] Yet if Faulkner "invented and peopled" a place of his
own creation, the "theme" of his Yoknapatawpha novels was "real": the
decline of the plantation aristocracy; the rise of the new men "descended
from carpetbaggers and bushwhackers"; the grinding poverty of white
farmers; the racial violence; and "the slow bleeding of the land itself
and the decomposition of a whole society." So profound was Faulkner's
love for his native Mississippi "that its misfortunes are almost more than
he can bear, when he tortures himself into presenting them." Thus, the
Faulkner that Cowley wished to present to midcentury American readers sought not to shock or titillate but rather to create his own "comédie
humaine." By judiciously selecting stories and excerpts that contributed
to Faulkner's Yoknapatawpha saga, Cowley ensured that the Balzacian—
and not the Caldwellian—Faulkner emerged.

As Cowley set about his work, he was guided by two concerns of
the wartime book industry. The first was the push to encourage Americans—those on the home front as well as those who served on the front
lines—to read. An educated citizenry was the nation's best defense
against fascism and totalitarianism, so the reasoning went. Both the Book
Publishers' Bureau and the Council on Books in Wartime jointly sponsored public events, including talks and author luncheons, produced
and syndicated radio programs such as *Books Are Bullets*, and published
pamphlets and broadsides, all designed to encourage wartime reading.
The publishing industry also distributed more than 35,000,000 copies of
fiction and nonfiction to military personnel free of charge, first from contributions raised by national book drives and later through the Armed
Service Editions.[11]

Viking created the *Portable* series to meet this demand. The idea
came from Alexander Woollcott, a book critic, radio personality, and
journalist who had had some success editing anthologies for Viking in
the 1930s. At the war's start, Woollcott proposed an anthology of American prose and poetry designed specifically for American troops overseas.
The anthology served the twin purposes of reminding troops why they
fought and providing sustenance to the homesick. As the back cover
announced, the anthology was Woollcott's "present to the troops."[12]

Woollcott's *Portable* appeared in March 1943 with the inelegant and
cumbersome title: *As You Were: A Portable Library of American Prose
and Poetry Assembled for Members of the Armed Forces and Merchant*

Marine. If the title alone were not enough to tie the volume into wartime publishing efforts, the book jacket's back flap hammered home the point. Here Viking advertised another one of its titles, *Opportunities in the Armed Forces*, an encyclopedic guide "for the benefit of officers, enlisted men, and those about to be inducted." Even before the publishing firm had a chance to fully realize the success of Woollcott's anthology—and it proved quite profitable—the second volume, *The Portable Steinbeck*, hit the market a mere four months later. As with Woollcott's volume, Viking designed the Steinbeck anthology for "the men in the fighting forces."[13] Even so, the trade recognized its likely popularity with the general reader and *Publishers' Weekly* touted the anthology's sales potential in its weekly "Forecast for Buyers" column. *The Portable Hemingway*, edited by Cowley, appeared in 1944, the same year he began work on *The Portable Faulkner*. By the end of the war, Viking had published more than a dozen titles in its *Portable* series and had established one of the most lucrative wartime publishing ventures in the industry.

Cowley envisioned a *Portable Faulkner* that would take its place in the successful franchise and elevate Faulkner's standing at the same time. The first part of the equation seemed easy enough to complete, although it did require a bit of politicking on Cowley's part. The second was trickier. Cowley was well aware of the changes to publishing wrought by the war. Even when he found certain trends discouraging, such as the decline in the publication of new fiction, he nonetheless understood the acute pressure faced by the publishing industry. As Cowley observed in late 1943, "The public is buying books," although "not always the books that critics think it ought to be reading."[14] The challenge was to make Americans want to read Faulkner. Cowley knew this would be a tough sell. His initial pitch to Viking conceded as much: "I wish to God I could do [a *Portable* on] Faulkner, but I suppose booksellers are too down on him at present to make it commercially feasible."[15] Alas, Viking's Marshall Best concurred, at least initially.[16] Cowley needed to convince Viking of his project's viability. He primed the pump by writing two profiles, one for the *New York Times Book Review*, the other for the *Saturday Review of Literature*.[17] Both called for Faulkner's greater visibility. "It is time," Cowley declared in the *Book Review*, "to make a plea for William Faulkner. . . . We haven't so many good novelists in this country that we can afford to neglect one of our most distinguished talents."[18] Both essays had Faulkner's blessing. "I would like very much to have the piece done," he wrote Cowley in the spring of 1944. "I think (at 46) that I have worked too hard at my . . . trade, with pride but I believe not vanity, with plenty of ego but with humility too . . . to leave no better mark on this our pointless chronicle than I seem to be about to leave."[19]

Equally important, the two essays, the first of which appeared eighteen months before the anthology, served notice to the publishing industry of Cowley's larger intent. The real effort would come with Cowley's magnum opus, *The Portable Faulkner*.

Cowley's *Portable* was equally influenced by a second wartime concern, the book industry's preoccupation with presenting the nation's diversity and heterogeneity as constitutive to America's development. Allied victory, the industry routinely emphasized throughout the war years, would signal the triumph of American values and institutions, best encapsulated by Roosevelt's Four Freedoms. American tolerance and liberty stood against European fascism and totalitarianism. In order for this understanding to serve the war effort, the publishing industry had to think hard about the ways in which it presented the South to national and international audiences. After all, the South of the 1930s was hardly free from want or from fear. Neither was it a haven for political or religious dissent. Yet the war effort demanded that the South no longer be presented as the nation's number-one problem.

In 1942 the *Saturday Review of Literature* took up the industry's call. In an open letter "To the Trade," its editors announced a new series that would "help in the cultural inventory" of the nation's regions. Over the next twelve months, the magazine would turn over eight of its issues "to guest regional editors. Their job," the announcement explained, "will be to tell their story to America, to tell it through their writers and artists."[20] The following year, Chapel Hill sociologist Howard Odum and Richmond newspaper editor Virginius Dabney coedited one of these regional issues in an effort to recast the South's image. In their deft hands, the South was transformed from a land of racial violence and repression into a region with a long history of championing liberal thought. The South did not stand apart from the rest of the nation, the two editors maintained. Instead, it had played a significant role "in the building of America's cultural heritage."[21] Cowley undertook a similar project, presenting the South as a variant of—but not an exception to—the dominant narrative of American development. In Cowley's estimation, then, Faulkner's southernness was crucial to the national culture-building of the 1940s.

In order to pull off this project, Cowley knew that he would need to downplay that for which Faulkner was perhaps best known, "the raw head and bloody bones" school of fiction.[22] It would not be easy. Cowley tinkered with potential selections and their arrangement, compiling broad themes and the stories or novels that might fit each heading. One such wry list included: "Pregnant Women Going to their Goal Blindly," "Murders," "Abortion," "Suicide," "Insanity and Idiocy,"

"Shotgun Weddings," "Bestiality," "Castration," "Rape," "Lynching," "Cannibalism," "Misanthropy," "Arson," and "Necrophilia."[23] Such a volume might have had traction had it appeared in the 1930s, for it would have pandered to what Caroline Gordon had summarized as "the eastern critics' desire for examples of Southern degeneracy."[24] But this was 1944, not 1934, and Cowley understood, perhaps better than most, that such a volume would not do for a nation at war. (No one proposed a *Portable Caldwell*.) Americans did not need a Faulkner who exoticized or pathologized the South. This was no time for "corn cob cavaliers" or "futilitarians," although Cowley always understood *Sanctuary* to be about something more than Popeye's sadism.[25] Cowley did not intend to put forward Faulkner as a regional writer. Rather, Cowley sought to parlay Faulkner's regional reputation into a national one by suggesting that Faulkner's South was America.

Consider, then, Cowley's efforts to connect Faulkner with another American writer—not one of his contemporaries, however, such as Hemingway or Fitzgerald, nor one from his region. Cowley argued in the *Portable*'s introduction that the American writer Faulkner most resembled was Hawthorne, an author from another century and from another region, albeit one known for its own literary renaissance. The comparison was odd, Cowley conceded readily. "They stand to each other as July to December, as heat to cold, as swamp to mountain, as the luxuriant to the meager but perfect, as planter to Puritan; and yet," he continued, "Hawthorne had much the same attitude toward New England that Faulkner has to the South, together with a strong sense of regional particularity." In this sense, Hawthorne's "'lump of earth'" had more in common with Faulkner's "little postage stamp of native soil" than one might suspect. For Hawthorne, "It was more than a lump of earth," Cowley wrote; "it was a lump of history and a permanent state of consciousness." The same held true of the fictional Yoknapatawpha County for Faulkner. What linked these two writers was their shared commitment to their respective regions. Thus both men created "moral fables" while elaborating regional "legends."[26]

Cowley explained his packaging of Faulkner in the original introduction: "It had to have an aim other than merely to select the best of Faulkner's work."[27] In fact, Cowley admitted in the editor's note that prefaced the final section, "Modern Times," that the excerpt from *Light in August* was "not the best passage in that powerful novel."[28] That's because Cowley was not compiling an anthology to be "dipped into." Rather, he hoped readers would "go through it from beginning to end," as "one continuous story" that "retained something of the organic unity of Faulkner's legend."[29]

To this end, Cowley set out to "write" a history of Yoknapatawpha County from its founding up through World War II. Anyone who has read through Cowley's correspondence with Faulkner knows how exasperating and tiresome Faulkner found the entire affair. He agreed with the presentation of his material in principle, but he never quite understood Cowley's slavishness to details. Cowley insisted on pinning each of the selections to a specific date.[30] Faulkner found this plan absurd. Inconsistencies abounded in his work—not because he was sloppy or inattentive but because, as he put it, he did not "care much for facts, am not much interested in them, you cant stand a fact up, you've got to prop it up, and when you move to one side a little and look at it from that angle, it's not thick enough to cast a shadow in that direction."[31] A rather protracted discussion of young Ikkemotubbe and the appearance of the first steamboat on the Mississippi bewildered Faulkner. "I realised some time ago you would get into this inconsistency and pitied you. I suggest you make dates . . . as vague as possible."[32] Yet Cowley needed precision—not because he was uptight or fastidious but because he needed to make the "Southern saga" an American story. Faulkner's saga needed touchstones. In a radical repositioning of the South, Cowley was, in essence, constructing American history through that of Yoknapatawpha.

The selections—each one self-contained and telling a particular episode—certainly made that point. So too did the editor's notes that prefaced each section. Here Cowley recounted the effects of European encroachment on the frontier, the repercussions of Jacksonian Indian policy, the buying and selling of human flesh, the dying away of an old order, and the attendant ills of mechanization and modernization. In the most basic sense, these stories could have been set in Anywhere, USA. Yet they were not—and that is Cowley's point, Granville Hicks and Alfred Kazin, two critics Cowley had singled out for their misreadings of Faulkner, be damned.[33] Yoknapatawpha is as central to Faulkner as New England to Hawthorne or Paris to Balzac. "More than any other writer of talent in this country," Cowley jotted in his notes, Faulkner had a sense of place, "a love for the land in which he was born, a love for and [an] understanding of the people on that land, and—this is the reason for his violence—a feeling that people and land are being oppressed, that the people are oppressing one another, and that the outcome will be some bloody and tragic outbreak."[34] What could be more American than that?

In the end, *The Portable Faulkner* did contribute to the resurrection of Faulkner's reputation, but this revival had as much to do with the Viking series as it did with Cowley's creativity and the critics' favorable reception. The *Portables* sustained literature at a time when books went out of print and when publishers were loath to maintain extensive backlists or order reissues. The average life of a book, whether a success or a flop, lasted a literary season, about five months. Literary reputations came and went. Viking's Marshall Best hedged when Cowley first suggested *The Portable Faulkner*, not simply because Faulkner was considered publishing suicide by the mid-1940s but because Viking was already taking a gamble on another author who had "passed his peak of popularity," F. Scott Fitzgerald.[35] Best asked Cowley to hold tight. "We are trying a . . . Fitzgerald this Fall and it may show us what we can do to revive interest in a contemporary or recent author." Best wanted to wait until the salesmen's book orders came in on *The Portable Fitzgerald* before he green-lighted Cowley's project. In the meantime, though, Best encouraged Cowley to finalize the table of contents while he looked into the status of copyrights.

The rest is, as they say, publishing history. Viking's genius rested in developing promotional plans that marketed the *Portable* series—and not just individual titles—to a postwar reading audience.[36] To be sure, some of the authors represented in the series had secure literary reputations. But for others, including Steinbeck, Hemingway, Fitzgerald, and, of course, Faulkner, the Viking series ensured that their works stayed in circulation and were read by a new generation of readers. And as the reviews of *The Portable Faulkner* make clear, Cowley's reputation was elevated, too. Cowley had tried to convince Faulkner to agree to a marketing campaign that promoted *The Portable Faulkner* as "a new work by William Faulkner." The Mississippi writer would have none of it. "It's not a new work by Faulkner," he objected pointedly. To clarify matters, he added that it was, however, "a new work by Cowley."[37] Certainly reviewers recognized Cowley's herculean effort. To Cowley went the "distinction" of providing the first comprehensive survey of Faulkner's work. It took Cowley, Caroline Gordon claimed, to recognize the "living pattern" that runs through the Yoknapatawpha saga—and not the published volumes—as Faulkner's "real achievement."[38] It also took Cowley, Gordon continued, to acknowledge Faulkner's autochthony. "No land less implacable and brooding could have given him his spiritual geography," she explained. Swept up in Cowley's argument, she concluded her review by declaring that Faulkner so loved his land "that he is fearful for the well-being of every creature that springs from it." Faulkner needed Cowley. Cowley needed Faulkner. And both men needed Viking.

NOTES

1. See, for example, Cowley to Faulkner, Gaylordsville, CT, 9 August 1945, and Cowley to Marshall A. Best, Gaylordsville, CT, 25 May 1945, both in the Malcolm Cowley Papers, Newberry Library. Subsequent references to the Cowley Papers will appear under the abbreviation MCP.

2. Malcolm Cowley, introduction to *The Portable Faulkner*, ed. Malcolm Cowley, rev. ed. (1946; New York: Penguin Books, 2003), xxvii. Subsequently cited as "Introduction" (2003).

3. Ibid., xiv.

4. Ibid.

5. Edmund Wilson, "Books," *New Yorker*, July 27, 1946, 65.

6. William Faulkner, "The Art of Fiction" (1955), in *The Paris Review Interviews*, vol. 2, ed. Philip Gourevitch (New York: Picador, 2007), 57.

7. Robert Penn Warren, "Cowley's Faulkner," *New Republic*, August 26, 1946, 237.

8. William Faulkner, "Address upon Receiving the Nobel Prize for Literature," in *The Portable Faulkner*, ed. Malcolm Cowley, rev. ed. (1946; New York: Penguin Books, 2003), 649.

9. Lawrence H. Schwartz, *Creating Faulkner's Reputation: The Politics of Modern Literary Criticism* (Knoxville: University of Tennessee Press, 1988), 37.

10. Malcolm Cowley, "William Faulkner's Human Comedy," *New York Times Book Review*, October 29, 1944, 4.

11. See, for example, Bernard Smith, "Books for Democracy," *Publishers' Weekly*, September 20, 1941, 1077–79; and Molly Gutpill Manning, *When Books Went to War: The Stories That Helped Us Win World War II* (New York: Houghton Mifflin Harcourt, 2014), 31–74.

12. Alexander Woollcott, introduction to *As You Were: A Portable Library of American Prose and Poetry Assembled for Members of the Armed Forces and Merchant Marine*, ed. Alexander Woollcott (New York: Viking, 1943), xi.

13. "P.W. Forecast for Buyers," *Publishers' Weekly*, July 3, 1943, 50.

14. Malcolm Cowley, "The Literary Business in 1943," *New Republic*, September 27, 1943, 417–19; Cowley, "Books by the Millions," *New Republic*, October 11, 1943, 482–85.

15. Cowley to Marshall A. Best, Gaylordsville, CT, 29 July 1944, MCP.

16. Marshall A. Best to Cowley, [New York, NY], 3 August 1944, MCP.

17. Cowley, "William Faulkner's Human Comedy"; Malcolm Cowley, "William Faulkner Revisited," *Saturday Review of Literature*, April 14, 1945, 13–16.

18. Cowley, "William Faulkner's Human Comedy."

19. Faulkner to Cowley, Burbank, CA, 7 May 1944, MCP.

20. Editors of the *Saturday Review of Literature*, "To the Trade," *Publishers' Weekly*, May 16, 1942, 1798–99.

21. Virginius Dabney and Howard Odum, "The Upper Old South; An Editorial," *Saturday Review of Literature*, January 23, 1943, 3.

22. Ellen Glasgow used this phrase to describe Faulkner's particular brand of the grotesque. See, for example, Ellen Glasgow, "Heroes and Monsters," *Saturday Review of Literature*, May 4, 1935, 3.

23. Malcolm Cowley, "Notes [1944]," MCP.

24. Caroline Gordon, "Mr. Faulkner's Southern Saga: Revealing His Fictional World and the Unity of Its Patterns," *New York Times Book Review*, May 5, 1946, 1.

25. For the wonderfully alliterative description of Popeye, see Ellen Glasgow to Irita Van Doren, Richmond, Virginia, May 23, 1935, in *The Letters of Ellen Glasgow*, ed.

Blair Rouse (New York: Harcourt, Brace, 1958), 154. For use of the term *futilitarian* to describe purveyors of the southern grotesque, see William Soskin, "Faith and Hunger in Virginia Hills," *San Francisco Examiner*, August 29, 1935, 11.

26. Cowley, "Introduction" (2003), xxvii.

27. Malcolm Cowley, introduction to *The Portable Faulkner*, ed. Malcolm Cowley (New York: Viking Press, 1946), 23–24. Hereafter cited as "Introduction" (1946).

28. Malcolm Cowley, "Modern Times," in *The Portable Faulkner*, ed. Cowley (New York: Viking Press, 1946), 652.

29. Cowley, "Introduction" (1946), 24.

30. See Cowley to Faulkner, Gaylordsville, CT, 2 November 1945, MCP.

31. Faulkner to Cowley, n.p, 18 February 1946, MCP.

32. Faulkner to Cowley, n.p., n.d., received 7 November 1945, MCP.

33. Cowley, "William Faulkner Revisited," 13–14. See Granville Hicks, *The Great Tradition: An Interpretation of American Literature since the Civil War* (New York: Macmillan, 1933), 262–68; and Alfred Kazin, *On Native Grounds: An Interpretation of American Prose Literature*, rev. ed. (New York: Harcourt, Brace, and Company, 1992), 453–67.

34. Malcolm Cowley, "Notes on an Introduction to Essay on Faulkner [1944]," 1, MCP.

35. Best to Cowley, New York, NY, 1 July 1945, MCP.

36. See, for example, "Choose Your Summer Reading" (advertisement), *New York Herald Tribune Books*, May 25, 1956, 17.

37. Cowley to Best, Gaylordsville, CT, 18 December 1945, MCP.

38. Gordon, "Mr. Faulkner's Southern Saga," 1.

Reading Faulkner's Readers: Reputation and the Postwar Reading Revolution

ANNA CREADICK

I have always been taught to bring a certain skepticism to William Faulkner's interviews, and like many teachers, I give my own students the same warning. Faulkner, I tell them, was notoriously slippery in interviews, famous for dodging, misleading, or contradicting himself in his own comments on his own works. The interviews, I tell my students, are dangerous.

Why do we say this? Is it a holdover of death-of-the-author critiques, a knee-jerk belief in the intentional fallacy? Whatever its source, this nervousness about the writer not falling into alignment with the criticism helps to keep critics at the center and authors—and *readers*—at the margins of deciding what books mean. But what if those interviews do tell the truth, or at least tell *a* truth, one to which we should attend? The truth, after all, is usually slippery, contradictory, and dangerous.

In the 2010 Norton Critical Edition of Faulkner's *As I Lay Dying*, editor Michael Gorra states, "Faulkner's work needs to be seen in two contexts at once. The first is that of international modernism. The second is that of the American South, and in part of what was called the Southern Renaissance."[1] Curiously, Gorra neglects altogether a third and equally significant cultural context: the publishing and revolution that, in the decades following the novel's 1930 publication, would shape how Faulkner was read. Gorra's omission is indicative of a larger tendency in Faulkner criticism: scholars have had to downplay the broader national story of shifting publishing and reading practices *in order* to frame Faulkner's career as strictly about modernism or regionalism.

Strong historical forces shaped the development of Faulkner's reputation. These forces included publishers, critics, and Faulkner's more general, everyday readers.[2] While the "machinery" of publishing and criticism has been to some degree addressed in Faulkner studies,[3] what has not been considered as closely is how he shaped and was shaped by the reading revolution through which he lived and wrote. Faulkner's career aligned exactly with tectonic shifts in the production and reception of books. From the 1930s through the early 1960s, the "paperback revolution" brought literature out of elite bookshops and into drugstores, dimestores, and newsstands, where increasing numbers of Americans could pick up a Faulkner novel for a quarter.[4] In the mid-1940s, when Faulkner had only $500 in the bank and the original trade edition of *As I Lay Dying* had sold only 540 copies, a start-up paperback publishing company decided to reprint *Sanctuary* (April 1947) and *The Wild Palms* (February 1948) in twenty-five-cent editions.[5] While only nine hundred bookstores nationwide had traditionally handled hardback fiction, these new paperback distribution networks sent Faulkner's works into about one hundred thousand outlets where they sold well: roughly half a million copies each.[6]

The translation of Faulkner's works into paperback not only increased his readership but affected his own aesthetics, priorities, and writing practices. For example, in January 1948, Faulkner set aside the long and still-incomplete World War I "fable" manuscript to begin a shorter "detective" novel he was "sure he could complete."[7] Four months later, *Intruder in the Dust* became Faulkner's first true bestseller and launched his commercial revival at Random House.[8] Other paperback editions of Faulkner's novels followed on into the 1960s, featuring vivid color covers, come-hither taglines ("Another POWERFUL and PASSIONATE Novel by the Author of SANCTUARY," promises the cover of the 1951 Signet paperback edition of *Soldiers' Pay*), and even movie tie-in editions (*The Sound and the Fury* in 1959, *Sanctuary/Requiem for a Nun* in 1961).[9] What did these new varieties of books mean for reading as a mark of American class distinctions?

The paperback publishing revolution was happening alongside and through the rise of literary modernism. It created new, broader communities of readers and changed what books meant culturally.[10] And it was an explosion that required a powerful critical discourse to "contain" it.[11] These historic shifts provided "good reading for the millions" but would also lead to increasingly rigid high/low literary distinctions.[12]

In the context of the paperback revolution, Faulkner's readership increased, and these "everyday" readers, I argue, became a critical force in the making of Faulkner's literary reputation.[13] Drawing on a previously neglected archive of reader response, this essay shows that Faulkner's midcentury readers, in their engagements with his works, both manufactured and tested the boundaries between "great" literature and trash, between modernism and pulp, between art and entertainment. In the end, the making of Faulkner's midcentury literary reputation would require the suppression of certain kinds of reading practices and the amplification of others.

Reconstructing historical reader response presents steep methodological challenges. Everyday readers do not typically read books then write diaries or letters about their experiences and leave those papers to archives. Fan correspondence can be one source, but surviving letters from readers to Faulkner are scarce, despite suggestive evidence that they did exist, and in great volume. Writer John Fante recalled evenings in Oxford with Faulkner where "there was a 100-gallon barrel full of fan mail that Faulkner would dip into only when he got very drunk, and then only to pull out an envelope and peer inside to see if there was any money. . . . [I]f not, he'd just toss the letter aside."[14] David Yalden-Thomson told Joseph Blotner a similar story of watching Faulkner sift through voluminous mail mainly to find free stamps.[15] Joseph Blotner also cites a letter Faulkner wrote to Jean Stein during the civil rights crisis: "I get so much threatening fan mail, so many nut angry telephone calls at 2 and 3 am from that country [the Delta]."[16] Why would William Faulkner disregard or destroy fan mail, as it seems he did? Perhaps he did not value audience response and did not think posterity would either. Other writers retained their correspondence from general readers among their papers, however. My sense is that Faulkner was enacting the paradox of the modernist career: he needed mass readers to make a *living* as a writer, but he needed the critics to make his *reputation* as a writer, so he managed to keep these streams separate. By effectively suppressing the voices of everyday readers, Faulkner could ensure that a different kind of discourse would define him. If one is received not by fans but by scholars, then one can claim space as a Great American Writer.[17]

In the absence of fan correspondence, where does one look to find Faulkner's everyday readers? In the winter of 1957 Faulkner arrived in Charlottesville for the first of two consecutive spring terms as the first writer-in-residence at the University of Virginia. In thirty-six separate readings and sessions, undergraduate and graduate literature students, reporters, engineering students, community members, psychology professors, and "law students' wives" asked Faulkner some fourteen hundred questions about his work and other subjects. University of Virginia English faculty Joseph Blotner and Frederick Gwynn, who largely organized and managed Faulkner's residence there, recorded these sessions on reel-to-reel tape and transcribed an abridged version of the recordings in their 1959 text *Faulkner in the University*, which has long been a resource for Faulkner scholars. Since 2010, through the joint efforts of University of Virginia professor Stephen Railton and the University of Virginia Library, those original reel-to-reel recordings have been

Faulkner and his readers, Rouss Hall. Photo by Ralph Thompson (Print #0218). Courtesy Faulkner at Virginia: An Audio Archive. © 2010 Rector and Visitors of the University of Virginia.

digitized and made available online in an audio-file format, with images, contextualizing materials, and searchable transcriptions. This trove of recorded sessions constitutes an archive that we have collectively overlooked: recordings of one cohort of midcentury readers talking about books, reading, and what reading meant to them. Unlike most scholars, then, I have been reading these interviews less for Faulkner's answers than for these midcentury readers' *questions*.

Editing the 1957–58 University of Virginia sessions for print publication required Blotner and Gwynn, as one reviewer noted, to "cut repetitious and occasionally trivial matter from 40,000 feet of tape recordings so as to bring the book [*Faulkner in the University*] down to reasonable size."[18] This necessary act began of a process of narrowing these rich conversations into a shape that would be most useful for the formalist criticism of the editors' day: opening and closing comments were cut; reader questions were tightened, omitted, or shortened; Faulkner's answers were consolidated into clearer monologues. Moreover, the *affect* that is part of the archive of these sessions—the laughter, which is so frequent, the awkward silences, the expressions of ethnic or gender difference, the meek stumblings or raw nerve of the readers—was left untranscribed at

the time. By excerpting Blotner and Gwynn's edited interviews in critical editions of Faulkner novels, scholars have continued to narrow what
happened at Virginia into still smaller nuggets. The interviews become
tools for close reading, "teachable" translations of difficult texts, offered
up in the author's own words. Listening to and looking more closely at
the Virginia sessions in the digital format, I have found a more complex
and subtle interchange between William Faulkner and his readership.

There were of course predictable patterns in the audience questions.
Readers asked the sorts of "advice to young writers" questions—about
habits, inspiration, motivation—that would likely surface at any public reading by any author at any time. Readers also asked Faulkner to
comment or prognosticate about politics and public affairs of the day:
questions about Joseph McCarthy, about civil rights, integration, and
the *Brown* decision, about the Holocaust and atomic bombs. Casting
Faulkner as a midcentury moralist, these questions reflect the readers' immersion in a midcentury culture of experts. In analyzing the
reader questions from the Virginia sessions more thoroughly, however,
I found that they coalesced into four surprisingly distinct patterns.
While Faulkner's literary works in the early paperback age were blurring the lines between pulp and modernism, these midcentury readers
were working through the contradictions. Faulkner's readers engaged
with cultural hierarchies, enacted formalist reading strategies, interrogated the function of literature, and dwelt upon matters of rank and
reputation. Taken together, these four dominant patterns in the Virginia
readers' responses reveal a moment in which midcentury readers were
helping to shape Faulkner's literary reputation, remaking him as the
Great American Modernist we recognize today.

The first pattern of reader response consisted of questions engaging high/low cultural distinctions. Across the late twentieth century,
Faulkner's works had shifted from somber cloth editions to sliced, diced,
and painted pulp editions and then to respectably bland collegiate paperback versions that encoded Faulkner into a genealogy of "great authors"
of the nation and, later, the world. While what was between the covers may not have changed (though in some cases it did), those exteriors
mediated changing relationships between books and readers.[19] Knowing
Faulkner in and through this paperback revolution, postwar readers at
Virginia thus readily crossed, or asked Faulkner to cross, what were then
called "brows": borders of cultural distinction in genre, medium, or form.
Often disregarding boundaries between popular and elite forms, readers
did not address Faulkner exclusively through his high-modernist literary production. They asked Faulkner about writing for film or television,
about writing stories versus novels, or about film adaptations of his work:

Unidentified [female] participant: Is the present movie [*The Long Hot Summer*, released in April 1958] a compilation of various episodes in different novels? I'm thinking of the horse particularly. Did that come from the "Spotted Horses," that's so much like it? (General Public, 23 May 1958)[20]

For the Virginia readers, William Faulkner was not a pure text but an adulterated one. While Faulkner, in his responses, usually reasserted the dominance of literature, his readers were navigating the novels, stories, and film adaptations simultaneously. As David M. Earle has argued, William Faulkner's midcentury success in paperback makes the commerciality of literary production unavoidable and deconstructs the idea of modernism as inaccessible to the masses.[21]

By the late 1950s, Faulkner's crossovers into magazine publishing, Hollywood screenwriting, genre novels, and film adaptations had produced a context in which readers could inquire about Faulkner's high modernist works in the same terms or in the same breath as what would become his more critically marginalized novels such as *Pylon*, *The Wild Palms*, *Intruder in the Dust*, *Sanctuary*, or the Snopes trilogy he was composing at the time:

> Unidentified participant: Mr. Faulkner, do you regard *Pylon* a serious novel and what were you driving at in that novel?

This audience member explicitly asks Faulkner to evaluate his works as "serious" or not, while Faulkner's response casts his pulpier works as somehow antidotes to the more "serious" or experimental works:

> William Faulkner: To me, they were a—a fantastic and—and bizarre phenomenon on the—the—the face of a—of a contemporary scene, of our culture at a particular time. I wrote that book because I'd gotten in trouble with—with *Absalom, Absalom!*, and I had to get away from it for a while, so I thought a good way to get away from it was to write another book, so I wrote *Pylon*.[22]

Readers pressed Faulkner about the violence in his work, about its obtuseness, and about writing for cash rather than for posterity. The fact that this practice was well established is evidenced by the 1957 University of Virginia student magazine comic showing Faulkner seated in a regal chair working at a typewriter, approached by a postman who holds out an envelope and states, "Your check from 'Dude Magazine' has arrived, Sir."

"Your check from 'Dude Magazine' has arrived, Sir."

A comic from a 1957 University of Virginia student magazine. *Virginia Spectator* 118.7 (April 1957), 16. Courtesy Faulkner at Virginia: An Audio Archive. © 2010 Rector and Visitors of the University of Virginia.

Like the comic, the cultural border-crossing questions frequently invoked laughter from the Virginia audiences. This laughter, transcribed in the new digital archive, is worth considering. Quite often Faulkner simply makes amusing remarks, but at other times the laughter seems a sign of audience discomfort with what a reader has asked or how a question has been answered:

> Unidentified participant: Sir, are there particular reasons why you do not go to the movies? [*audience laughter*]
>
> William Faulkner: Yes, sir. They come at the wrong time of day. [*audience laughter*] That's the time of day I like to have two or three drinks and eat supper and then sit down and smoke and read. If the—if they had moving pictures—well, I don't know, I'd have something else better to do any time

of day. [*audience laughter*] I think maybe I'd rather read it than listen to it. I'd rather read Shakespeare than see his plays.[23]

Here the laughter seems a sign of anxiety, as the questioner asks Faulkner (a great writer) about film (his potential competition in the marketplace) and his response (that he'd rather "read" or find "something else better to do") reasserts a hierarchy of cultural value in which books trump movies. To emphasize the point, Faulkner even says he values Shakespeare on the page over Shakespeare onstage.

A second pattern that emerges in the Virginia archive is that these readers, particularly and not surprisingly the college students, repeatedly modeled or enacted a formalist engagement with Faulkner's work, dwelling especially on questions of symbolism, characterization, or entanglements of plot. These careful close-reading questions famously flummoxed Faulkner, who often could not recall his own works in enough detail to respond effectively. He apparently even reread *Absalom, Absalom!* between his two terms as writer-in-residence in order to improve his performance.[24] In this category of response, readers seek clues about and translations of the text, as these examples illustrate:

> Unidentified participant: I am interested in the—in the symbolism in *The Sound and the Fury*, and I wasn't able to figure out exactly the significance of the shadow symbol with Quentin.[25]
>
> Unidentified participant: In *Sanctuary*, Mr. Faulkner, is the character of Popeye emblematic of evil in a materialistic society, or what would he stand for?[26]
>
> Unidentified participant: Who is the central character of *Absalom, Absalom!*? It seems so obviously to be Sutpen, yet it's been said that it's also the story of Quentin, and I was wondering just who is the central character?[27]
>
> Unidentified participant: Sir, in *Light in August*, the central character Joe Christmas had most of his troubles and his persecutions and in his search to find himself was based on his belief that he was part Negro, and yet it's never made really clear that he is. Was he supposed to be part Negro, or was this supposed to add to the tragic irony of the story?[28]

In seeking validation or verifications of their close readings, these readers try to squeeze Faulkner's texts into the logics of New Criticism, seeking a "central character" for *Absalom, Absalom!* or symbolism for Popeye, or a function for the racial ambiguity of Joe Christmas. The readers' deference even extends to asking the author to define appropriate reader response: "Sir, in the same book [*Absalom*], I was wondering what is supposed to be the reader's attitude towards Mr. Coldfield, the father of Ellen?"[29]

In this vein, Faulkner's readers also revealed criticism as a dominant lens through which they read. Quoting newspapers, journals, or individual critics by name, they asked Faulkner to function as an arbiter of the critical discourse. While Faulkner seemed happy to judge fellow writers, he responded to these lines of questioning with firm statements that he did not read criticism. The boundary Faulkner erected between writer and critic was one the readers were left struggling to traverse. Without criticism, one reader asks, "What gives you the sense of having failed or succeeded in a book?"[30]

Formalist engagement with Faulkner did not simply emerge as a preferred reading practice; it was actively promoted by Faulkner's hosts. Professors Blotner and Gwynn modeled, shaped, or directly assigned such inquiries. An excerpt from the beginning of one session, content that would be cut from the published *Faulkner in the University* volume, features Professor Gwynn opening the session by directing readers to ask questions "having to do with [Faulkner's] own work and on anything that people want to consider about the problems of writing in general."[31] A lengthy silence follows this introduction before the first question is asked, perhaps indicating an intimidated, nervous group. Throughout this session and others, both the readers and William Faulkner often sweetly stammer, hesitate, or clear throats, seeming to struggle for words in the face of the fame of the man at the podium.

Most surprising to me, then, were the moments when several readers boldly confronted William Faulkner with what they saw as a self-conscious and deliberate difficulty of style. One woman reader "confessed" how deeply she struggled with *The Sound and the Fury* in both its form and its content.[32] Another reader, South Asian by birth, admitted how he wrestled with what he hesitatingly described as Faulkner's "lyrical" writing style:

> Unidentified participant: Sir, I come from India, and I've been trying to read a good many of your books. [I am finding] it extremely difficult to follow the narrative method that you adopt. Is it true to say that you adopt a lyrical method to a narrative, and [a novel is also a] narrative of certain events and what the characters do, what happens to them? We find that in a novel like *As I Lay Dying* or *The Sound and the Fury* or the *Sanctuary* [sic] that it's difficult to follow the event. Is it true to say that you follow the lyrical method while trying to tell a story? Am I correct?[33]

Another male reader quite directly pointed to the divergence between those texts Faulkner lauds and those his "average reader" enjoys:

(Continued on page 9)

ACORN

6

THE VIRGINIA SPECTATOR

Virginia Spectator 118.7 (April 1957), 6. Courtesy Faulkner at Virginia: An Audio Archive. © 2010 Rector and Visitors of the University of Virginia.

> Unidentified participant: Sir, why is it that most of your short stories and hunting stories are so clear and simple like the one you just read, yet—yet some of your novels that you think are your finest, are, you know, [have] to be so mixed up psychologically in that they're hard for the average reader to—to understand?[34]

Confronting Faulkner with the fact that his more experimental writing frustrates readers, this midcentury reader articulates an emergent bifurcation in Faulkner's canon, in which his high-modernist Yoknapatawpha novels are set apart from works that had found a more mass audience, likely through popular magazines, pulp paperback format, or even via film. In this way, the readers both acknowledged and enacted a division between what we might call mod-Faulkner and pop-Faulkner.

In response to such reader resistance, Faulkner was sometimes stutteringly apologetic but usually deflected these criticisms by resorting to the third person and saying "the writer" must tell the story the way the story requires. In such moments, Faulkner aligned difficult with "good," a response that set up writing as aspirational and implied that reading should be as well. But again, the student newspaper the *Virginia Spectator* delighted in lampooning this theory. In a four-panel comic strip called *Acorn*, the artist shows a young reader settled on a street curb with a thick book of Faulkner's "Works" opened to read. Frowning, the figure turns the Faulkner tome diagonally, then upside-down, and finally just walks away, leaving the book spread down on the curb, unfinished.

A third pattern in reader response consisted of questions in which readers struggled to theorize literature's function. Approaching Faulkner through the lens of criticism, these inquiries arrived most frequently at the universalizing philosophies of literary value articulated in Faulkner's Nobel speech. Readers asserted (or invited Faulkner to assert) proper ways of reading, reasons for reading, even philosophies of reading. Repeatedly, almost without exception, and even where the question was on another matter, Faulkner's answers pointed to grand claims about literature as timeless, as universal, or as art, with a purpose to probe the "human heart in conflict with itself."[35] This response, articulated by both Faulkner and his readers, was a fundamentally individualist and depoliticized one, but it suggests that the humanist function of reading literary fiction was emerging as a dominant one by midcentury.

When readers pointed to alignments between Faulkner's plots or characters and contemporary cultural politics, for example, the author often pushed them past the local or national allegory toward the timeless, the universalized, the "human":

> Unidentified [female] participant: Mr. Faulkner, although you primarily write about the South and southern people, are you striving for universality, [that people who live in another locality can use it]?[36]

This reader both understood and tested the theory that universality is the mark of great literature. Through such questioning, she participated in shifting of Faulkner's reputation from southern writer to national or even world writer. Faulkner, in his answer, affirmed her instincts, brushing off his southernness as "locale" that was simply "most familiar" and convenient: he just "writes about what he knows."[37] This move occurred again in a press conference session, but this time it was Faulkner who performed a fascinating rhetorical distancing of himself from Mississippi and the South in order to recast his works as universal:

> Unidentified participant: Do you feel that if you had been born and grown up someplace else, you would've written pretty much the same kind of book [. . .] or do you think Mississippi is particularly strong in bringing out the—these conditions in the human race?
>
> William Faulkner: No, no, the imagination would be the same. The observation we—would be different and assuming that—that the experience, the—the books were—were Russian books or French books, that would be a little different.
>
> Unidentified participant: I mean—
>
> William Faulkner: But the people I write about are the same people. People haven't changed that much. The—the locale is—is just incidental. The writer uses that because that's easier.
>
> Unidentified participant: You wouldn't say there's anything significant about—

William Faulkner: No.

Unidentified participant:—about [. . .] Mississippi beyond—

William Faulkner: No, it's just because it's there. That's easier. If I wrote about another locale, I'd have to do some research or risk somebody saying, "Uh-uh, that's wrong." [*audience laughter*]

Unidentified participant: Do you feel you would have been influenced also probably to write the same type of thing?

William Faulkner: Yes, people are the same. People don't change that much. Their problems are the same problems.[38]

Emphatic in his claim to universality, Faulkner says "no" four times and interrupts the reader three times, to guide his audience toward the conclusion that "people are the same."

A final pattern of reader response saw readers engaged or inviting Faulkner to engage in the ranking of authors and literary works. A critical mass of questions emerged on themes related to reading and reputation:

Unidentified [female] participant: I would like to know what you think of Ernest Hemingway as a writer, what is your opinion of him?[39]

Unidentified [male] participant: Mr. Faulkner, I wondered what's your opinion of John Steinbeck now?[40]

Inserting Faulkner into an imagined genealogy of "greats," the readers actively engaged in midcentury canon-formation. Seeking the affirmation of a shared aesthetic, they asked Faulkner's assistance in determining a hierarchy of American authors. They asked him to list his "favorite books," to name *his* "greatest book," and to chart the "great books" of all time, and they readily employed words like "classic" and "tradition":

Unidentified [female] participant: Mr. Faulkner, I have been trying to trace a tradition in your work, and I'm curious to know whether you read Sir Walter Scott to any extent in the time previous to writing your novels.[41]

When readers asked Faulkner to "rank" or to evaluate his own works or the works of other writers, he rarely hesitated to do so. He was unabashed about the thievery writers practice as they borrow from those who preceded them. But in his replies to the canon-formation questions, Faulkner often equivocated. Sometimes he rattled off lists of highbrow texts no modern(ist) library would be without, such as Shakespeare, Homer, Cervantes, Dickens, Dostoevsky, Flaubert, Conrad, Wolfe (though not Woolf), and Dos Passos. At other times, however, Faulkner would say or suggest that he did not read, or that he had not read a new novel in decades, or that he read indiscriminately[42]:

> Unidentified participant: What specifically in your memory did you—you read that helped you more than anything else?
> William Faulkner: Everything I ever read, from the telephone book up and down. Trash. The good stuff. All of it.[43]

An interesting tension emerges between Faulkner's comment here and his refusal elsewhere to accept the mantle of reader, choosing instead to identify as a writer, one for whom the greatest "virtue" in finishing a book is that he will "never have to read" it again.[44] Such sentiments recur often and reveal Faulkner's occasional broad, populist reading practices. Faulkner's repeated advice to young writers was to watch people without judgment and to read, it seems, without discretion.

One woman reader in the final general public session in May of 1958 asks the author an interesting question:

> Unidentified [female] participant: Do you think that there's a particular order in which your works should be read [. . .]? Many people have offered a sequence. Do you think there's a particular sequence that your books should be read in?[45]

Implicit in her wish for an authoritative order in which to read is the notion that reading is a duty, an assignment. One reads not for pleasure, by choice, or by whim. Faulkner didn't hesitate to answer: "Probably to begin with a book called *Sartoris*. That has the germ of my apocrypha in it."[46] In so doing, he effectively validated the idea that there is indeed a "way" one "should" read Faulkner. In these and other questions about which writers influenced him, which writers he still read, and which living writers he favored or felt were worth their salt, the Virginia readers were not only asking what to read, they were asking *how* to read.

The 1951 Signet paperback edition of *Pylon* features two yellow banners on its jacket. The wide one at the top beckons, "By the author of 'Sanctuary,'" while the narrow one at the bottom reassures, "By the winner of the Nobel Prize for Literature."[47] Faulkner's readers, like the larger mass of midcentury readers, were left to navigate the space between those competing claims.[48] The fact that these claims appear on the cover of the same text reveals at least one secret of Faulkner's postwar success: he could tap into all the emergent hierarchies of American reading at once. Faulkner was pulp, he was middlebrow, and he was high-modernist, and he invited his readers to cross such boundaries,

Faulkner in Rouss Hall. Photo by Ralph Thompson (Print #0222). Courtesy Faulkner at Virginia: An Audio Archive. © 2010 Rector and Visitors of the University of Virginia.

sometimes even in the same text. The affordability and portability of paperback fiction marked a changing relationship to books, to authors, and to reading. Making Faulkner "portable" meant pocketing him, owning him.

Richard Brodhead writes, "the Faulkner we possess . . . is always and necessarily one his readers have helped to make."[49] This essay has worked to refocus attention on the everyday people of the 1950s who played a role in *making* Faulkner simply by *reading* Faulkner. The transformation of Faulkner's reputation by the late 1950s was a result, at least in part, of more readers finding more editions of Faulkner novels and stories, reading them, and believing them significant enough to be worth the struggle. While Faulkner kept to a fairly narrow script in his answers, the readers' questions at the University of Virginia regularly drifted into territories that Faulkner studies has increasingly begun to mine: civil rights, the Cold War, whiteness, print culture, and Hollywood. But the question of reputation was a focal one for Faulkner and his readers in 1957–58 at Virginia.

A literary "reputation" cannot be forged by the author alone; rather, it is a triangulation between publisher, author, and readers, critics included. The sessions at Virginia constituted a moment when Faulkner both went public and acquired a public. As a writer-in-residence, William Faulkner became Faulkner in the University, or Faulkner at the lectern, the place where he is *still* most fully remembered. Yet closer attention to the reading practices evident in this archive reveals a moment in which the hierarchies through which we continue to assess literary value were highly unstable: complex, muddy, and in flux. The boundaries of taste in reading that emerged at midcentury were not simply reflective but con-stitutive of shifting American class distinctions. In their focus on matters of reading, rank, and status, the repeating threads in the Virginia read-ers' responses therefore constitute remarkable evidence of what I would call dominant ways of reading at midcentury. Readers were engaged in making Faulkner's reputation, but they were also working to enhance their own reputations.

In an evocative photograph taken at the end of one of the Virginia ses-sions, a blurred mass of readers exits the Rouss Hall classroom in which Faulkner has just finished a reading and discussion. One woman reader stops by the doorway to greet the author. Glancing adoringly at him, she touches her white-gloved hand to his as the camera draws Faulkner's pleased expression into crisp focus. At a time when the democratization of print was colliding with the shaping of an American literary canon, Faulkner's reputation was changing hands—from the realm of critics to the realm of readers. While some might say that by the late 1950s Faulkner had found his readers, I would counter that by the late 1950s these readers had also "produced" Faulkner.

NOTES

My gratitude to Jay Watson, Sarah E. Gardner, and Kevin Dunn for their assistance as I revised this essay for publication, to David Earle for doing so much groundwork, and to Jaime Harker, endlessly, for that class. I also wish to thank Stephen Railton and the University of Virginia Library for the digitized archive that makes this work possible.

1. Michael Gorra, "Cultural Context," in *As I Lay Dying*, by William Faulkner (New York: Norton, 2010), 203.

2. The term "readers" is of course inadequate, since critics are readers, as are friends and fellow writers. My aim is to try and discern and discuss that aggregate of people vari-ously described as "average" readers, as "everyday" readers, as "educated readers," as "mass readers," or, by some scholars, as the "reading class." The University of Virginia readers were clearly not a cross-section of "average readers." They were college students, teachers, staff, professors' spouses, journalists, and community members. Most were already part of an educated elite. As people who chose to come hear Faulkner, they were likely somewhat fearless readers, aspirational readers unintimidated by challenging liter-ary fiction. Many were writers or aspiring writers themselves. I would venture to say, how-ever, that the Faulkner readers did in this way comprise *one segment* of the midcentury "reading class."

3. Jane Tompkins writes of the "machinery of publishing and reviewing [through] which an author is brought to the attention of his audience" in *Sensational Designs: The Cultural Work of American Fiction 1790–1860* (New York: Oxford University Press, 1985), 23. Examples of such work in Faulkner studies range from the 1960s to the present and include Floyd C. Watkins, "Faulkner and His Critics," *Texas Studies in Literature and Language* 10.2 (Summer 1968): 317–29; Lawrence H. Schwartz, *Creating Faulkner's Reputation: The Politics of Modern Literary Criticism* (Knoxville: University of Tennessee Press, 1988); Susan Donaldson, "Reading Faulkner Reading Cowley Reading Faulkner: Authority and Gender in the Compson Appendix," *Faulkner Journal* 7 (Fall 1991/Spring 1992): 27–39; Stacy Burton, "Rereading Faulkner: Authority, Criticism, and *The Sound and the Fury*," *Modern Philology* 98.4 (May 2001): 604–28; and Roland Végsö, "Faulkner in the Fifties: The Making of the Faulkner Canon," *Arizona Quarterly* 63.2 (Summer 2007): 81–107.

4. Kenneth C. Davis writes that the "marriage" of cheap paper publishing technology to magazine and newspaper distribution networks is what "paved the way" for the paperback revolution in the United States. See Davis, *Two-Bit Culture: The Paperbacking of America* (Boston: Houghton Mifflin, 1984), 47.

5. Joseph Blotner cites the figure for Faulkner's bank account in 1946 in *Faulkner: A Biography* (New York: Random House, 1984), 1205. By 1946, total sales of Faulkner's modernist masterpiece *The Sound and the Fury* had reached only 2,990 copies, and *As I Lay Dying* had sold just 540 copies. See Schwartz, *Creating Faulkner's Reputation*, 223n51.

6. Schwartz, *Creating Faulkner's Reputation*, 57.

7. Ibid., 61.

8. Ibid., 61, 56. At the University of Virginia, Faulkner makes the pulp influence explicit in his response to a question about the origin of *Intruder* in the English Department Faculty and Wives Session, 13 May 1957. The audience laughs as he acknowledges the tropes of the genre: "William Faulkner: Well, [*Intruder*] began with the notion—there was a tremendous flux of detective stories going about at that time, and my children were always buying them and bringing them home. I'd stumble over them everywhere I went. And I thought of an idea for one would be a man in jail, just about to be hung [*sic*], that would have to be his own detective. He couldn't get anybody to help him. Then the next thought was, the man for that would be a Negro. Then the character of—of Lucas—Lucas Beauchamp came along. And the book came out of that. It was the notion of a man in jail who couldn't hire a detective, couldn't hire one of these tough guys that slapped women around [*audience laughter*] and took a drink every time he couldn't think of what to say next. [*audience laughter*] But once I thought of Beauchamp, then he took charge of the story, and the story was a good deal different from the idea that—of the detective story that I had started with." See "English Department Faculty and Wives, 13 May 1957," *Faulkner at Virginia*, University of Virginia, http://faulkner.lib.virginia.edu/display/wfaudio13 (accessed December 11, 2015). See also Thomas L. McHaney, "What Faulkner Read at the P.O.," in *Faulkner at 100: Retrospect and Prospect: Faulkner and Yoknapatawpha, 1997*, ed. Donald M. Kartiganer and Ann J. Abadie (Jackson: University Press of Mississippi, 2000), 180–87; and David M. Earle, "Yoknapatawpha Pulp, Or, What Faulkner *Really* Read at the P.O.," in *Fifty Years after Faulkner: Faulkner and Yoknapatawpha, 2012*, ed. Jay Watson and Ann J. Abadie (Jackson: University Press of Mississippi, 2016).

9. William Faulkner, *Soldiers' Pay* (New York: Signet/NAL, 1951); Faulkner, *The Sound and the Fury* (New York: Signet Classics, 1959); Faulkner, *Sanctuary* with *Requiem for a Nun* (New York: Signet, 1961).

10. See David M. Earle, "Faulkner and the Paperback Trade," *William Faulkner in Context*, ed. John T. Matthews (Cambridge, UK: Cambridge University Press, 2015).

11. See David M. Earle, *Re-Covering Modernism: Pulps, Paperbacks, and the Prejudice of Form* (Burlington, VT: Ashgate, 2009) and Earle, "Pulp Magazines and the Popular Press," in *The Oxford Critical and Cultural History of Modernist Magazines: Volume II*, ed. Peter Brooker and Andrew Thacker (Oxford: Oxford University Press, 2012), 197–216. See also Sarah E. Gardner's essay in this volume, as well as her forthcoming monograph, *Reviewing the South: The Literary Marketplace and the Making of the Southern Renaissance*, from Cambridge University Press.

12. Kurt Enoch and Victor Weybright, New York managers of US publishing for Penguin (London), arranged with Random House to print *Sanctuary* in paperback (April 1947). They then formed the New American Library of World Literature, which licensed *The Wild Palms* in February of 1948. The phrase "good reading for the millions," according to Enoch, was not just the firm's slogan but its philosophy (qtd. in Schwartz, *Creating Faulkner's Reputation*, 57).

13. As David M. Earle has argued, "It is safe to say that more readers were introduced to Faulkner in paperback than in any other form, however much the academy has derided and ignored such fare" ("Faulkner and the Paperback Trade," 232).

14. Richard Collins, *John Fante: A Literary Portrait* (Toronto: Guernica, 2000), 164.

15. Blotner, *Faulkner*, 686.

16. Faulkner to Stein, 28 or 29 November 1955, in *Selected Letters of William Faulkner*, ed. Joseph Blotner (New York: Random House, 1977), 388.

17. Disdainful comments Faulkner made about his reading public might lead one to this same conclusion, although his constant, patient kindness toward readers across the Virginia sessions challenges this view.

18. Charles Anderson, rev. of *Faulkner in the University: Class Conferences at the University of Virginia, 1957–1958*, by Frederick L. Gwynn and Joseph L. Blotner, *Modern Language Notes* 76.1 (January 1961): 72.

19. See Earle, *Re-Covering Modernism*, 151–217. Matthew Vaughn notes that American modernist writers Djuna Barnes, Gertrude Stein, and William Faulkner all turned to pulp writing during a period in their careers when they were "anxious that their aesthetic would be compromised by any attempt to make it sellable to middlebrow readers" ("Radical Pulp: Popular Print Culture and the Anxiety of Modernist Authorship" [PhD diss., University of Tulsa, 2012], iv).

20. Faulkner responds, "I don't know, ma'am, because I'm not a moving picture-goer. I haven't seen [the movie]. [*audience laughter*] I really don't know. My experience with moving pictures is that they have almost any reason for buying the book except to make it. [*audience laughter*]."

21. Earle, "Faulkner and the Paperback Trade."

22. William Faulkner, "The English Club, tape 2, 7 March 1957," *Faulkner at Virginia*, University of Virginia, http://faulkner.lib.virginia.edu/display/wfaudio02_2 (accessed December 11, 2015).

23. William Faulkner, "General Public, 23 May 1958," *Faulkner at Virginia*, University of Virginia, http://faulkner.lib.virginia.edu/display/wfaudio32 (accessed December 11, 2015).

24. See Stephen Railton, "Faulkner at Virginia: An Introduction," *Faulkner at Virginia*, University of Virginia, http://faulkner.lib.virginia.edu/page?id=essays&section=intro (accessed December 11, 2015). See also Frederick L. Gwynn and Joseph L. Blotner, eds., *Faulkner in the University: Class Conferences at the University of Virginia 1957–1958* (Charlottesville: University Press of Virginia, 1959), viii.

25. William Faulkner, "Gwynn's Literature Class, 15 February 1957," *Faulkner at Virginia*, University of Virginia, http://faulkner.lib.virginia.edu/display/wfaudio01_1 (accessed December 11, 2015).

26. William Faulkner, "Blotner and Gwynn's Classes, tape 1, 13 April 1957," *Faulkner at Virginia*, University of Virginia, http://faulkner.lib.virginia.edu/display/wfaudio06_1 (accessed December 11, 2015).

27. Ibid.

28. Ibid.

29. Ibid.

30. William Faulkner, "General Public, tape 1, 15 May 1957," *Faulkner at Virginia*, University of Virginia, http://faulkner.lib.virginia.edu/display/wfaudio14_1 (accessed December 11, 2015).

31. Faulkner, "Blotner and Gwynn's Classes, tape 1, 13 April 1957."

32. Ibid.

33. Ibid.

34. Faulkner, "General Public, tape 1, 15 May 1957."

35. Faulkner used the phrase "human heart" in "conflict" on at least eleven separate occasions before a variety of audiences in 1957 and 1958, ranging from engineering students to undergraduate literature students to local and public community sessions. As the search function of *Faulkner at Virginia* reveals, the phrase "human heart" occurs in thirty-five separate comments.

36. William Faulkner, "Law School Wives, 16 May 1957," *Faulkner at Virginia*, University of Virginia, http://faulkner.lib.virginia.edu/display/wfaudio15 (accessed December 11, 2015).

37. Ibid.

38. William Faulkner, "Press Conference, 20 May 1957," *Faulkner at Virginia*, University of Virginia, http://faulkner.lib.virginia.edu/display/wfaudio17 (accessed December 11, 2015).

39. Faulkner, "General Public, tape 1, 15 May 1957."

40. Ibid.

41. Faulkner, "General Public, 23 May 1958."

42. It is likely that the question of "how to read" was a fraught one for Faulkner, who, according to biographer Philip M. Weinstein, "did not grow up in a reading household," and though his mother "encouraged him to read widely in canonical western literature," his father read only the "funny papers" and the occasional western (Weinstein, *Becoming Faulkner*, 38–39). Faulkner's own life as a reader is a rich and relevant resource that reflects shifting meanings of reading across the twentieth-century United States. Though I cannot delve into this aspect of the story here, it is part of my current work in progress on midcentury reading. See also David Wyatt, "Faulkner and the Reading Self," in *Faulkner and Psychology: Faulkner and Yoknapatawpha, 1991*, ed. Donald M. Kartiganer and Ann J. Abadie (Jackson: University Press of Mississippi, 1994), 272–87; and McHaney, "What Faulkner Read at the P.O.," 180–87.

43. Faulkner, "Press Conference, 20 May 1957."

44. Faulkner, "General Public, tape 1, 15 May 1957."

45. Faulkner, "General Public, 23 May 1958."

46. Ibid.

47. William Faulkner, *Pylon* (New York: Signet/New American Library, 1951).

48. As Earle observes, "the physicality of a book—the dust-wrapper, illustrations, typeface, quality of paper, where it is bought, the price paid, etc.—all play a part in the initial interpretation of a book, all are integrally linked to the author and publisher's intended, even constructed audience, how it is read by the individual as well as the public en masse" (*Re-covering Modernism*, 158).

49. Richard H. Brodhead, qtd. in Jackson R. Bryer, *Sixteen Modern American Authors, Vol. 2: A Survey of Research and Criticism Since 1972* (Durham, NC: Duke University Press, 1989), 234.

"The Paper Old and Faded and Falling to Pieces": *Absalom, Absalom!* and the Pulping of History

BROOKS E. HEFNER

For all its minute obsession with the legacy of southern history, William Faulkner's *Absalom, Absalom!* has some fairly well-documented historical problems. Whereas the particulars of Thomas Sutpen's family life in Yoknapatawpha County are keyed to the most intricate details of ante- and postbellum Mississippi history, Sutpen's backstory contains a rather glaring error. Drawn to the West Indies, "a place . . . to which poor men went in ships and became rich," Sutpen effects a personal transformation, from poor-white mountain man to nascent dynasty builder, largely though the symbolic subjugation of what appears to be a Haitian slave rebellion.[1] Of course, as many critics (including Richard Godden, Maritza Stanchich, Chris Bongie, and others) have already noted, this involves an oversight (perhaps intentional, perhaps not) regarding Caribbean history: the Haitian Revolution had ended slavery a number of decades before Sutpen's arrival there.[2] This historical problem has taken a more central role in criticism of the novel in recent decades as critics have puzzled through the ideological implications of the novel's apparent inaccuracies.[3] In this essay, I offer an alternative route into understanding the novel's relationship to history. With its many narrators, its multiple tellings and retellings, and the increasingly sensationalistic qualities that Sutpen's story takes on, *Absalom, Absalom!*'s relationship to history is fluid and flexible. In effect, the novel enacts what I term a "pulping" of history, self-consciously destroying, recycling, and repurposing the historical record. This treatment of history is encoded in the novel's metacommentary, when Mr. Compson describes the main figures in this drama as "like a chemical formula exhumed along with the letters from that forgotten chest, carefully, the paper old and faded and falling to pieces, the writing faded, almost indecipherable, yet meaningful, familiar in shape and sense" (80). Characters become not just embodied in the text but transformed into metonymic and ephemeral paper records, falling apart, continually reconstituted through the act of narration.

At the same time, I'd like to extend this notion of the pulping of history to the text's narrative and ideological levels. Faulkner had a long and complex history with popular literary production during his career. Friends with pulp writer Dashiell Hammett, Faulkner certainly thought of some of his output as inhabiting the same cultural sphere as popular genre writing. For example, he called *Sanctuary* (1931) "a cheap idea . . . deliberately conceived to make money," and *Pylon* (1935), as David M. Earle has noted, operates as a meditation on the early 1930s popularity of aviation pulps.[4] Both *Sanctuary* and *Pylon*—two relatively popular Faulkner novels that became even better known after their reprinting in sensationalized popular paperback forms in the 1940s—caused critic Granville Hicks to wonder whether Faulkner was "in danger of becoming a Sax Rohmer for the sophisticated," a reference to the sensational writer known for creating the sinister Fu Manchu and inspiring innumerable copies of this stereotypical figure.[5] Hicks's concern—voiced more strongly in the 1935 revised edition of *The Great Tradition*—immediately anticipates the publication of *Absalom, Absalom!* and indicates the degree to which cultural arbiters of the era saw Faulkner as veering dangerously close to the style and subject matter of sensational fiction.

During this period, Faulkner even conceptualized some of his own work as "pulp." While he was working on *Absalom*, he supported himself with the stories that would comprise the novel/story cycle *The Unvanquished* (1938), something Faulkner himself characterized as a "pulp series," even though most of the pieces appeared in the well-paying middlebrow magazine the *Saturday Evening Post*, one of the "slick" magazines the pulps defined themselves against.[6] The fact that this "pulp series" effectively underwrote the composition of *Absalom* is nothing new; but how might the latter novel—often characterized as Faulkner's most difficult modernist masterwork—be connected to the unabashedly lowbrow world of mid-1930s pulp fiction? This pulping of history I have described entails not only a form of narrative recycling but also an increasingly sensationalized image of the past. In *Absalom, Absalom!*, the narrators—from Rosa Coldfield and Mr. Compson to Quentin and Shreve—increasingly layer the narrative and ideological tropes of pulp fiction over Sutpen's history. The resulting narrative, while formally quite difficult, depends on—and even revels in—scenarios common in mid-1930s pulps: from criminal masterminds to heroic Anglo-Saxon adventurers, from racial conspiracies to *femme fatales*, *Absalom*'s pulping of history extends beyond mere narrative recycling to what might be understood as the broader ideological framework of pulp fiction.

In a sense, the novel's slippery relationship with history anticipates the poststructural historiography of Hayden White, whose 1973 volume *Metahistory* promoted the idea of literary or generic "emplotment" as a principle narrative strategy for historians more generally. "Emplotment," White writes, "is the way by which a sequence of events fashioned into a story is gradually revealed to be a story of a particular kind."[7] Following Northrop Frye, White conceives of historical emplotment as taking on a variety of generic forms or "modes": Romance, Tragedy, Comedy, and Satire. These generic modes of emplotment intersect with argument and ideology to produce different kinds of historical visions. James M. Mellard's detailed reading of *Absalom* explicitly tracks the novel's use of what White called "tropics" and associates the novel's individual narrators with White's four forms of emplotment.[8] Even without reference to White's *Metahistory*, however, critics of *Absalom, Absalom!* have long discussed its peculiar emplotment of history, with most characterizing the novel's visions of history as partaking in a variety of generic conventions. Eric Sundquist, for example, emphasizes "the gothic tragedies" of the novel's principal characters, while other critics point to the narrative modes of melodrama or romance and even suggest that the novel's various narrators each draw on distinct story forms.[9] Doubtless *Absalom* has deep roots in these nineteenth-century literary modes and structures. However, many of the novel's thematic and ideological reference points simultaneously suggest a form of sensational fiction contemporary with its publication, namely the interwar pulp magazine, the generic conventions of which present twentieth-century transformations of modes like the gothic.

In the process of attempting to master Sutpen's history, to emplot it convincingly, the narrators produce characters that are unlike "real" historical figures, instead taking on larger-than-life qualities, becoming like characters in a story. Mr. Compson meditates on the results of this kind of historical narration, calling the characters in Sutpen's history

> "people too as we are and victims too as we are, but victims of a different circumstance, simpler and therefore, integer for integer, larger, more heroic and the figures therefore more heroic too, not dwarfed and involved but distinct, uncomplex who had the gift of loving once or dying once instead of being diffused and scattered creatures drawn blindly limb from limb from a grab bag and assembled, author and victim too of a thousand homicides and a thousand copulations and divorcements." (71)

These "simpler" and "more heroic" people of the past exhibit the qualities of pulp fictional creations rather than the "diffused and scattered creatures" common in high-modernist fiction.[10] This trend toward fictional enlargement and sensationalization is all the more visible in the language Rosa Coldfield uses to represent Sutpen and others. For example, Rosa views Sutpen as "man-horse-demon" (4) and "an ogre or a djinn" (16), a figure of monstrous and nearly supernatural evil on whom the loss of the Confederacy might even be blamed. Rosa's language conjures up images associated with horror and supernatural fiction, one of the more successful and influential genres of pulp fiction published in the 1930s. The success of titles like *Weird Tales* led to an explosion of what were called "shudder pulps" in the 1930s: featuring a mixture of what Robert Kenneth Jones described as "Gothicism, sadism[,] and weird menacism," fiction in these magazines often thrived on the perceived threat nonwhites presented to white womanhood.[11] In this sense, shudder pulps shared a significant ideological orientation with Jim Crow–era notions about monstrous black sexuality.

In this pulp figuration, Sutpen occupies two opposing positions: he is simultaneously the demonic threat to southern ideals and the Anglo-Saxon protector of them. An "ogre or a djinn" in Rosa's estimation, Sutpen—outsider in Jefferson and Yoknapatawpha County—poses a sexualized, monstrous, and quasi-foreign threat, first to Rosa's sister (whom he marries) and later to Rosa herself (whom he nearly marries). Rosa's rather vicious narration is clouded by a long-standing attraction/ repulsion to Sutpen, heightened by the indecent proposal that ends her short engagement to him. But Rosa's narration also anticipates—if only fleetingly—an alternative Sutpen, not the mysterious and dangerous interloper in the world of white Jefferson but the heroic white warrior defending against racial threats. This emphasis first appears in Rosa's description of Sutpen fighting with his own slaves at Sutpen's Hundred:

> "Ellen seeing not the two black beasts she had expected to see but instead a white one and a black one, both naked to the waist and gouging at one another's eyes as if their skins should not only have been the same color but should have been covered with fur too. Yes. It seems that on certain occasions, perhaps at the end of the evening, the spectacle, as a grand finale or perhaps as a matter of sheer deadly forethought toward the retention of supremacy, domination, he would enter the ring with one of the negroes himself." (20–21)

Sutpen's hand-to-hand combat with these slaves would seem, at first, to call Sutpen's race into question. For Rosa such behavior means that "their skins should not only have been the same color but should have been covered with fur too." Certainly this characterization partakes in distressing and pernicious uses of evolutionary theory to justify racial hierarchies; it also recalls the numerous stories of atavism that populated pulp titles like *Weird Tales* and *Amazing Stories.*[12] But this image is also echoed in the later description of Sutpen's experience during the Haitian slave rebellion, another instance of interracial, hand-to-hand combat: "something had to be done so he put the musket down and went out and subdued them," protecting his (presumably) white employer and the employer's (presumably) white daughter from (presumably) terrible fates (204). Sutpen's demonstration of physical superiority is described and speculated upon at length:

> "he just put the musket down and had someone unbar the door and then bar it behind him, and walked out into the darkness and subdued them, maybe by yelling louder, maybe by standing, bearing more than they believed any bones and flesh could or should (should, yes: that would be the terrible thing: to find flesh to stand more than flesh should be asked to stand); maybe at last they themselves turning in horror and fleeing from the white arms and legs shaped like theirs and from which blood could be made to spurt and flow as it could from theirs and containing an indomitable spirit which should have come from the same primary fire which theirs came from but which could not have, could not possibly have." (204–5)

In scenes like these, scenes saturated with racial violence and "naked to the waist" displays of physical superiority, *Absalom* reveals that it is not the nineteenth-century conventions of melodrama and the gothic that completely dominate the novel's "emplotment." Rather, the twentieth-century tropes of pulp fiction suddenly emerge as central to the novel's structure and ideological work.

Sutpen's superhuman strength—as demonstrated by his single-handedly subduing a group of rebellious slaves "maybe . . . turning in horror and fleeing from the white arms and legs"—remains rather unbelievable in the novel; however, it would be right at home in the pages of any number of mid-1930s pulps that emphasized a virile and triumphant white masculinity. Characters like Robert E. Howard's Conan, who first appeared in *Weird Tales* in 1932, consistently battled racialized threats and defeated enemies in superior numbers through brute strength. By the mid-1930s, characters like Conan began to populate the "hero pulps," titles devoted to the exploits of a single character. These single character pulps emerged first in 1931 with *The Shadow*, but soon over twenty single-character pulps could be found on newsstands, with the hero pulp phenomenon beginning to subside, according to pulp historian Robert Sampson, around 1935, the year Faulkner composed *Absalom.*[13] Along with *The Shadow*, the most recognizable of these "hero" pulps

"Traitress! What game are you playing?"

Jewels of Gwahlur

By ROBERT E. HOWARD

The tale of a weird, jungle-hidden palace and a strange weird people— and the marvelous sacred jewels that were known as the Teeth of Gwahlur.

1. Paths of Intrigue

THE cliffs rose sheer from the jungle, towering ramparts of stone that glinted jade-blue and dull crimson in the rising sun, and curved away and away to east and west above the waving emerald ocean of fronds and leaves. It looked insurmountable, that giant palisade with its sheer curtains of solid rock in which bits of quartz winked dazzlingly in the sunlight. But

299

Joseph Doolin, illustration for Robert E. Howard's "Jewels of Gwahlur," *Weird Tales*, March 1935. Special Collections, Carrier Library, James Madison University.

was likely Lester Dent's *Doc Savage* (begun in 1933), which carried on the tradition of foreign exploration and adventure into a contemporary setting, with an announcement in the first issue promising that the near superhuman Doc and "his five adventurous companions" would, in each issue, "fight their battle in a locale far from the previous contacts."[14] Central to the Doc Savage stories—as was the case with much pulp adventure fiction—was the use of exotic settings that allowed their heroic white protagonists (Savage is described as "the man of bronze" in his first adventure) not only the romance of foreign travel but the opportunity to demonstrate physical and mental superiority in locales generally figured as racially nonwhite.

The violent, heroic, white masculinity exhibited by these pulp figures has been described by Christopher Breu, in his insightful *Hard-Boiled Masculinities*, as "wearing the black mask," a nod to the influential crime pulp *Black Mask*. In Breu's reading,

> the hard-boiled male . . . borrowed in implicit ways from the iconography of black masculinity. He defined himself against a Victorian morality that constructed white middle-class manliness in virtuous opposition to the figure of the black savage or rapist. Here the hard-boiled male, as a version of twentieth-century working-class masculinity, finds its shadowy double in the figure of the transgressive and primitivized black male.[15]

Although Breu's chapter on Faulkner locates a particular version of this phenomenon in Joe Christmas from *Light in August*, I would argue that the fight scene that so haunts Rosa is an even more effective demonstration of this notion of "wearing the black mask," for Sutpen's staged battle with his own slaves involves an explicit racial performance ("their skins should not only have been the same color") in which Sutpen reinscribes racial difference through a pure brute force already associated with the slaves he is fighting. But the stakes of this contest are deadly: Sutpen's masculinity—certainly a version of "hard-boiled masculinity" Breu describes—is an ideological feedback loop, embodying the racist stereotypes of the other to ensure the other's subjugation, echoing Richard Godden's powerful Hegelian reading of the novel. After all, it is a battle that Sutpen cannot lose, for what would his white spectators do to the slave that defeated him?

As Breu's argument suggests, a particularly powerful strain in the pulps consisted of the continual reenactment of racial and sexual threats; covers of a large number of pulps of the 1930s routinely featured sexualized threats posed to scantily clad white women by menacing nonwhites. Sean McCann, likewise, has seen in the pulps—specifically in the genre

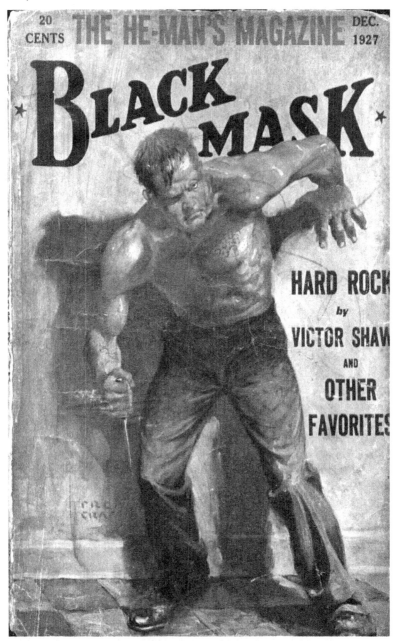

Fred Craft, cover art, *Black Mask*, December 1927. Pulp Holdings, Department of English and World Languages, University of West Florida.

of adventure or "exotic fiction"—"a recurrent battle between insidi-
ous miscegenation and an imperiled, domestic homogeneity."[16] These
concerns—pitting domestic stability against a racialized threat to sexual
purity—are at the core of a number of the competing (and complementary) narratives about Thomas Sutpen. For if Sutpen is figured by some
in the narrative as nearly superhuman ("integer for integer, larger, more
heroic"), his battles are almost always figured as racial ones. Whether
it is the "naked to the waist" staging of "the retention of supremacy" in
the fights with his own slaves, the single-handed subjugation of a slave
rebellion in Haiti, or the more subtle battle with Charles Bon over his
family legacy, in *Absalom, Absalom!*, Sutpen's narratives are consistently
in accord with the racial obsessions of the pulps, figuring the enemies of
Sutpen's own domestic design as nonwhite threats.

   Absalom, Absalom!'s other man of mystery, the biracial Charles Bon,
likewise exhibits strong affiliations with these complex pulp dynamics.
In one of the novel's first extended descriptions of Bon, Mr. Compson
describes him as a foreign, decadent aesthete, "reclining in a flowered,
almost feminised gown, in a sunny window in his chambers—this man
handsome elegant and even catlike and too old to be where he was,
too old not in years but in experience, with some tangible effluvium of
knowledge, surfeit: of actions done and satiations plumbed and pleas-
ures exhausted and even forgotten" (76). Even Henry (in Mr. Compson's
telling) sees Bon as "a hero out of some adolescent Arabian Nights." The
danger Bon poses to the Sutpen legacy is ultimately racial (or so Quentin and Shreve's speculative narration tells us), but in this initial textual
encounter, the stronger danger appears to be that of a sensuous and
seductive foreignness. This foreignness is clearly associated with New
Orleans, "that city foreign and paradoxical, with its atmosphere at once
fatal and languorous, at once feminine and steel hard" (86), while the
novel characterizes Henry as a "grim humorless yokel out of a granite
heritage" associated with Protestantism, Puritanism, and "Anglo-Saxons"
(92). Although Bon's foreignness is explicitly linked to the powerful
influences of French culture and Roman Catholicism in New Orleans,
the association of Bon with "Arabian Nights" links his decadence with an
Orientalist strain of representation common in the pulps, for the ethnic
groups most frequently vilified across horror and science fiction pulps
were undoubtedly Asian.[17]

   Pulp titles contemporary with the writing and publication of *Absalom,
Absalom!* include *Oriental Stories* (1930–34), *The Mysterious Wu Fang*
(1935–36), and *Dr. Yen Sen* (1936). Drawing explicitly on Yellow Peril
narratives popularized by Sax Rohmer in his Fu Manchu series, these
stories drew on stereotypes of inscrutability and longstanding anti-Asian

sentiment in the United States, as documented in John Kuo Wei Tchen and Dylan Yeats's recent *Yellow Peril! An Archive of Anti-Asian Fear*.[18] In the pulps, Fu Manchu and others were what Robert Sampson calls "emperors of evil," engineers of plots, schemes, and conspiracies.[19] Moreover, popular pulp stories featuring anti-Asian sentiment often opposed "virile" Anglo-Saxon masculinity to a weak, feminized Asian threat. Central to this opposition was the depiction of Orientalist tropes of exotic luxury. For example, in Philip Francis Nowlan's early *Amazing Stories* contributions (featuring the first appearance of a character later known as Buck Rogers), the "modern, virile American race" is opposed to the "effete" Asiatic Han empire, with its "magnificently luxurious and degraded scheme of civilization."[20]

"Luxurious and degraded" would certainly be one way of describing the threat Charles Bon ("a hero out of some adolescent Arabian Nights") poses to Sutpen's design—not to mention to Sutpen's "Anglo-Saxon" son Henry, who is enamored with the "effete" Bon from the outset. These pulp parallels become even clearer in Shreve McCannon's narrative invention of the broad conspiracy perpetrated by Charles Bon's mother (named Eulalia in the novel's genealogy but never named in the novel's text) and facilitated by "that lawyer who maybe had the secret drawer in the secret safe and the secret paper in it . . . all of the notations in code" (241). Shreve's version of the South, already a larger-than-life vision populated by Guineveres (142) and Launcelots (256) and figured as a "fairy tale" (255) and "better than Ben Hur" (176), assumes an even stronger degree of sensationalism through his invention of a New Orleans lawyer conspiring with the beautiful and biracial Eulalia, "plotting and planning" to destroy the dream of Anglo-Saxon supremacy embodied in the story of Sutpen's design (241). Richard Godden has argued that Eulalia's name points toward the combination of the Greek for *joy* (Eula) and an "obscuring" of the word *liar*, an indicator of her deception.[21] This sexual-racial conspiracy positions Eulalia as a conspicuously absent *femme fatale*, a figure associated, according to Greg Forter, with "a seductively excessive and dangerous pleasure."[22]

Highlighting *Absalom, Absalom!*'s pulping of history not only offers the opportunity to see individual characters as variations on pulp types transported into the antebellum South; it also allows the novel's conclusion to be read as a meditation on pulp obsessions with racial conflict and racial warfare. In this sense, Henry's murder of Bon at the gate of Sutpen's Hundred operates as an extension of Sutpen's efforts as an Anglo-Saxon protector of white women. Vanquishing the "elegant" foreign threat that Bon poses to his sister out of a blind adherence to his "granite heritage" of Anglo-Saxonism, Henry becomes the (perhaps reluctant) hero in a story about the dangers of miscegenation. In the climax of this novel, by a writer Granville Hicks feared was becoming the "Sax Rohmer of the sophisticated," Henry vanquishes the sinister threat of Bon's racialized conspiracy. Likewise, Shreve's flippant prediction that "in time the Jim Bonds are going to conquer the western hemisphere" (302) not only speaks to anxieties about racial extermination stoked by nativists like Madison Grant and Lothrop Stoddard; it also evokes the numerous science fiction texts of the 1920s and 1930s that imagine the future as a racial battleground.[23]

If Quentin and Shreve's narrative speculation about Sutpen's history partakes in the ideological contents of pulp magazine fiction, the process of their narration echoes the immersive and escapist experience of pulp reading. This appears most explicitly in their lengthy co-narration in chapter 8, when "it was not two but four of them riding the two horses through the dark over the frozen December ruts of that Christmas eve: four of them and then just two—Charles-Shreve and Quentin-Henry" (267). As the two roommates tell the story to each other, it assumes the quality of an immersive experience, one strongly associated with the reading habits of the pulp audience. In 1937, veteran pulp editor Harold Hersey described pulp readers as "all the multitude of men and women, young and old, who have discovered a way through the pulpwoods to an evanescent world of dreams, where all one has to do is open a page and be transported on a magic carpet to the frontiers of fantasy," also noting that these readers "automatically place themselves in the roles of the hero and the heroine."[24] This popular reading practice differs significantly from that associated with literary modernism, which values critical distance and an interpretive pose that produces what Richard Poirier once described as "grim readers."[25] As Quentin and Shreve tell and hear themselves tell the "fairy tale" of Henry and Bon, they lose themselves in the romance of a story "better than Ben Hur," placing themselves in these roles. In opposition to the difficulty readers encounter with a tangled text like *Absalom*, Quentin and Shreve's experience becomes that typically associated with popular reading practice, centering on fantasy, escapism, and wish-fulfillment.[26]

The difficult text of *Absalom*, however, has elicited a long and productive critical history that situates the novel in a host of 1930s contexts. From linking Sutpen's background to the plight of the Depression-era poor to more recent work contextualizing Sutpen's story against the rise of Fascism in Europe, critics have emphasized the novel's deep concern with issues of the period. My emphasis on the novel's pulping of history allows these disparate arguments to be layered on top of one another in a complementary fashion. Cleanth Brooks's early and seminal reading of the novel, for example, emphasizes Sutpen as an embodiment of "the innocence of modern man"; such innocence was strongly associated with the readers of pulp magazine fiction, who were routinely characterized as innocent, naïve, and childlike.[27] Likewise, critics like Dirk Kuyk Jr. and Charles Hannon see the novel as intricately intertwined with Depression-era concerns over labor and the New Deal; unsurprisingly, such concerns resonate across pulp genres of the period, as the working class constituted their primary readership.[28] More recently, Ted Atkinson, Daniel Spoth, and Jeanne A. Follansbee have emphasized the novel's concern with the rise of power, paralleling the rise of Fascism in Europe.[29] If anything, the novel's echoes of "virile," Anglo-Saxon adventure fiction and Yellow Peril narratives not only warn of the dangers of such power but also mirror the ideological work of a Fascist movement that sought to elevate the pulp vision of the Anglo-Saxon "superman" onto the world stage. As such, *Absalom, Absalom!*'s pulping of history provides a crucial intersection for many of the novel's meaningful threads. It also shows the rich interpenetration of cultural and ideological material between the most degraded and ephemeral of cultural forms and one of the most difficult and canonized texts of American modernism.

Finally, I'd like to return to the novel's obsession with the ephemerality of history. As anyone who has worked closely with pulp magazines knows, these physical objects quite literally crumble in your figures as you read them. Printed on some of the cheapest paper available at the time, pulps were—and continue to be—like Mr. Compson's vision of history: "paper old and faded and falling to pieces, the writing faded, almost indecipherable, yet meaningful, familiar in shape and sense" (80).[30] Contemporary commentators and critics of pulp fiction echoed this, emphasizing both the naïveté and ephemerality of the pulp form. In 1928, Henry Morton Robinson ended a rather vicious article on the pulp market by claiming that "[n]o library files copies of wood-pulp. Of the millions of words the wood-pulp writer grinds out, of the hundreds of plots he concocts, nothing remains but ephemera, shades—dead wood-pulp with an old date on the cover."[31] If, after their instant consumability, pulps ultimately produce "ephemera, shades," then *Absalom, Absalom!*'s notion of history is most certainly a pulp vision of the past. For the novel constantly invokes the ephemerality of the very story it tells. Whether the paper record is "old and faded and falling to pieces" or the historical record is being compared to "a block of stone with scratches on it" (101), history becomes a series of dream-like shadows, ephemeral and constantly in danger of being forgotten. This is not to say that *Absalom, Absalom!* should be read as a pulp text, as critics have done with texts like *Sanctuary*, for the novel's style and aesthetic mode are quite at odds with the easily consumable popular fiction published in the pulps. Rather, the novel exhibits a pulp relationship to the historical narrative it tells: recycling and repurposing narrative material out of the crumbling and ephemeral texts of the past, figuring history as a site of sensational action and adventure, *Absalom, Absalom!* transforms history itself into a kind of pulp fiction.

NOTES

I would like to thank David M. Earle, Sean McCann, Sarah E. Gardner, and Anna Creadick for comments on an earlier draft of this essay.

1. William Faulkner, *Absalom, Absalom!* rev. ed. (1936; repr., New York: Vintage International, 1990), 195. Subsequent references to this edition will be cited parenthetically in the text.

2. Richard Godden, *Fictions of Labor: William Faulkner and the South's Long Revolution* (New York: Cambridge University Press, 1997); Maritza Stanchich, "The Hidden Caribbean 'Other' in William Faulkner's *Absalom, Absalom!* An Ideological Ancestry of US Imperialism," *Mississippi Quarterly* 49 (Summer 1996): 603–18; Chris Bongie, *Islands and Exiles: The Creole Identities of Post/Colonial Literature* (Stanford, CA: Stanford University Press, 1998).

3. John T. Matthews has suggested that this "famous central anachronism" might be merely another one of "the products of Sutpen's ignorance," and that his dealings in Haiti were with mixed-race "jaunes" all along. See Matthews, *William Faulkner: Seeing through the South* (Malden, MA: Wiley-Blackwell, 2009), 193, 192. However, this reading does not quite account for the Creole-speaking (and presumably Haitian) slaves Sutpen brings with him to Yoknapatawpha County.

4. William Faulkner, *Novels 1930–1935* (New York: Library of America, 1985), 1029n179.1; David M. Earle, *Re-Covering Modernism: Pulps, Paperbacks, and the Prejudice of Form* (Burlington, VT: Ashgate, 2009), 200. See also Walter Wenska, "'There's a Man with a Gun over There': Faulkner's Hijackings of Masculine Popular Culture," *Faulkner Journal* 15.1–2 (1999): 35–60, and Doreen Fowler and Ann J. Abadie, eds., *Faulkner and Popular Culture: Faulkner and Yoknapatawpha, 1988* (Jackson: University Press of Mississippi, 1990).

5. Granville Hicks, *The Great Tradition: An Interpretation of American Literature since the Civil War* (1933; New York: Macmillan, 1935), 268. I am indebted to Sarah E. Gardner for pointing me to this reference.

6. Joseph Blotner, ed., *Selected Letters of William Faulkner* (New York: Random House, 1977), 84. On pulp self-definition, see Erin A. Smith, *Hard-Boiled: Working-Class Readers and Pulp Magazines* (Philadelphia: Temple University Press, 2000), 18–42.

7. Hayden White, *Metahistory: The Historical Imagination in Nineteenth-Century Europe* (Baltimore: Johns Hopkins University Press, 1973), 7.

8. James M. Mellard, *Doing Tropology: Analysis of Narrative Discourse* (Urbana: University of Illinois Press, 1987), 91–141.

9. Eric Sundquist, *Faulkner: The House Divided* (Baltimore: Johns Hopkins University Press, 1983), 99. See also Philip J. Egan, "Embedded Story Structures in *Absalom, Absalom!*," *American Literature* 55.2 (1983): 199–214, Walter Brylowski, *Faulkner's*

Olympian Laugh: Myth in the Novels (Detroit: Wayne State University Press, 1968), 22–27, and Peter Lurie, "'Some Trashy Myth of Reality's Escape': Romance, History, and Film Viewing in *Absalom Absalom!*," *American Literature* 73.3 (2001): 563–97.

10. Of course, Faulkner has it both ways here, emphasizing the heroic dimensions of the past relative to the scattered present while blurring the lines between the two and demonstrating that Sutpen's history is more scattered than Mr. Compson likely believes.

11. Robert Kenneth Jones, *The Shudder Pulps* (West Linn, OR: FAX Collector's Editions, 1975), 7. For a discussion of Faulkner's *Sanctuary* in light of the shudder pulps, see Matthew R. Vaughn, "Radical Pulp: Popular Print Culture and the Anxiety of Modernist Authorship" (PhD diss., University of Tulsa, 2012), 135–91.

12. On intersections between modernist fiction and atavism, see Dana Seitler, *Atavistic Tendencies: The Culture of Science in American Modernity* (Minneapolis: University of Minnesota Press, 2008).

13. Robert Sampson, *Glory Figures*, vol. 1 of *Yesterday's Faces: A Study of Series Characters in the Early Pulp Magazines* (Bowling Green, OH: Bowling Green University Popular Press, 1983), 19–21.

14. "Announcement," *Doc Savage Magazine*, March 1933, 2.

15. Christopher Breu, *Hard-Boiled Masculinities* (Minneapolis: University of Minnesota Press, 2005), 36.

16. Sean McCann, *Gumshoe America: Hard-Boiled Crime Fiction and the Rise and Fall of New Deal Liberalism* (Durham, NC: Duke University Press, 2000), 65.

17. See John Cheng, *Astounding Wonder: Imagining Science and Science Fiction in Interwar America* (Philadelphia: University of Pennsylvania Press, 2012), 147–78, and Nathan Vernon Madison, *Anti-Foreign Imagery in American Pulps and Comic Books, 1920–1960* (Jefferson, NC: McFarland, 2013).

18. John Kuo Wei Tchen and Dylan Yeats, *Yellow Peril! An Archive of Anti-Asian Fear* (New York: Verso, 2014).

19. Robert Sampson, *From the Dark Side*, vol. 3 of *Yesterday's Faces: A Study of Series Characters in the Early Pulp Magazines* (Bowling Green, OH: Bowling Green State University Popular Press, 1983), 4–26.

20. Philip Francis Nowlan, "The Airlords of Han," *Amazing Stories*, March 1929, 1106, 1118; Nowlan, "Armageddon—2419 a.d.," *Amazing Stories*, August 1928, 422.

21. Godden, *Fictions of Labor*, 70.

22. Greg Forter, *Murdering Masculinities: Fantasies of Gender and Violence in the American Crime Novel* (New York: New York University Press, 2000), 33. While the figure of the *femme fatale* dominates pulp fiction (and film) more prominently in the 1940s and 1950s, seminal texts such as Hammett's *The Maltese Falcon* (1930) and James M. Cain's *The Postman Always Rings Twice* (1934) provided early examples. The 1920s trope of the "vamp" also anticipates this generic formation.

23. In addition to Nowlan's fiction, see also Cheng, as well as David H. Keller, "The Menace," *Amazing Stories Quarterly* (Summer 1928): 382–91, and George S. Schuyler, *Black Empire*, ed. Robert A. Hill and R. Kent Rasmussen (1936–1938; repr., Boston: Northeastern University Press, 1991).

24. Harold Brainerd Hersey, *Pulpwood Editor: The Fabulous World of the Thriller Magazines Revealed by a Veteran Editor and Publisher* (New York: Frederick A. Stokes, 1937), 9, 7.

25. Richard Poirier, "The Difficulties of Modernism and the Modernism of Difficulty," in *Images and Ideas in American Culture: The Functions of Criticism; Essays in Memory of Philip Rahv*, ed. Arthur Edelstein (Hanover, NH: Brandeis University Press, 1979), 130.

26. Michael Denning not only describes the working-class readers of dime novels (nineteenth-century precursors to the pulps) as engaging in a politicized form of wish-fulfillment; he also, following Antonio Gramsci, characterizes dime-novel reading practices as "social, familial[,] and communal." See Denning, *Mechanic Accents: Dime Novels and Working-Class Culture in America* (London: Verso, 1987), 66, 69. Critics of pulp magazines also emphasized the qualities of these fictions as dreams and wish-fulfillments. See for example Marcus Duffield, "The Pulps: Day Dreams for the Masses," *Vanity Fair*, June 1933, 26+.

27. Cleanth Brooks, *William Faulkner: The Yoknapatawpha Country* (1963; Baton Rouge: Louisiana State University Press, 1990), 297. For Duffield, pulp readers were "those who move their lips when they read" (26); for Hersey, they are adults in a "second childhood" (7). For Alvin Barclay, pulps are "magazines for morons" that "are edited for mental children" ("Magazines for Morons," *New Republic*, August 28, 1929, 42). For Margaret MacMullen, pulps are "edited for a mental age of perhaps eleven years" ("Pulps and Confessions," *Harper's Magazine*, June 1, 1937, 94).

28. Dirk Kuyk Jr., *Sutpen's Design: Interpreting Faulkner's "Absalom, Absalom!"* (Charlottesville: University Press of Virginia, 1990), 21–22; Charles Hannon, *Faulkner and the Discourses of Culture* (Baton Rouge: Louisiana State University Press, 2005), 76–103. On pulps and New Deal–era labor concerns, see McCann.

29. Ted Atkinson, *Faulkner and the Great Depression: Aesthetics, Ideology, and Cultural Politics* (Athens: University of Georgia Press, 2006), 162–72; Daniel Spoth, "Totalitarian Faulkner: The Nazi Interpretation of *Light in August* and *Absalom, Absalom!*," *ELH* 78 (2011): 239–57; Jeanne A. Follansbee, "'Sweet Fascism in the Piney Woods': *Absalom, Absalom!* as Fascist Fable," *Modernism/Modernity* 18.1 (2011): 67–94.

30. Hersey's description of the process is evocative: "The stock used for the ordinary seven-by-ten pulpwood magazine is made from watery wood pulp. I have never tired of watching the mixture pour into a long, mysterious machine, gradually become transformed into a wide sheet, and issue forth as a roll of paper" (15).

31. Henry Morton Robinson, "The Wood-Pulp Racket," *Bookman*, August 1928, 67.

Massachusetts and Mississippi: Faulkner, History, and the Problem of the South

NATALIE J. RING

> I can move these people around like God, not only in space but in
> time too. The fact that I have moved my characters around in time
> successfully, at least in my own estimation, proves to me my own
> theory that time is a fluid condition which has no existence except
> in the momentary avatars of individual people. There is no such
> thing as *was*—only *is*.
>
> —*William Faulkner*

The theme of the conference this year is "Faulkner and History," and
I found myself asking the following questions: how does one begin to
understand a southern fiction writer from the perspective of a southern historian? How does one understand Faulkner's historical intent?
More specifically, how much of Faulkner is rooted in the "real" history
of Mississippi, and does that even matter? I begin with my own personal history and sense of regional identity, locate myself in relationship
to Faulkner's characters in *Absalom, Absalom!* and *The Sound and the
Fury*, situate these novels in the historical context of the "real" Harvard University, consider how Faulkner's own historical background
might have influenced his narrative choices, and then engage in a bit
of fictional imagination myself with regard to Quentin Compson. Part
of my choice to engage with Faulkner as a southern historian through
more unconventional means is rooted in the overwhelming synchronicity between my childhood regional identity, my college experience, my
research interests as a historian, and Faulkner's fiction.

The first time I read William Faulkner I was nineteen years old and
a freshman at a small liberal arts college in Massachusetts. As an American studies major I took a required introductory course, "The South as
a Literary Landscape," taught by literature professor Barry O'Connell.

Described as "an intensive investigation of the South as an imagined world," it focused exclusively on Mississippi in the nineteenth and twentieth centuries, looking at fiction, folk art, music, history, and geography.[1] Faulkner figured heavily in the syllabus. The second required American studies course I enrolled in was "Revolution and Counter-Revolution: Shays' Rebellion and the Making of the Constitution" with Professor Robert Gross. Shays' Rebellion began in 1787 in central and western Massachusetts, when incensed insolvent farmers responded to high land taxes initiated by elites in power. Daniel Shays and his conspirators were disillusioned with the inequities of the political and social landscape that had developed in the wake of the American Revolution and made an unsuccessful attempt to seize the federal arsenal at Springfield, Massachusetts. Later the regulators were shut down by the state militia when the legislature declared martial law.[2] The course was designed "to mark the bicentennials of Shays' Rebellion and of the U.S. Constitution," using the insurgency "as a case study for agrarian rebellion in a countryside undergoing radical unsettlement."[3] This post–Revolutionary War revolt occurred just miles down the road from where I grew up and attended college.

Each course (on Shays' Rebellion and the cultural landscape of Mississippi) made up two halves of the required set of courses for the American studies major. North and South. Massachusetts and Mississippi—the former taught by a history professor, the latter taught by a literature professor. It turns out that the course on Mississippi was the outlier in a sea of courses on New England or "the North" as America writ large. I was in college in the 1980s, when the New England–centric/ Perry Miller model fully dominated the American studies curriculum. Despite Professor O'Connell's acknowledged effort to challenge the prevailing model by offering a course on southern literature, overall my alma mater's American studies program, even if unintentionally, represented the South to me as "the Other"—something exotic and fundamentally peculiar. The curriculum at Amherst College evoked the sentiment of Faulkner's character Gavin Stevens, who noted that the North had a peculiar "gullibility: a volitionless, almost helpless capacity and eagerness to believe anything about the South not even provided it be derogatory but merely bizarre enough and strange enough."[4]

Even more telling is the fact that "The South as a Literary Landscape" focused explicitly on Mississippi. Mississippi is a state burdened by a deeply entrenched mythology that insists it is the most distinctive of all the southern states. Often the state is used as a metonym for "the South."[5] In the wake of Medgar Evers's death, Roy Wilkins, executive director of the NAACP, stated bluntly: "We view this as a cold, brutal, deliberate killing in a savage, uncivilized state; the most savage, the most uncivilized state in the entire fifty states. There is no state with a record that approaches that of Mississippi in inhumanity, murder, brutality, and racial hatred. It is absolutely at the bottom of the list."[6] New Englanders, or outsiders, have always needed the South as a foil, to serve as the antipode of the North. This practice extends as far back as the eighteenth century and involves portraying the South as a backward, alien land that stood apart from the rest of the nation.[7] Likewise, New England, in particular the state of Massachusetts, holds symbolic meaning for many Americans. It was a religious refuge for the Pilgrim settlers, served as the incubator of the American Revolution, and had a reputation as a hotbed of antislavery radicalism in the antebellum period. It also is home to the first university in the United States, Harvard College.[8] Massachusetts, then, is a metonym of the North. The course I took on the significance of Shays' Rebellion and the US Constitution captured the essence of Massachusetts and could not exist without the course on Mississippi standing in as a synecdoche of the South.

The pairing of Massachusetts and Mississippi in the two required introductory American studies courses reflects a familiar literary trope. In the novel *The Bostonians* (1886), Henry James relates the story of Basil Ransom, a former Confederate veteran and lawyer from Mississippi working in New York, who visits his cousin Olive Chancellor, a radical feminist in Boston described by her sister Mrs. Luna as a "female Jacobin" and "a nihilist." Basil becomes enamored with Olive's feminist protégée, Verena Tarrant, a Bostonian of "the best New England stock," whom he meets at a political meeting. Basil and Olive compete for the affections of Verena throughout the course of the novel, pitting the sensibilities of Mississippi against Massachusetts.[9] In this novel a displaced Mississippian who cannot seem to create a prosperous life for himself in the North fantasizes about attending Harvard like many southerners before him, and he is inexplicably drawn to a northern woman with ambitions to seize the political possibilities and freedoms available to her in Boston.

William Faulkner's Compson novels—*The Sound and the Fury* and *Absalom, Absalom!*—also underscore the way in which Massachusetts and Mississippi stand in opposition to each other yet are indelibly intertwined. As in *The Bostonians*, Harvard stands in as the chief emblem of Massachusetts and the North. Mr. Compson sells a parcel of the family land in order to pay for daughter Caddy's wedding and son Quentin's education at Harvard, a university that Quentin tells himself was "mothers dream since you were born."[10] Quentin arrives in the fall of 1909, meeting his Canadian roommate, Shreve. In both Compson novels

Quentin fails to acclimate to New England and is situated as an interloper in Massachusetts. Even those southerners he runs into on the Harvard campus read him as idiosyncratic; ironically the authenticity of his
southernness is called into question in the context of the Massachusetts
environment when he crosses paths with Spoade, Gerald Bland, and
Mrs. Bland. While at Harvard, Quentin is tenuously connected to Mississippi, belonging to neither the South nor the North yet simultaneously
existing in the southern past and the northern present, only perhaps still
rooted in Mississippi through his efforts to connect to the southern past
via the story of Thomas Supten. Before Quentin leaves for Harvard,
Rosa Coldfield reminds him that he will find it difficult to retain his
ties to the South, that whatever trace of southernness might exist now
in the present has been destroyed by northern interference in the past.
"So I dont imagine you will ever come back here," Rosa tells Quentin,
"and settle down as a country lawyer in a little town like Jefferson since
Northern people have already seen to it that there is little left in the
South for a young man."[11] Heading North to Harvard puts Quentin at
risk of forgetting where he comes from, as if Massachusetts can erase the
existence of Mississippi, particularly if Quentin chooses never to return
home to the South (as opposed to Gavin Stevens).

Quentin does not live long enough to give a full written account of
the South, but he engages with Shreve in a verbal reconstruction of
the meaning of the region. In *Absalom, Absalom!* Quentin and Shreve
scheme, conjecture, and recreate the Sutpen narrative together, with
Quentin obsessively retrieving the memories of Rosa Coldfield and his
father and Shreve embellishing and concocting even more details as they
proceed. In the context of the Sutpen narrative Shreve stands in as the
outsider; although he is from Canada, he embodies the northern view
of the South as an exotic dysfunctional place populated with curious
outlandish characters. At one point Shreve exclaims, "Jesus, the South
is fine, isn't it. It's better than the theatre, isn't it. It's better than Ben
Hur, isn't it. No wonder you have to come away now and then, isn't it."[12]
Shreve's fascination with the Sutpen story and his demand that Quentin
"tell about the South" are not unexpected literary choices on Faulkner's
part, given that the fictional Shreve likely would have consumed magazines, newspapers, and books discussing the nationally known "southern
problem."[13]

Faulkner's choice to use Harvard as the site where Shreve and Quentin face the ghosts of the southern past is a deliberate one, as both Mississippi and Massachusetts serve as metonyms of the regions that went
to war in 1861. It is accepted wisdom among Faulkner scholars, though,
that Quentin and Shreve's Harvard is really Yale University because

of Faulkner's strong ties to Oxford resident Phil Stone, who attended Yale for his BA and law degree.[14] Stone mentored Faulkner, encouraged him to read American literary classics, and housed Faulkner in New Haven in 1918. Afterward, Faulkner decided to enter the Canadian Royal Air Force. Because of Faulkner's close friendship with Phil Stone and his stint in the RAF, scholars often presume the Compson novels are informed by Faulkner's experiences with Yale and Canada. Shreve's Canadian citizenship reflects his outsider relationship to the South, and the Shreve-Quentin attempt to comprehend the southern past in the context of a northern university suggests that Faulkner could have modeled his fictional Harvard after Yale. However, the literary pairing of Massachusetts and Mississippi in *Absalom, Absalom!* and *The Sound and the Fury* is not accidental.[15] Harvard is the key academic institution associated with the Union cause. Harvard as an icon of the North and abolitionism serves more straightforwardly as a foil to the burdens of the South (Mississippi) than Yale. The symbol of Harvard is critical to Faulkner's texts as the destination of both Quentin Compson and Gavin Stevens. Within the context of the history of the New South, Harvard, as an emblem for Massachusetts, plays an important role.

In 1905 Albert Bushnell Hart, an alumnus of and history professor at Harvard University, announced in the first sentence of the New York City–based *Independent Magazine*, that "no Northern visitor crosses Mason and Dixon's line without realizing there is a Southern problem." In his short exposition, Hart informed his readers that any northerner who spent more than a few months in the South would become, like his fellow southerners, "infected with this uneasy sense of a destiny unfulfilled, of a civilization anxious for its own future."[16] Visitors choosing to spend time in the "real Southern South" far away from the industrial and tourist areas of the "Northern South" might discover a foreign land in the heart of America, lending credence to W. J. Cash's assertion almost forty years later that the South "was not quite a nation within a nation, but the next thing to it."[17] Hart observed, "As time passes the inquirer becomes aware that he is in an unfamiliar environment, population is diffused, resources are scanty, commercial enterprise is sluggish, labor is uncertain; and above all and through all is an antagonism of races which broods over the whole community."[18]

In the late nineteenth and early twentieth centuries, discussion of the existence of a general "southern problem" typically followed three lines of inquiry: "the race question" or "race problem," the problem of economic development, and the problem of illiteracy and lack of education in the South. In addition, Americans identified a whole variety of other southern problems, including lynching, street violence, dueling, disease, moonshining, religious intolerance, political stagnation, miscegenation, demagoguery, one-crop agriculture, illiteracy, and poor whites. In truth, the list was endless. Consequently, the phrase the "southern problem" could be elusive in meaning, but at the turn of the century most Americans recognized it. The expression called up an image of a backward, stagnant, uncivilized region that was distinct from the rest of the United States. As historian Larry J. Griffin argues, over time "the region itself— rather than the objective conditions—became commonly understood as the 'real' problem."[19]

Beginning in 1880 an array of institutions and people, including national and local journalists, progressive reformers, social scientists, clergymen, politicians, federal officials, and intellectuals promulgated the image of the South as a regional, national, and even global problem. This was not the first time that Americans and foreigners had set the South apart and at odds with the rest of the nation. During the antebellum period, abolitionists, free labor Republicans, and travelers to the South often depicted the region negatively, emphasizing its backwardness, licentiousness, and abject poverty. However, at the turn of the century the problem of the South elicited far greater national attention than it ever had before, with the possible exception of Reconstruction. Hundreds of books, journal articles, lectures, sermons, and academic presentations drew national attention to the defects of the region, touching on a vast array of southern topics.[20]

It is altogether likely, then, that William Faulkner would have been familiar with this phenomenon, given the pervasiveness of the subject. Interest in the "southern problem" was not specific to the North, as sympathetic southern liberals fashioned the image as well in an effort to solicit help for progressive reforms. Conversation on the "southern problem" was the talk of the day. Shreve's interrogation of Quentin in the Harvard dormitory room parallels the avid interest in the Problem South percolating at the turn of the century. In short, Quentin and Shreve fashion their own narrative about the "southern problem" in Yoknapatawpha County, focusing on the weight of the southern past that continues to haunt Quentin's psyche. As Cleanth Brooks notes, "*Absalom, Absalom!* is a persuasive commentary upon the thesis that much of 'history' is really a kind of imaginative construction . . . and if we are to hope to understand it in any way, we must enter into it and project ourselves imaginatively into the attitudes and emotions of the historical figures."[21] Likewise, although Albert Bushnell Hart was trained to be a professional historian in the German tradition at the University of Freiburg, much of his work on the South involved contemporary observation fused with the actual history of the region. It involved an "imaginative construction" in the vein of Quentin and Shreve; it was not quite fiction in its own right but incorporated Hart's own personal experience as a northerner, an interest in determining the historical relevance of the region, and a desire to impart meaning to place through resourceful observation.

Ironically, Hart's education is strikingly similar to that of Gavin Stevens who condemned the North for its naiveté and its inclination to believe grotesque stories about the South. Although Stevens is an attorney, not a historian, he attended Harvard University as an undergraduate and studied at the University of Heidelberg, a German institution, before receiving a law degree from the University of Mississippi. *Light in August* describes Stevens's friendship with a former classmate from Harvard who is a professor at a "neighboring State University" that likely stands in as the University of Mississippi.[22] In fact, Hart maintained friendships with two University of Mississippi professors, Franklin L. Riley of the history department and Thomas P. Bailey of the psychology and education department. In both Yoknapatawpha County and the historical context of the early twentieth century, Harvard, standing in for Massachusetts, reaches into Mississippi and back again.

Seeking southern stories, Albert Bushnell Hart undertook more than a dozen trips to the South (from days to months long) over many years, including a thousand-mile journey by horseback and wagon in the winter of 1907–8, riding from North Carolina all the way to Texas, where he connected with Franklin L. Riley and Thomas P. Bailey. Hart viewed himself as continuing in the tradition of Frederick Law Olmsted, another New Englander who in the 1850s made two journeys through the South and published three volumes of social analysis on the region. The Harvard professor published over thirty articles on his southern visits in scores of newspapers and magazines (twelve articles appeared just in the *Boston Transcript* alone, and several appeared in Virginia and North Carolina papers), and he also gave public speeches on what he called the "real South" at such places as the Lowell Institute in Boston, the Brooklyn Institute in New York City, and the Massachusetts Historical Society. Eventually he published *The Southern South* (1910) based on the material he had collected on his various excursions.

During the 1907–8 winter trip, Hart visited Mississippi, connected with Riley in Oxford, toured the countryside, and traveled to Jackson to speak to the Mississippi Historical Society (MHS) at Riley's invitation. On January 10, 1908, at the decennial meeting of the MHS, Hart gave his invited lecture "What a Historical Society Should Accomplish" before a crowd that included members of the state legislature. Since Hart's address was "ex tempore" there is no record of his talk, although Riley reported that the Harvard professor discussed the "negro problem" and his "observations with reference to our economic, social, and political problems." Hart's address, Riley claimed, "was replete with sentiments of good will to the people of Mississippi" and showed "appreciation of the good work" accomplished by the MSH.[23]

Hart's performance was seemingly a triumph, but what Riley did not note in his official report is the commotion that preceded and followed Hart's arrival. The tumult later came to be known as the "Mississippi incident," as described by George Petrie of Alabama Polytechnic Institute, and the "row at Jackson," as referred to by Hart and Leroy Percy, plantation owner, lawyer, future senator, and father of William Alexander Percy.[24] Several days before Hart's lecture a number of Mississippi newspapers, from both sides of the political spectrum, printed editorials questioning why he had been invited to speak before the MHS. The *Winona Times*, colored by what Thomas P. Bailey called a "strong tincture of Vardamanism," was the first to draw attention to the Harvard professor's visit.[25] The *Columbus Dispatch* christened Hart "a Traducer of the South," blamed him for propagating "false impressions" of the region, and concluded that "he should kindly send his regrets or get lost in the shuffle."[26] Southern demagogue James K. Vardaman, who assumed the governorship in 1903 and held the nickname "The Great White Chief," offered the state a populist message infused with virulent racist proclamations. He campaigned on the slogan "A VOTE FOR VARDAMAN IS A VOTE FOR WHITE SUPREMACY, THE SAFTEY OF THE HOME, AND THE PROTECTION OF OUR WOMEN AND CHILDREN."[27] Vardaman supporters would not have taken kindly to a Harvard professor who criticized the South publicly.

Even newspapers known to be hostile to Governor Vardaman condemned Hart's visit to Mississippi. The *Jackson Evening News* led with the scathing headline "The Venom of Dr. Albert Hart" and said it was a mistake to allow the traveling Harvard professor to "tell the people of Mississippi how to run a historical society" given the "outrageous calumny" he had written about the South.[28] The paper pointed to a particular section of Hart's 1905 "southern problem" article for the *Independent* in which he wrote, "The sanctity of womanhood (that is, of course, of *white* womanhood) is in the South an article of faith, and good people rarely make laborious distinction between the man who is guilty and the man who looks like a criminal: between shooting him in his tracks or burning him at the stake; between burning the guilty man or burning his innocent wife; between a quiet family inferno, with only two or three hundred spectators, and a first-class advertised *auto-da-fé*, with special trains and the children of the public schools in the foreground."[29] Hart's reference to the spectacle of the southern lynch mob and his sardonic note that only white women (not black women) were presumed to be virtuous inflamed the *Jackson Evening News*, which called him a "blue abdomened [*sic*] miscreant," "an infamous calumniator," and a man who would "willfully falsify the record in order to vent his spleen against any and all people who happen to live south of Mason and Dixon's line."[30]

Albert Bushnell Hart was not off the mark and rather prescient in his critique of the frenzy and spectacle of the lynch mob. Exactly eight months from the day the *Jackson Evening News* issued its scathing editorial regarding Hart, a group of men in Oxford stormed down the doors of the jail, seized African American murder suspect Nelse Patton, and lynched him for allegedly slicing a white woman's throat. Joe Christmas in William Faulkner's *Light in August* commits a similar crime, murdering and nearly decapitating his white paramour Joanna Burden before being killed by townspeople. In Faulkner's 1931 short story "Dry September," he explores the escalating white southern anxiety about black men raping white women that leads to a subsequent lynching.[31] Faulkner was just shy of eleven years old on September 8, 1908, the day Patton was lynched in Oxford. Although Faulkner once said in a conversation with *Vanity Fair*, "I never saw a lynching and so couldn't describe one," it is hard to imagine that the lynching of Patton did not leave an imprint on him, since it would have been all anyone could talk about in a small town.[32] Faulkner lived around the corner from where Patton's mutilated body hanged in the town square for several days. Likewise, Faulkner was ten years old when Albert Bushnell Hart visited Oxford several months before the lynching, and it's possible the dust-up over Hart's critique of the white southern obsession with race, sex, and violence, as well as the address he gave at the MHS, also had invaded Faulkner's mind.

Faulkner's family, who had been in Oxford since 1885, must have spoken often of political and educational affairs. Many of the Falkners attended the University of Mississippi. William Faulkner's grandfather, John Wesley Thompson Falkner, served in the Mississippi House of Representatives and Senate and on the university's board of trustees. He also led Oxford, Mississippi's Vardaman Club, once introducing Vardaman before a crowd of 5,000 when William Faulkner was thirteen years old. William Faulkner's uncle, John W. T. Falkner Jr., joined the family law practice with his father in 1909, served as a Democratic Party organizer, rallied for another demagogic politician, Governor Theodore Bilbo, and later was appointed as a judge. When Faulkner was a young man he drove his uncle to political rallies.[33] Faulkner came of age in the early twentieth-century South when fear of the "black beast rapist" dominated the political discourse.[34] It is difficult to imagine that the arrival of a northerner as outspokenly critical of southern demagogues as Albert Bushnell Hart did not register with the community of Oxford and the Falkner family. As Doyle writes, "No one knows how this historical knowledge surrounding Faulkner might have filtered into his consciousness. . . . It would have been difficult, especially for a man of Faulkner's curiosity about the past, to be alive in this environment and *not* become familiar with the past that enveloped him."[35]

Just two months before Faulkner's fictional Quentin Compson commits suicide by drowning himself in the Charles River, Albert Bushnell Hart published his travelogue *The Southern South*. "Every year opens out some new unexplored field which must be taken into account," he declares in the opening pages, "if one is to hope for anything like a comprehensive view of the subject."[36] One purpose of the book was to bring together northern and southern reformers who were interested in rehabilitating the region. Hart did not entitle the book "The Southern Problem," likely because his two 1905 essays in the *Independent* elicited a flood of personal letters from white southerners protesting his characterization of the region. These letters ranged from polite complaint to searing contempt. Hart answered each one, sometimes establishing a back-and-forth correspondence involving many pages and occasional retractions. In fact, the *Independent* provided a forum for Mrs. H. L. Harris of Rockport, Georgia, who published numerous articles lamenting the North's unfair treatment of the South. Less than a year after publication of Hart's articles she wrote in the same magazine, "Perhaps nothing is more offensive to the Southern people than the impressions which Northern visitors often receive of the South. I do not know who is to blame . . . but I do know that it is very like laying a fuse across Mason and Dixon's line when some Yankee, gifted with the critical spirit and the missionary instinct, comes down here to see what is the matter with us and to propose a remedy which is utterly foreign to our tastes and to the emergencies of the situation."[37]

The year before *The Southern South* was published, the Southern Historical Publication Society issued the first volume of *The South in the Building of the Nation* (1909) in an attempt to counteract northern propaganda and write the first "true history of the South." The editors included an array of southern academics, intellectuals, and writers such as Hart's friend Franklin L. Riley, Walter Lynwood Fleming, Samuel Chiles Mitchell, Edwin Mims, and Thomas E. Watson. In an introductory section titled "The South Misunderstood," they wrote that much of southern history has been written by "men of the North, who in many instances faithfully and consistently tried to be fair," but who, because they were not raised in the South, "have been biased by the environments of their youth and by their residence without being aware of the fact."[38] They specifically singled out three known historians and Massachusetts residents: James Ford Rhodes, a corporate capitalist who made his fortune in iron, steel, and coal in Cleveland, Ohio, before writing history; John Fiske, a Harvard alumnus who taught at both Harvard University and Washington University; and Albert Bushnell Hart. The belief that Massachusetts was the birthplace of erroneous historical interpretations of the South was taken as fact by many southern academics. Several years before *The South in the Building of the Nation* was published, Ulrich B. Phillips, professor at Tulane University and later contributor to this southern manifesto, groused that "the history of the United States has been written by Boston and largely written wrong."[39]

For many white southerners, Albert Bushnell Hart, the son of an abolitionist and a leading professor at Harvard, was the perfect symbol of how New England, and in particular Massachusetts, continued to write sectional histories biased against the South. Indeed, Dunbar Rowland, the director of the Mississippi Department of Archives and History, acknowledged in an apologetic letter written to Hart after the "row at Jackson" that "every one [sic] believes that Hart and Harvard mean the same thing."[40] In the late nineteenth and early twentieth centuries the discipline of history was moving toward professionalization. Peter Novick explains, "there was, in the genteel culture of the turn of the century, a widespread distaste for sharp controversy and criticism."[41] Yet creating a national history and incorporating regional viewpoints into a universal patriotic American understanding of the past was difficult and marked by moments of sectional antagonism that threatened to imperil the entire project. Albert Bushnell Hart viewed himself as a historian, but his interest in contemporary southern problems threatened to endanger his sense of professional objectivity and push him into the realm of sociology or anthropological practice. For the southern historians associated with *The South in the Building of the Nation*, Hart's writings on the New South might as well have been fiction.

However, Hart's assessment of the South was more nuanced than his baser critics gave him credit for. While he was overly critical of the South's lack of civilization, he often struggled with the paradox of the New South, oscillating between optimism and despondency in his writing. The same year he published the two pieces on the "southern problem" in the *Independent* he wrote companion pieces for the *Richmond Times-Dispatch* with the headings "The South's 'Backwardness'" and "The South's Progress." Hart frequently corresponded with Edgar Gardner Murphy, a clergyman and educational reformer residing in Alabama who had written *The Problems of the Present South* (1904). He admired

Murphy's work and believed the two could study the "southern problem" collaboratively and write independent reports with similar conclusions that might sway negative opinion about the region.[42]

Murphy, though, was a prickly, outspoken man. Although he was not as venomous as the more reactionary white southerners who lashed out at Hart's early journalistic pieces, shortly before the professor embarked on his thousand-mile journey through the South from December 1907 to January 1908, Murphy chastised him for his decidedly northern bias and sloppy methodology. "How far are the supposed Southern peculiarities really Southern, in a local or sectional sense, and how far are they merely rural?" he queried Hart.[43] Murphy took issue with Hart's choice of language and scolded the professor for work that bordered on fiction. "I am frankly sorry that you are to base a book to be called 'The Real South' upon such a journey or on the aggregate of this and other similar experiences," he declared, because "it will strike the minds of many of our best men both North and South as just another adventure in extemporaneous sociology. . . . You have not known, and—in such a journey—cannot begin to know the 'The Real South'—anymore than I can claim to know the 'Real North' though."[44] Murphy described Hart's social analysis as written "merely from the tourist point of view" and insisted that a deeper study crafted by a transplanted northerner living permanently on southern soil would clearly yield a more accurate study than one written by a traveler briefly passing through.[45]

In short, Murphy suggested that Hart's portrait of "the Real South" was an entirely fictional construction based on a patchwork of flimsy impressions and preconceived ideas. He challenged Hart's authority as a historian, alluding to its propagandistic nature. In the same way that Quentin and Shreve create an "imaginative construction of history," so Albert Bushnell Hart tried to frame his historical inquiry into the significance of the South. In a curious inversion, with southerner questioning northerner, Murphy might have asked Hart, "Why do you hate the South?" Hart may not have despised the South, but his credentials as a historian might be questioned given that he was writing on a current topic. In addition to Hart's quick jaunts to the South, his understanding of the region likely was shaped by interactions with southern students at Harvard, abolitionist memories passed down from his father, conversation with southern expatriates living in New England, and collaborations with historians at southern universities when he served on the board of and as president of the American Historical Association.

Thus the unremitting struggle to describe the South in the early twentieth century involved a universal tension between fact and fiction, history and imagination. Edgar Gardner Murphy might not have been off the mark in his accusation that Albert Bushnell Hart's identification of the "Real South" was a fable. In December of 1909 Hart gave his annual address as president of the American Historical Association and provocatively titled it "Imagination in History." Hart began with what initially appeared to be a celebration of the objective model of practicing history in the pursuit of truth. "What we need is a genuinely scientific school of history," he proclaimed, "which shall remorselessly examine the sources and separate the wheat from the chaff; which shall critically balance evidence; which shall dispassionately and moderately set forth results."[46] A good portion of the speech glorified and worshipped facts found in archives and evident in the behavior and personalities of great men. Hart understood the needs and expectations of his audience, a room teeming with historians on the cusp of the discipline's professionalization. But not surprisingly, Hart ended with a more humanistic plea for creating historical scholarship. "There is no great history without larger imagination, any more than there is painting, or, for that matter scientific discovery. Of all the writers of time not one has clearly seen this task of the historian more than the American sage Emerson."[47] Hart was referring to Massachusetts native and Harvard alumnus Ralph Waldo Emerson's 1841 essay "History," which claimed that an individual could successfully locate the entire past within himself. Past and present merge as well as fact and fiction. Emerson wrote that "all inquiry into antiquity . . . is the desire to do away with this wild, savage, and preposterous There or Then, and introduce in its place the Here and Now."[48] Shreve and Quentin's quest to reconstruct the Sutpen narrative and Hart's own writing also reflect the tension between the weight of the past and its present consequence.

For years at Harvard Professor Albert Bushnell Hart taught a general undergraduate course during the fall semester on American political and constitutional history known as History 13. I like to imagine Quentin and Shreve were enrolled in this course their first semester at Harvard since it was known to be an exceedingly popular choice. The only identified course they take is psychology. On the morning of his suicide, Quentin moves slowly and Shreve nags him about getting to class by 8:00 A.M. It is tempting to envision that William James taught Quentin and Shreve's psychology class, but the renowned psychologist and philosopher retired from teaching in 1907 and passed away in August of 1910. However, given the content of Hart's class and the timeline of Quentin and Shreve's attempt to uncover the story of Thomas Sutpen, it is entirely conceivable they took Hart's class. Faulkner writes that "the two of them who four months ago had never laid eyes on one another yet who since had slept in the same room and eaten side by side of the same food and used the same books from which to prepare to recite in the same freshman courses" were indelibly tied together in the here and now.[49]

According to Hart's teaching assistant Samuel Elliott Morison, who worked for him in the fall of 1910, the professor was frequently late to class after trudging across the college yard with a hefty green bag laden with notes "closely followed by a perspiring assistant, bearing an even greater bag stuffed with supplementary data." With the remaining forty-three minutes left in class, Hart then proceeded to deliver what Morison called a "rapid, brilliant, and witty commentary on the subject of the day."[50] Quentin and Shreve might have listened to these lectures intently since the professor often invited guests who were there to serve as a living monument of the past. Hart's classroom visitors included a radical abolitionist named Franklin B. Sanborn, who was a member of the Secret Committee of Six that funded John Brown's raid on Harper's Ferry, and a retired Union officer named Colonel Thomas Leonard Livermore. Hart required two written papers, one at the midway point and one at the end of the semester. For the first assignment the professor asked each student to fill out "an elaborate questionnaire about his father's profession, home, ancestors, etc., with a view to finding a biographical subject which would give him a personal identification with American history."[51] For the second assignment Hart circulated a self-authored handbook listing hundreds of themes on the history of slavery that students could choose to write on: the American slave system, pro-slavery arguments, antislavery arguments, the abolitionist movement, the slave trade, and the experience of African Americans in the United States.[52]

Quentin's compulsion to respond to Shreve's demand that he "tell about the South" might have been magnified by his experience in Hart's classroom researching Compson genealogy, listening to abolitionists, and debating the morality of slavery. Perhaps their discussion in the dorm room against the January backdrop of the "strange iron New England snow" grew out of topics in Professor Hart's course.[53] Shreve would have researched his own Canadian background, but curiosity about the assignment might have prompted him to insist not just that Quentin "tell about the South" but that he explain "What's it like there. What do they do there. Why do they live there. Why do they live at all."[54] In 1909 Quentin and Shreve certainly would have been aware of Albert Bushnell Hart's particular fascination with the South, including his interest in poor whites, rural poverty, race relations, miscegenation, and general southern backwardness. In addition, between 1909 and 1913 an acrimonious debate erupted over whether Confederates who were Harvard

alumni would be honored with a campus Civil War memorial. During
the early 1870s wealthy alumni funded the construction of Memorial
Hall, a building designed to honor those who had fought for the Union
cause. Should Confederate alumni, including the son of Robert E. Lee,
be offered a separate monument or integrated into Memorial Hall? Former graduates wrote countless letters, many calling for no recognition at
all for former Confederates, and debated the question within the pages
of the Harvard *Bulletin* and *Graduate's Magazine*. Northern schools
such as Yale and Princeton ultimately combined Confederate and Union
names, but Harvard never once paid tribute to Confederate soldiers.[55] In
its failure to memorialize men who fought for the South, the university
clung to its abolitionist and Union past, underscoring Massachusetts as
the state most emblematic of the North. It is not hard to imagine why
"Quentin Compson preparing for Harvard in the South, the deep South
dead since 1865 and peopled with garrulous outraged baffled ghosts,"
might find himself especially conflicted about "old ghost-times" when he
attended Harvard from 1909 to 1910.[56]

In Faulkner's novels, Massachusetts and Mississippi exist in the realm
of "only *is*" and not "*was*." My own personal experience with Massachusetts and Mississippi in the first two years of college, the ties between
Harvard University professor Albert Bushnell Hart and his cohorts at the
University of Mississippi during Faulkner's childhood, the give and take
between Shreve McCannon and Quentin Compson in a Harvard dorm
room, the possibility that two fictional freshmen named Shreve and
Quentin might have taken a real introductory history course with Professor Hart in the fall of 1909, and the release of Hart's book *The Southern
South* shortly before Quentin Compson's suicide in June of 1910 reflect
a parallelism born out of coincidence. These moments demonstrate the
Emersonian and Faulknerian indefiniteness of time, coupling fact and
fiction, history and literature. In the hour before his death, in a discon-
nected reverie, Quentin notes, "A quarter hour yet. And then I'll not
be. The peacefullest words. Peacefullest words. *Non fui. Sum. Fui. Non
Sum* [I was not. I am. I was. I am not]. Somewhere I heard bells once.
Mississippi or Massachusetts. I was. I am not. Massachusetts or Mississippi."[57] In reading Faulkner I am reminded that the study of history is
not only influenced by one's past and molded by the present but might
be sharpened through the use of imagination borne out of synchronicity.
Faulkner once wrote that "by sublimating the actual into apocryphal I
would have complete liberty to use whatever talent I might have to its
absolute top."[58] As a historian, considering the apocryphal when writing
about the actual, I hope for similar liberties.

NOTES

James B. Meriwether and Michael Millgate, eds., *Lion in the Garden: Interviews with William Faulkner, 1926–1962* (New York: Random House, 1968), 255.

1. *Amherst College 1986–1987 Catalog*, 73–74, Amherst College Digital Collections, Archives and Special Collections, Amherst, MA, https://acdc.amherst.edu/view/asc:455356 (accessed September 10, 2015).

2. For a useful history of Shays' Rebellion, see Leonard L. Richards, *Shays' Rebellion: The American Revolution's Final Battle* (Philadelphia: University of Pennsylvania Press, 2001). For a history of similar revolts involving taxation and issues of governance in the post-Revolutionary period, see Woody Holton, *Unruly Americans and the Origins of the Constitution* (New York: Hill and Wang, 2008) and Terry Bouton, *Taming Democracy: "The People," the Founders, and the Troubling End of American Democracy* (New York: Oxford University Press, 2009).

3. *Amherst College 1987–1988 Catalog*, 80–81, Amherst College Digital Collections, Archives and Special Collections, Amherst, MA, https://acdc.amherst.edu/view/asc:424554 (accessed September 10, 2015).

4. William Faulkner, *Intruder in the Dust*, rev. ed. (1948; repr., New York: Vintage International, 2011), 149–50.

5. See Joseph Crespino, "Mississippi as Metaphor: Civil Rights, the South, and the Nation in the Historical Imagination," in *The Myth of Southern Exceptionalism*, ed. Matthew D. Lassiter and Joseph Crespino (New York: Oxford University Press, 2010), 99–120.

6. "Mississippi: Is This America? (1962–1964)" transcript, *Eyes on the Prize: America's Civil Rights Movement 1954–1985*, Public Broadcasting System, http://www.pbs.org/wgbh/amex/eyesontheprize/about/pt_105.html (accessed August 25, 2015).

7. See James Cobb, *Away Down South: A History of Southern Identity* (New York: Oxford University Press, 2005); Jennifer Rae Greeson, *Our South: Geographic Fantasy and the Rise of National Literature* (Cambridge, MA: Harvard University Press, 2010); and Natalie J. Ring, *The Problem South: Region, Empire, and the New Liberal State, 1880–1930* (Athens: University of Georgia Press, 2012).

8. Dona Brown, *Inventing New England: Regional Tourism in the Nineteenth Century* (Washington, DC: Smithsonian Institution, 1995), and Margot Minardi, *Making Slavery History: Abolitionism and the Politics of Memory in Massachusetts* (New York: Oxford University Press, 2010).

9. Henry James, *The Bostonians* (New York: Random House, 2003), 5, 12, 64, 221, 232, 234.

10. William Faulkner, *The Sound and the Fury*, rev. ed. (1929; repr., New York: Vintage International, 1990), 178.

11. William Faulkner, *Absalom, Absalom!*, rev. ed. (1936; repr., New York: Vintage International, 1990), 5.

12. Ibid., 176.

13. For a history of the idea of the South as a problem, see Ring, *The Problem South*, and Larry J. Griffin and Don H. Doyle, eds., *The South as an American Problem* (Athens: University of Georgia Press, 1995).

14. James G. Watson, *William Faulkner: Self-Presentation and Performance* (Austin: University of Texas Press, 2002), 61.

15. Faulkner scholar Patrick Samway writes in his minute-by-minute reconstruction of Quentin Compson's last day of life before his suicide in *The Sound and the Fury* that Faulkner's "uncanny sense of direction" when it comes to Cambridge and Boston might

suggest he had visited. Samway argues that Boston is to William Faulkner what Dublin was to James Joyce. See Patrick Samway, "June 2, 1910: An Historic Day," in *Faulkner and History*, ed. Javier Coy and Michel Gresset (Salamanca: Ediciones Universidad de Salamanca, 1986), 111–12. Charles Chappell doubts Samway's assertions, since there are contradictions between *The Sound and the Fury* and the "Appendix Compson: 1699–1945" that Faulkner wrote in 1945 for Malcolm Cowley for *The Portable Faulkner*. Chappell argues it is not clear whether the death occurred in Boston or Cambridge. See Charles Chappell, "Quentin Compson's Scouting Expedition on June 2, 1910," *Essays in Literature* 22 (Spring 1995): 113–22.

16. Albert Bushnell Hart, "Conditions of the Southern Problem," *Independent* 58 (March 23, 1905): 644.

17. Ibid.; and W. J. Cash, *The Mind of the South* (Garden City, NY: Doubleday, 1941), viii.

18. Hart, "Conditions of the Southern Problem," 644.

19. Larry J. Griffin, "Why Was the South a Problem to America?" in Griffin and Doyle, *The South as an American Problem*, 14.

20. See Ring, *The Problem South*, for a detailed analysis of this phenomenon.

21. Cleanth Brooks, *William Faulkner: The Yoknapatawpha Country* (1963; repr., New Haven, CT: Yale University Press, 1991), 311–12.

22. William Faulkner, *Light in August*, rev. ed. (1932; repr., New York: Vintage International, 1990), 444. For a discussion of Gavin Stevens's significance to Faulkner's work, see Lori Watkins Fulton, *William Faulkner, Gavin Stevens, and the Cavalier Tradition* (New York: Peter Lang, 2011), and Claude Pruitt, "What's in a Name," unpublished manuscript in author's possession.

23. "Notes and News," *American Historical Review* 13 (April 1908): 703; and Franklin L. Riley, "Proceedings of the Decennial Meeting of the Mississippi Historical Society," in *Publications of the Mississippi Historical Society*, ed. Franklin L. Riley (Oxford, MS: Mississippi Historical Society, 1909), 9–12.

24. George Petrie to Peter J. Hamilton, 12 January 1907, Albert Bushnell Hart Papers, Folder "Southern Trips 1902–1908 #3," Box 2, Harvard University Archives, Cambridge, MA. Alabama Polytechnic Institute later came to be known as Auburn University. Also see Albert Bushnell Hart to Leroy Percy, 4 February 1908, Albert Bushnell Hart Papers, Folder "Southern Trips 1902–1908 #4," Box 2, Harvard University Archives, Cambridge, MA; Leroy Percy to Albert Bushnell Hart, 8 February 1908, Albert Bushnell Hart Papers, Folder "Southern Trips 1902–1908 #4," Box 2, Harvard University Archives, Cambridge, MA.

25. Thomas P. Bailey to Dear Friend, 14 January 1908, Albert Bushnell Hart Papers, Folder "Southern Trips 1902–1908 #3," Box 2, Harvard University Archives, Cambridge, MA.

26. "A Traducer of the South," *Columbus Dispatch*, January 15, 1908, 4.

27. See David M. Oshinsky, *"Worse Than Slavery": Parchman Farm and the Ordeal of Jim Crow Justice* (New York: Free Press, 1996), 90.

28. "The Venom of Dr. Albert Hart. Reprinted from the Jackson, Miss. Daily News, January 8, 1908," typescript, Albert Bushnell Hart Papers, Folder "Southern Trips 1902–1908 #3," Box 2, Harvard University Archives, Cambridge, MA.

29. Hart, "Conditions of the Southern Problem," 648.

30. "The Venom of Dr. Albert Hart," 1.

31. For a discussion of this lynching in the context of William Faulkner's life, see Don H. Doyle, *Faulkner's County: The Historical Roots of Yoknapatawpha* (Chapel Hill: University of North Carolina Press, 2001), 321–26; and Joel Williamson, *William Faulkner and Southern History* (New York: Oxford University Press, 1993), 157–61.

32. William Faulkner quoted in Barbara Ladd, *Nationalism and the Color Line in George W. Cable, Mark Twain, and William Faulkner* (Baton Rouge: Louisiana State

University Press, 1996), 157. Doyle, *Faulkner's County*, 326, also argues that the lynching of Nelse Patton likely would have been on Faulkner's radar in spite of his young age.

33. See Doyle, *Faulkner's County*, 292; Williamson, *William Faulkner and Southern History*, 73, 194, and A. Nicholas Fargnoli, Michael Golay, and Robert W. Hamblin, eds., *Critical Companion to William Faulkner: A Literary Reference to His Life and Work* (New York: Facts on File, 2008), 452.

34. See Joel Williamson, *The Crucible of Race: Black-White Relations in the American South since Emancipation* (New York: Oxford University Press, 1984), and Diane Miller Sommerville, *Rape and Race in the Nineteenth-Century South* (Chapel Hill: University of North Carolina Press, 2004), 223–60.

35. Doyle, *Faulkner's County*, 14.

36. Albert Bushnell Hart, *The Southern South* (New York: D. Appleton, 1910), 4.

37. Mrs. H. L. Harris, "A Southern Woman's Impressions of New York City," *Independent*, February 22, 1906.

38. *The South in the Building of the Nation* (Richmond, VA: Southern Historical Publication Society, 1909), xxi–xxii.

39. Ulrich B. Phillips quoted in John David Smith, "DuBois and Philipps—Symbolic Antagonists of the Progressive Era," *Centennial Review* 24 (Winter 1980): 94.

40. Dunbar Rowland to Albert Bushnell Hart, 7 March 1908, Albert Bushnell Hart Papers, Folder "Southern Trips 1902–1908 #3," Box 2, Harvard University Archives, Cambridge, MA.

41. Peter Novick, *That Noble Dream: The "Objectivity Question" and the American Historical Profession* (New York: Cambridge University Press, 1988), 58.

42. Albert Bushnell Hart to Edgar Gardner Murphy, 1 June 1905, Edgar Gardner Murphy Papers, Southern Historical Collection, Wilson Library, University of North Carolina at Chapel Hill.

43. Edgar Gardner Murphy to Albert Bushnell Hart, 8 October 1907, Albert Bushnell Hart Papers, Southern Question, Folder "Southern Trips 1902–1908, #2," Box 2, Harvard University Archives, Cambridge, MA.

44. Ibid.

45. Ibid.

46. Albert Bushnell Hart, "Imagination in History," *American Historical Review* 15 (January 1910): 230.

47. Ibid., 250–51.

48. Ralph Waldo Emerson, "History," in *The Essential Writings of Ralph Waldo Emerson*, ed. Brooks Atkinson (New York: Modern Library, 2000), 6.

49. Faulkner, *Absalom, Absalom!*, 208.

50. Samuel E. Morison, "Albert Bushnell Hart, 1889–1939," *Proceedings of the Massachusetts Historical Society*, Third Series, 66 (October 1936–May 1941): 436.

51. Samuel Eliot Morison, "A Memoir and Estimate of Albert Bushnell Hart," *Proceedings of the Massachusetts Historical Society*, Third Series, 77 (1965): 39.

52. Ibid.

53. Faulkner, *Absalom, Absalom!*, 141.

54. Ibid., 142; emphasis removed.

55. Helen P. Trimpi, *Crimson Confederates: Harvard Men Who Fought for the South* (Knoxville: University of Tennessee Press, 2009), xvi.

56. Faulkner, *Absalom, Absalom!*, 4.

57. Faulkner, *The Sound and the Fury*, 174.

58. Interview with Jean Stein vanden Heuvel, 255.

"Saturated" with the Past: William Faulkner, C. Vann Woodward, and the "Burden" of Southern History

JAMES C. COBB

On October 2, 1954, C. Vann Woodward was checking out of the Algon-quin Hotel in New York and on his way to England to assume his duties as Harmsworth Professor of American History at Oxford. With four highly regarded books already in print, the forty-five-year-old Johns Hopkins historian was well on his way, as Richard H. King put it, not only to revolutionizing "the established views of Southern history from the end of the Civil War to World War I" but to creating what King called "a new paradigm . . . a new way of looking at Southern history." For all his accomplishments, however, Woodward confessed to be feeling more than a little apprehensive about what awaited him over at Oxford as he stood in line to pay his bill, when, by his account, "a small man just in front of me . . . turned a profile and I immediately recognized him. I could have said that I was sorry to have missed him when Jim Silver took me to his house in Oxford. . . . And that I needed his blessing just now. But No." Nearly twenty-five years earlier, Woodward had botched a similar opportunity to meet another literary idol, Thomas Wolfe, and as he stood but inches away from William Faulkner, once again, he admit-ted, "My nerve failed me, and I never met another of my heroes."[1]

Unbeknown to Woodward at the time, he had caught Wolfe's atten-tion even before he fluffed his chance to meet him, and he and Robert Penn Warren had long since forged a mutually admiring relationship. Yet it is more than doubtful that the most acclaimed southern novelist of the twentieth century, who read very little, if any, southern history, would have even recognized, much less welcomed an advance from, the man who would become the region's most influential historian over the same span. The chance non-encounter seems regrettable nonetheless, in light not only of Woodward's oft-acknowledged intellectual debt to William Faulkner but of his career-long effort to transfuse the study of southern history with the same determination to challenge the past and explore its power over the present that flowed through the works of Faulkner, Wolfe, Warren, and other key figures in the literary awakening that began to flower in the South at the end of the 1920s.

Born in 1908, eleven years after Faulkner and 130 miles away in northeast Arkansas, as the son of a teacher, principal, and later school superintendent, Comer Vann Woodward grew up in a household steeped in the importance of formal education, though he would later insist that, like his literary idol, most of what he learned that was of real importance to him came at his own initiative. A voracious reader, even as a teenager, he developed a fascination with Henry James, and he feasted on Russian and British literature as well. After he had devoured most of the shelf content of the local Carnegie library, this passion for the written word would follow him to Henderson Brown College, a tiny Methodist liberal arts school in Arkadelphia, Arkansas. He quickly became a fixture in the college's literary society, and his English teacher recalled that he was "much more interested in English and writing" than history and that his compositions suggested he had all the makings of "a great novelist."[2]

After two years, the budding young writer moved on to Emory University, where despite his apparent aimlessness, he eventually earned Emory's first baccalaureate degree in philosophy in 1930. Truth be told, however, good literature, and increasingly, the art of writing it, remained Woodward's consuming interest, and here again the most critical relationships he formed revolved around the campus literary magazine, the *Phoenix*, where he not only contributed material but became fast friends with its business manager, Glenn W. Rainey, and its editor, Ernest Hartsock. Though Rainey was studying southern politics, he was a young man of a decided literary bent who would go on to translate a volume of Chaucer and, as an aspiring poet, see his verse published not only in the *Phoenix* but in the *New York Times*. Hartsock, meanwhile, was already widely recognized as a poet of proven talent and even greater promise. Not unlike other young intellectuals of his generation, Hartsock had declared war on the old, sterile romantic tradition in southern letters, and he not only anointed the *Phoenix* as "an oasis" in what H. L. Mencken decried as the "Sahara of the Bozart," but when he went on to launch his own magazine of verse, he dubbed it *Bozart*.[3]

Hartsock's untimely death in 1930 left Woodward and Rainey to soldier on dutifully in pursuit of "a literary style" by immersing themselves in the works of renowned writers such as James Joyce and Marcel Proust—in the latter case, Rainey explained, to give Proust "a chance to influence me while I am in the process of becoming a novelist." Woodward would later recall reading Faulkner "in college . . . without knowing what he was saying but without ever a doubt that he was saying it to me and that it changed everything." In reality, although it had been love at first read with Thomas Wolfe, Faulkner was more of an acquired taste for Woodward. He did not finish *The Sound and the Fury*, and aping a snide New York critic in 1938, he would even castigate Faulkner for appearing to "draw most of his subjects out of abandoned wells." He had revised his estimate dramatically four years later, however, when, eager to secure a copy of *Go Down, Moses*, he anointed its author as "tops of contemporaries—a high sense of tragedy and humor as rich as W. Shakespeare and more so than Mark Twain's."[4]

After graduating from Emory and coasting through the next year teaching English at Georgia Tech, Woodward was off, courtesy of a Rosenwald Fellowship, to pursue a master's degree at Columbia in 1931, where his biggest excitement came in briefly rubbing shoulders with Langston Hughes and other members of the New York literati. Though generally disinterested in his classes, he finally opted, more or less by default, to study political science. After writing his thesis on the notorious Alabama white supremacist, Sen. J. Thomas Heflin, he returned to Georgia Tech pondering a book about several contemporary southern demagogues before settling eventually on a single biographic account of the compelling, if deeply disturbing, life and career of Georgia's fiery Populist leader, Thomas E. Watson. Watson had begun his Populist career as a fierce champion of the South's oppressed rural masses, white and black, daring even to preach the heretical doctrine of black-white political cooperation. With the demise of the politically outgunned Populists in 1896, however, much as Dr. Jekyll gave way to Mr. Hyde, Watson sank to the depths of vitriolic Negrophobia and religious bigotry, the latter culminating in his role as a primary instigator of the lynching of Leo Frank in 1915.[5]

Woodward was still very much of a literary persuasion, and determined to tell what he repeatedly described as Watson's personal "story" in all the fullness of its pathos and tragedy. Approaching the project more like a novelist than a historian, he began writing with no "academic purpose in mind" and only "the faintest formal preparation" in American history, acquired in a single, exceedingly dull course at Emory that had "been more than enough to discourage further curiosity." A massive budget cut cost Woodward his job at Georgia Tech in 1933, however, and after researching for a year and writing four chapters of his Watson biography, his depleted finances persuaded him that "the best hope of completing the book seemed to be in getting a fellowship for graduate work in history and offering the book as a dissertation." Fortunately for him, through family and friends he met renowned University of North

Carolina sociologist Howard Odum, through whose offices he received a Rockefeller Foundation stipend for PhD study in history at UNC at Chapel Hill, which, propitiously enough, had recently secured Watson's private papers for its new Southern Historical Collection archive.[6]

For all his excitement about ready access to the Watson papers, he was less than thrilled about the prospect of graduate study in southern history, and as it turned out, utterly devastated by the reality. When he arrived at UNC in 1934, "at the peak and crest of the Southern Renaissance," he had at least expected to encounter some semblance of the "explosion of creativity" that had key figures in southern fiction, poetry, and drama "writing about the same things historians were writing about and making the whole world of letters at home and abroad . . . ring with their praise." Instead, he was sorely disappointed to find "no renaissance here, no surge of innovation and creativity, no compelling new vision." Even in the reputed "oasis in the Sahara of the Bozart" that was Chapel Hill, the masters of southern history were, by and large, simply recycling the "received wisdom" that had long sustained "the present order, the system founded on the ruins of Reconstruction known as the New South."[7]

Woodward's characterization found a perfect embodiment in J. G. de Roulhac Hamilton, the first director of the Southern Historical Collection, where the Watson papers were to be housed. Hamilton's writings on Reconstruction praised the Ku Klux Klan, and his classroom orations, much to Woodward's chagrin, were replete with racist references. Hamilton's selection as an archivist and collector was entirely in line with the thinking of University of Georgia historian E. Merton Coulter. In 1935 Coulter used the inaugural presidential address to the newly formed Southern Historical Association to rebuke his fellow white southerners for losing sight of the fact that, since the Civil War, history had emerged as the white South's "last stronghold . . . not for the defense of its nationality but for the protection of something more clear and sacred, its reputation." As a case in point, Coulter pointed approvingly to the Southern Historical Society, formed in 1869 by prominent ex-Confederates intent on collecting the appropriate historical documents to comprise "a complete arsenal from which the defenders of our cause may draw any desired weapon."[8]

With the eager assistance of the United Daughters of the Confederacy and numerous other Confederate memorialist groups, there quickly emerged a remarkably pervasive popular and academic historical justification of white southerners' actions before, during, and after the Civil War. The critical foundation of this mythic metanarrative lay in an utterly idyllic vision of an elegant and genteel Old South ruled by an enlightened and benevolent plantation aristocracy and described by a postbellum novelist as shining with "beauty . . . purity . . . grace" and "a charm that passes all language at my command." Though the leaders and sworn protectors of this veritable heaven on earth ultimately failed to repulse the subsequent Yankee invasion, their heroic defense of state rights and regional honor in the face of the overwhelmingly superior numbers had not only validated but sanctified their "Lost Cause." In the wake of its defeat, however, "under the euphemism of reconstruction," as Thomas Nelson Page put it, the white South, which had been both womb and cradle to the American republic itself, had been "dismembered, disfranchised, [and] denationalized" by the leaders of that same republic.[9]

What one scholar called this "tragic legend" of Reconstruction became another vital pillar of a comprehensive New South historical creed, but the critical link between a heroic but ultimately vanquished past and a "can-do/kick-butt" vision of the future lay in an adoring portrayal of the Redeemers, so named for their bravura performance in bringing the horrors of Reconstruction to an end. Somehow, without sullying in the least the honorable traditions of their planter-aristocrat forebears, these men had brazenly stuffed ballot boxes, terrorized would-be black voters, and murdered or set to flight a good number of Republican politicians of both races, thereby rescuing the white South from the living hell of Yankee tyranny and black rule. That accomplished, in their wisdom, the Redeemers had eagerly embraced the New South vision of industrial progress, determined, as historian David Goldfield noted, "to beat the Yankees at their own game," vowing steadfastly all the while to "build factories and cities" without "corrupt[ing] the morals of the people or upset[ting] racial, gender, and social balances derived from the vanished civilization." Accordingly, postbellum proponents of thoroughly industrializing and commercializing the region forfeited no opportunity to pay homage to what Henry Grady called the glorious "civilization" of the Old South, "which has not been surpassed, and perhaps will not be equaled among men," and to insist in virtually the same breath, as Grady did, that the New South would simply be "the Old South under new conditions."[10]

As in numerous cases of identity-construction across time and space, the prophets of a New South proclaimed undying fealty to a lost golden age of yore, while promising a future golden age that would not simply reclaim, but eclipse, the glories of the first, and New South dogma demanded a prematurely triumphant vision of regional self-resurrection. As Paul M. Gaston noted, early-twentieth-century professional New South historians focused on "the concept of triumph over adversity, of steel will and impeccable character overcoming staggering problems, often against what seemed impossible odds."[11] W. Fitzhugh Brundage noted that despite their propensity for exaggeration the emerging turn-of-the-century generation of young professionals pursuing southern history as an academic career separated themselves from their untrained amateur contemporaries largely by claiming a more scientific and ostensibly objective approach rather than by challenging "conventional attitudes" or advancing "unorthodox interpretations of hallowed themes."[12]

The New South historical creed presented such a formidably seductive synthesis of a glorious past, a reassuring present, and a glittering future that historians inclined to criticize or challenge any aspect of it did so at their peril. A case in point was the founder of the *Sewanee Review*, William P. Trent, whose criticism of such Old South and Confederate icons as John C. Calhoun, William Gilmore Simms, and Jefferson Davis led some Sewanee trustees to brand him "a dangerous religious and political heretic." With some of his more pious faculty colleagues also praying fervently for his "spiritual regeneration," Trent ultimately opted for a one-way ticket to New York and Columbia University.[13]

The quickest route to an "enforced resignation," maintained Randolph Macon historian William E. Dodd not long before he took off for the University of Chicago himself in 1908, lay in "suggesting that the revolt from the union in 1860 was not justified." Foolishly presuming that, a half century after Fort Sumter, some "calm history" might be in order, University of Florida professor Enoch M. Banks naively posited in 1911 that the root cause of secession was not state rights, but slavery and that, on balance, "the North was relatively right and the South was relatively wrong." When the ensuing outcry reached the point of threats to withhold the university's funding, Banks was compelled to resign.[14]

All of this is to suggest that, in its broad outlines and social and political implications, academic writing and commentary on the South's history differed but little from deeply embedded and jealously guarded popular perceptions even in the mid-1930s when Woodward arrived for his professional training in Chapel Hill. This raises some intriguing questions about the potential influence of more formal academic historical training on a thirty-seven-year-old Mississippi writer who had already mined his region's past quite effectively in several novels and short stories at that juncture, even though his last and most systematic instruction about that past had come in seventh grade. William Faulkner acknowledged that a college education could "save the writer a good deal of trouble . . . in simply learning about . . . the recorded history of man . . . which otherwise he has got to get out and dig for himself." Yet he also cautioned that in pursuing his craft, the real fiction writer "don't get out and do any research" in the formal sense but "collects his material all his life from everything he reads, from everything he listens to, everything he sees," all to be filed away in his mind and retrieved later when he needs to "throw the flashlight on the particular moment."[15]

Faulkner's own virtual file cabinet bulged with material plucked from an incessant swirl of legendary battlefield exploits, recycled hearsay, exaggeration, and, especially for him, the bitterly resentful harangues of his "maiden spinster aunts [who] had never surrendered." There was also no shortage of gossip about once-high-and-mighty slaveholding families fallen on hard times and rough-edged arrivistes on the make. Nor was Faulkner isolated from the staged or performed past, including striking visuals of wobbly Confederate veterans who, he recalled, "would get out the old shabby grey uniforms and . . . the old battle-flag on Decoration [or] Memorial Day." Stashed away in his personal historical memory file and later infused with his imagination, these observations and recollections became the stuff of a far more compelling narrative than any traditional archive might have offered at that or perhaps any point. At any rate, it seems fair to say that had Woodward's literary hero joined him when he began graduate study at the University of North Carolina, he would have confronted an approach to writing and teaching southern history that might have enhanced his factual knowledge while not only blinding him to historical reality but, worse yet, stifling his curiosity about historical truth.[16]

Writing in 1938, Donald Davidson pointed out that every major piece of writing about the region in the last fifteen years had explored "the historian's question—What the South was?—and the related question— What the South is?" Yet in reality no group of intellectuals had proven more reluctant at that point to ask the historian's questions about the South than its historians themselves. Not so for its writers, however, including not only such historical inquisitors as Faulkner, Thomas Wolfe, and Ellen Glasgow, but none other than Margaret Mitchell. Mitchell's insistence that she had undertaken *Gone with the Wind* with no "intention of writing about Cavaliers" certainly resonates in Gerald O'Hara, a largely illiterate Irish bogtrotter whose obsessive hunger for wealth and position served him much better than Thomas Sutpen's as he rose meteorically into the planter aristocracy, winning even the lordly Mrs. Wilkes's anointment as "a gentleman." Mitchell's challenge to the Cavalier myth was largely lost in Hollywood's rush to romanticize the Old South in the celluloid version of her novel. The film's producers did better, however, by her more openly critical treatment of the greedy New South as it was captured in the impoverished Scarlett O'Hara's vow to go to Atlanta where there was "still plenty of money to be made by anyone who isn't afraid to work—or to grab." Scarlett is afraid to do neither, nor to mock the Old South gender conventions, preserved and practiced in Mitchell's youth by Confederate widows and spinster aunts, like Faulkner's, who clung to the foolish notion that it was somehow possible to "be a lady without money." Mitchell was actually quite conversant with the relevant historiography when she began the book, and although her oft-criticized depictions of slavery, Reconstruction, and black-white relations departed but little from the prevailing scholarly orthodoxy, her scathing portrayal of the New South actually went further than any but a very few of her academic contemporaries in southern history were willing to go in the mid-1930s.[17]

Woodward's dissertation-turned-book on Watson would eventually prove him an exception, of course, but only after showing such disdain for what a fellow graduate student called "the facts of history" that he almost failed his PhD orals and admitting that he had yielded "only when I had to" when adviser Howard Beale urged him to provide more of the "transitions, summaries, etc." that would assist readers in grasping the details and broader historiographical implications of his study. Woodward's preference for a more novelistic approach came through in his observation that the entire Watson saga "would make as powerful stuff" as Wolfe's *Look Homeward Angel*, "drunken, raw, and full of passion." In the end, his effort to do justice to Watson's story simply confirmed for him "the sheer inadequacy of biography vs. fiction." Even as it went to press, he worried that "the book would have been better . . . if I had been prey to all the pangs of a literary conscience—instead of sometimes mearley [sic] the PhD conscience which is something else."[18]

Readers consistently applauded Woodward's literary achievement in *Tom Watson: Agrarian Rebel* (1938), but though he later claimed that the book attacked the prevailing historiographical view of southern Populism as both economically irrational and politically irrelevant, this challenge was clearly more apparent to Woodward in retrospect than to the great majority of his initial readership. Reacting to a reviewer who praised the book but totally misread its implications, he sounded more like a temperamental artist than a scholar when he airily declared that he was "not surprised that it is not understood. I did not expect it to be." He also insisted that "sometimes there is virtue in lack of clarity" because "the reader should do some of the work . . . and appreciates more what is not spoonfed." Yet, by focusing so intently on the story of the man rather than the movement he led, while scarcely even hinting at the possibility of political and economic motivations for Watson's otherwise mysterious turn to the dark side after 1896, he left most reviewers free to see the book primarily as the tragic story of a white southern liberal taken down by the self-destructive racism that plagued his people or, more broadly, as a metaphor for the entire region.[19]

Whether it was interpreted precisely as Woodward intended, the
Watson biography brought its author notice. In February 1939, Woodward was invited to write volume four, covering the period 1877 to 1913,
in the recently announced History of the South series, a project funded,
ironically enough, by Major George Littlefield, C.S.A., a wealthy Texan
intent on securing a version of southern history that offered "the plain
facts concerning the South . . . fairly stated in order that the children
of the South may be properly taught." Littlefield's vision had been captured quite well in the first volume published in the series. E. Merton
Coulter's *The South during Reconstruction, 1865–1877*, which appeared
in 1947, amounted, so claimed a sarcastic detractor, to "an impartial history from the Southern point of view" that fairly reeked of the very New
South historical orthodoxy that Woodward was by then determined to
overturn.[20]

To that end, he immediately shelved plans for another biography and
leapt at the opportunity "to have my say about the period. . . . To lay
down the main lines of interpretation and to do something fairly definitive." Despite his contention that readers should not be "spoonfed" and
perhaps already mindful that his Watson book had only struck the historiographical establishment a glancing blow, Woodward was determined
that there would be no "intentional obscurity" in *Origins of the New
South, 1877–1913*. He invited those who read his chapter drafts to "give
me hell for it." Rainey and Howard Beale proved especially obliging.
The former thought Woodward's "thread of thought was somewhat tangled" and called for "clear summaries of interest and accomplishment at
the start and the close, and plain unadorned transitions within the chapters!" Meanwhile, Beale chided him for repeatedly assuming "too much
intelligence and imagination on the part of the reader" and pointed to
specific passages where "you could state it much more explicitly than you
do without spoiling the artistic effect of it as it is."[21]

Woodward's newfound receptivity to such criticism paid off hand-
somely. Although World War II and other intervening factors delayed
its publication until 1951, *Origins of the New South, 1877–1913* was a
sweeping and altogether brilliant narrative that also amounted to what
Woodward saw as "a sort of historiographical black mass in the eyes of
the believers." As his first heresy, Woodward attacked the notion that
the Redeemers and their New South descendants could trace their
roots to the old Cavalier order, when, in fact, they were "of middle class,
industrial, capitalistic outlook with little but nominal connection with the
old planter regime." After attacking the Redeemers' claims to ancestral
legitimacy, Woodward went on to question their virtue and leadership,
arguing that Redeemer governments were no more honest or fiscally

responsible than those of the Reconstruction era and that they had systematically starved the South's schools and public services. Shackling the region with a ruthlessly exploitive colonial industrial economy controlled by the moneyed interests of the Northeast, they had also abandoned the vast majority of its rural population of both races to the seemingly endless and hopeless cycle of tenancy, dependency, and debt that was the sharecropping and crop-lien system. Complicit in all this, of course, were the Redeemers' New South protégés who, for all their promises of a New Canaan awash in milk and honey and lots of money, had instead delivered an outdated and unjust economic system that offered little more than "juleps for the few and pellagra for the crew."[22]

For Woodward, Charles A. Beard's vision of history as the story of the successive conflicts of competing economic systems or interests seemed altogether appropriate to explain the demise of the Populists and the rise of the Redeemers and their would-be modernizer New South successors. It is doubtful, to say the least, that Faulkner ever read Beard, but historian Sheldon Hackney's observation that the overarching Beardian narrative Woodward offered in *Origins* would "provide a familiar context for many of Faulkner's characters" raises the question of how the perspectives and approaches of two of the South's ablest interpreters may have complemented, supplemented, or contradicted each other as they examined a common time and place.[23]

Though Woodward made no secret of his sympathies for the down-and-out Georgia farmers who rallied to the banner of Populism in the 1890s, he generally assumed their interests and yearnings were faithfully depicted in the public rhetoric of Tom Watson, who at that point was one of the state's wealthiest farmers and a landlord to hundreds of tenants. Largely ignoring potential differences in political and economic aims between landlord and tenant and writing in an era when evidence of the day-to-day lives of poor southerners of either race was admittedly hard to come by, Woodward also lacked the kind of personal experiences and associations that would have offered a richer sense of them as anything more than victims. Simply put, the contents of his virtual file cabinet would not have sustained anything remotely akin to Faulkner's brilliant evocation of landlord-merchant Will Varner's deftly negotiated relationship with an unwitting constituency of fiercely independent "Protestants and Democrats and prolific" yeomen to whom he managed to convey without the appearance of command what he would "like for [them] to do if [he] was able to make [them] do it."[24]

Although Woodward was born in a county named for one Confederate forebear and in a village named for another, no spectral ancestral presence hovered about as he wrote southern history. Still, though he wrote relatively little about the antebellum planter regime, when he did, his treatments seemed more understanding and respectful than might be expected of someone committed to overthrowing the historiographical order. Part of this disposition may be checked off to the influence of a Beardian vision of the Civil War as a conflict between the rising industrial behemoth of the North and the outmanned and out-factoried agrarian interests of the South. Not only did such an approach cast the old planter class as underdogs, but its focus on conflicting regional economies helped to subsume their specific identification with slavery to their broader affiliation with agrarianism. As Louis D. Rubin surmised, Woodward clearly saw antebellum planters as "a distinctive landed gentry with a set of values and attitudes qualitatively different from the finance-capital-dominated plutocracy of the Northeast." Beyond this, however, for all his self-proclaimed aversion to Old South romanticism, Woodward's tendency to empathize with the old, presumably anticapitalist planters suggests that, as a close friend noted, he might well believe "there was a genuine aristocracy," and "he feels this aristocracy thing more than he lets on."[25]

For Faulkner, meanwhile, the long shadow of his legendary great-grandfather, William Clark Falkner, "the Old Colonel," clearly fell across many of the pages that he wrote. His personal yearnings after at least a "performed aristocracy," manifested in his late-in-life efforts to insinuate himself into the Virginia hunting set, may also have complicated his struggle to come to terms with the rapid deterioration of the finest old families as the postbellum South moved toward modernity. Like his own "Old Colonel," Faulkner's Colonel John Sartoris passed into legend as an aristocratic and dashing Confederate who became an equally brazen and bold Redeemer as likely to shoot a carpetbagger as to look at him. Faulkner generally adhered to the legend of the colonel's wartime bravery, but in the dirty business of restoring white supremacy and Democratic rule, he is shown more transparently as ruthless, rigid, power-mad, and ultimately self-destructive. The latter characteristics become increasingly pronounced in his male descendants, whose ongoing unrequited struggle to reconnect with the family's aristocratic tradition and efforts to situate themselves within it culminate with young (and truly bad-news) Bayard Sartoris, who scores a "two-fer" in effecting not only his own demise but his grandfather's as well.[26]

Faulkner would likewise chronicle the progressive implosion of the patrician Compsons in *The Sound and the Fury* and elsewhere, giving particular emphasis to failed Confederate general Jason Lycurgus Compson II's decision to mortgage the square mile comprising the family's holdings to "a New England carpetbagger" in 1866 (in just the sort of sellout for which Woodward would roundly lambaste his less aristocratic version of the Redeemers). Faulkner would more than once allude to the willingness of successive generations of Compsons to renege, bit by bit, on their obligations to the land until the general's embittered, thoroughly materialistic namesake, Jason Compson IV, would be reduced to clerking in a farm-supply store and cynically observing that "pride" was simply beyond his means.[27]

Faulkner flashes back in *Absalom, Absalom!* to the days when the Compsons were still among the principal gatekeepers of polite society in Jefferson. In the novel, General Compson attributes Thomas Sutpen's failure to secure entrée to that society to his belief that social acceptance and standing require only a big house, lots of land and slaves, and the right wife who could give him a male heir to whom it all might be passed. Yet Faulkner also reveals the first Compson who arrives in Mississippi is the son of a traitor and a totally ruthless man who comes as "a free forester to grasp where and when he could and wanted to, and established what should have been a princely line." In scarcely three generations that line had, in fact, produced a governor, Quentin MacLachan Compson II, who would stand, by Faulkner's reckoning, as "the last Compson who would not fail at everything he touched save longevity or suicide."[28]

By that point, Thomas Sutpen is already on the scene in Jefferson, of course, and the fact that, employing an approach much like Sutpen's, Jason Lycurgus Compson I had succeeded where Sutpen did not might suggest that the latter's failure reflected not simply his ignorance of an unwritten social and class compact but the local elite's discomfort with a latecomer forced to scratch, kick, and claw his way up in full view of more established families who doubtless preferred not to think about the ugly details of their own clan's still relatively recent ascent.

Beyond his allusions to the emotional devastation inflicted by their defeat in war, Faulkner shied away from a broad explanation of how a class of such people who had shown themselves so valorous and strong in the antebellum era could so easily lose their grip on the levers of power and influence thereafter. Certainly, his fiction frequently suggested that, however genuine their dedication to honesty and honor, the old planter-cavaliers were simply ill equipped to cope with encroaching modernity. He was hardly the first southern writer to explore this theme, of course. John Pendleton Kennedy had even hinted ever so gently of such doubts in his 1832 novel *Swallow Barn*, and by the middle of the nineteenth century, William Gilmore Simms was observing that, however honorable and proud, the men of the old planter elite were often of little use in a real crisis. "In disastrous periods," Simms complained, "they fold their arms, in stupid despair." For Simms, the hesitant and indecisive planter was but a latter-day embodiment of Shakespeare's Hamlet, "whose native hue of resolution / Is sicklied o'er with the pale cast of thought."[29]

Faulkner was certainly not alone among writers and intellectuals of his era in setting the demise of those old planter aristocrats within a broader regional declension narrative in which they invariably profited by comparison with the regime that displaced them. Utterly contemptuous of the contemporary South's Babbitry and cultural sterility as the 1920s drew to a close, H. L. Mencken even bemoaned the "calamity of Appomattox" as the death knell for "a civilization of manifold excellences," effectively reduced to rubble by the rabble after the "old aristocracy went down the red gullet of war," leaving "the poor white trash . . . now in the saddle." Whatever Thomas Wolfe's distaste for the enduring romantic vision of the Old South, he could find even less good in the New, as he revealed in his absolute disgust with his booming hometown of Asheville, which in 1922 he found awash in "greed, greed, greed—deliberate crafty and motivated." Meanwhile, as Robert Penn Warren noted, though Faulkner "knew, hated and wrote about it," his general "outsideness" relative to modern America was even more pronounced with respect to the New South, which Faulkner famously declared was really "not the South" at all but "a land of immigrants" intent on rebuilding Dixie in the image of "the towns and cities in Kansas and Iowa and Illinois."[30]

Woodward's personal distaste for the exploitive greed and coarse materialism of the New South movement was not difficult to discern in *Origins of the New South*, where he clearly made good on his personal conviction that "besides teaching people what to hate and what to cherish . . . education should equip them with proper heroes and villains." In this case, he was trying to show that, by embracing the Redeemers and scoffing at their Populist challengers, white southerners had actually been applauding the villains and booing the heroes. As Hackney and others have suggested, though sweepingly Beardian in its emphasis on economic conflict, *Origins* was also imbued with a slightly less fatalistic but still decidedly Faulknerian vision of southern history. Woodward himself allowed that in its materialistic desecration of traditional southern values, the New South meant "the Compsons going to work for the Snopeses." As in Faulkner's fiction, heroes in Woodward's history were few and flawed, with Tom Watson a case in point. Yet where Faulkner's villains were typically complicated and even occasionally sympathetic, Woodward's (comprising the Redeemers and New South prophets and profiteers alike) were noticeably more one dimensional and much easier to despise. In his view, this demonization was more than justified because at the middle of the twentieth century, southern politicians still spared no effort in casting themselves as the second coming of the old Redeemer captains, swearing to save the South from any semblance of a Second Reconstruction that would once again seek to destroy white supremacy.[31]

Woodward would make his most striking and far-reaching attempt at historically conscious social engineering in *The Strange Career of Jim Crow*, which appeared less than a year after the historic 1954 *Brown v. Board of Education* desegregation decision. Intent on undermining segregation's guardians and jolting those who simply acquiesced to it, Woodward insisted that, widespread popular belief notwithstanding, the South's rigid system of racial separation and discrimination was no ancient, immutable custom. Indeed, black-white relations had shown remarkable fluidity from the end of the Civil War until racial separation was written heavy-handedly into law, beginning only at the end of the nineteenth century. Contrary to those who foresaw insurmountable difficulties in implementing the *Brown* decree, if Woodward was correct, as a practice created by law, and relatively recently at that, segregation must surely be susceptible to destruction by the same means.[32]

Meanwhile, Faulkner's widely quoted World War II letter to his stepson declaring that "[a] change will come out of this war" and expressing his personal hope that "there will be a part for me, who cant do anything but use words, in the re-arranging of the house" seemed largely in keeping with Woodward's historical activism. It was, however, decidedly out of character for someone who, as Warren observed, previously "had no truck with any obvious program for social salvation," and Faulkner's subsequent halting and often awkward, if not embarrassing, efforts to do his part by commenting personally on the struggle for racial justice in the South seemed to generate more confusion and controversy than anything else. Much the same was true when his invigorated sense of social purpose appeared to creep into his fiction, most notably perhaps in *Intruder in the Dust*. Here, the muddled mystery surrounding the murder that threatens to get an elderly black man, Lucas Beauchamp, lynched competes for the reader's attention with long-winded lawyer Gavin Stevens and his incessant bloviating about southern whites being allowed to clean up the racial mess they have made without interference from meddling Yankee "outlanders."[33]

In the end, *Intruder in the Dust* was, as Richard Gray put it, "a register of the confusion of the time when it was written and the man who wrote it." Thus some critics considered the book to be a Faulknerian "counterblast" aimed at the emerging civil rights agenda revealed in the 1948 Democratic presidential platform, while others tended to see the story as "an expression of hope that the South may extricate itself from the swamps of hatred and violence." Others challenged the plausibility of a tale where a white teenager manages, with only the assistance of a black counterpart and a free-spirited white matron, to thwart the male white southerner's historic impulse to rush without judgment to lynch any black man accused of murdering a white man. In reality, of course, the very improbability of this tiny little victory underscored the power of a past that is an almost palpable presence throughout the book.[34]

Faulkner's consistent focus on what one admirer called the "impossible load of the past" might seem to suggest a connection with Woodward through the title of Woodward's 1960 collection of essays, *The Burden of Southern History*. Although the final edition of Woodward's book (1993) would offer an essay addressing Faulkner's "Burden," the title is ultimately and perhaps unwittingly ironic because the two most widely read pieces in the collection, "The Irony of Southern History" and "The Search for a Central Theme," both written in the 1950s, argued that for all its suffusion with brutality, suffering, and defeat, the southerner's historical legacy need not be entirely burdensome. If the South's record of failure and humiliation denied southerners a share in the exhilarating national legend of invincibility and moral certitude savored by other Americans, it just as surely gave them something in common with practically all the other peoples of the known world. As the only Americans to whom history had actually "happened" at that point, they held claim, therefore, to a distinctive regional identity that required no further clinging to white supremacy as the very cornerstone of "the southern way of life." In addition, properly understood, their peculiarly un-American encounter with defeat might inspire them to caution their fellow Americans against an uncritical embrace of the reckless messianism and megalomania that gripped their nation in the midst of the Cold War.[35]

The idea that southerners might suddenly recognize and embrace the lessons within their own history—and even share them with the Yankees—would likely have been a hard sell to William Faulkner, who generally found the substance of the past less user-friendly than did Woodward. Certainly, this was true by the early 1960s, when, with Parchman bulging with Freedom Riders and a defiant latter-day, race-baiting Clarence Snopes at the helm in Mississippi, Faulkner's final novel struck some as simply an admission that he had lost the heart for further struggle against a resurgent and still intractable past. In *The Reivers*, he chose to construct a much different past, situated not in the actual first decade of the twentieth century, marked by nearly eight hundred lynchings, but in an imagined one, featuring a congenial, communal society where race and class distinctions needed no blunt enforcement and where an eleven-year-old boy could emerge as one of the few of Faulkner's males of aristocratic lineage who ultimately proves worthy of the challenges he faces. Disappointed liberals might see the author sifting here through the past one last time and suggesting rather wishfully that perhaps we should give the southern upper crust another whirl at saving our present from our past. It is fair enough, by literary standards, to assess *The Reivers* as "Faulkner Lite," but there is also a very real sense in which this judgment also imposes the standards of the historian on the novelist who, in this case, is not granted the license simply to do what novelists do by probing his memory and imagination for one final rollicking good story.[36]

At the very least, this reaction should remind us that, while what William Faulkner wrote *made* history, it was often *made into* history by others, some of whom then proceeded to judge him as a historian when, in reality, as Warren suggested, his objective was not to add to the crust of formally recorded history but to explore "the moral reality beneath it." Surely no one understood this better than Woodward, who hung Faulkner's picture behind his desk at Yale because he had come to realize that Faulkner "was always a powerful influence on me, although I didn't always know it." This did not mean that he saw the Yoknapatawpha novels that so inspired him offering a sense of "southern history in microcosm" or "any very consistent ideas or theories about Southern history." Yet Woodward fully appreciated that Faulkner's observation that he "never read about" the South's history but was simply "saturated" with it was the key to his genius for helping us "know" the past as other humans experienced it, rather than as a mere collection of fact and detail subjected to stringent scholarly analysis. Woodward also understood that in their acute awareness of the imposing and enduring power of the past in the present, Faulkner and the best of his southern literary contemporaries had far outstripped their historian counterparts in "[giving] history meaning and value and significance as events never do merely because they happen."[37]

NOTES

1. Richard H. King, *A Southern Renaissance: The Cultural Awakening of the American South, 1930–1955* (New York: Oxford University Press, 1980), 257; and Woodward to David H. Donald, 17 June 1984, folder 176, box 16, C. Vann Woodward Papers, Manuscripts and Archives, Sterling Memorial Library, Yale University.

2. John Herbert Roper, *C. Vann Woodward, Southerner* (Athens: University of Georgia Press, 1987), 1–30; Ellen Boulware et al., interview by John Herbert Roper, 18 March 1984, transcript, folder 20, box 1, John Herbert Roper Papers, Southern Historical Collection, Louis Round Wilson Library, University of North Carolina, Chapel Hill; and Roger Adelson, "Interview with C. Vann Woodward," *Historian* 54 (September 1991): 3.

3. James C. Cobb, "On the Pinnacle in Yankee Land: C. Vann as a [Southern] Renaissance Man," *Journal of Southern History* 67 (November 2001): 715–16.

4. Glenn W. Rainey to Woodward, 16 September 1929, folder 2, box 22, Glenn Weddington Rainey Papers, Special Collections, Robert W. Woodruff Library, Emory University; Woodward to Rainey, 19 October 1942, folder 1, box 22, Rainey Papers; Woodward to Robert Penn Warren, 8 April 1966, folder 703, box 59, Woodward Papers; and C. Vann Woodward, "The South in Search of a Philosophy," *Phi Beta Kappa Addresses at the University of Florida* (1938), 15.

5. Woodward to Rainey, 20 October 1931, folder 1, box 22, Rainey Papers; n.d., folder 3, box 22, Rainey Papers; C. Vann Woodward, "J. Thomas Heflin, the Nativist" (Master's thesis, Columbia University, 1932); and Roper, *C. Vann Woodward*, 52, 76.

6. C. Vann Woodward, *Thinking Back: The Perils of Writing History* (Baton Rouge: Louisiana State University Press, 1986), 20–21.

7. Ibid., 22–23.

8. Joseph Grégoire de Roulhac Hamilton, *Reconstruction in North Carolina* (New York: Columbia University Press, 1914); and E. Merton Coulter, "What the South Has Done about Its History," in *The Pursuit of Southern History: Presidential Addresses of the Southern Historical Association, 1935–1963*, ed. George B. Tindall (Baton Rouge: Louisiana State University Press, 1964), 14–17.

9. George W. Bagby, quoted in David R. Goldfield, *Still Fighting the Civil War: The American South and Southern History* (Baton Rouge: Louisiana State University Press, 2002), 21; and Thomas Nelson Page, *The Old South: Essays Social and Political* (Chautauqua, NY: Chautauqua Press, 1919), 41, 45, 4.

10. Goldfield, *Still Fighting the Civil War*, 22; Paul M. Gaston, *The New South Creed: A Study in Southern Mythmaking*, rev. ed. (1970; repr., Montgomery, AL: New South Books, 2002), 181, 173.

11. Paul M. Gaston, "The New South," in *Writing Southern History: Essays in Historiography in Honor of Fletcher M. Green*, ed. Arthur S. Link and Rembert W. Patrick (Baton Rouge: Louisiana State University Press, 1965), 321.

12. W. Fitzhugh Brundage, *The Southern Past: A Clash of Race and Memory* (Cambridge, MA: Harvard University Press, 2005), 128–29.

13. William P. Trent, *William Gilmore Simms* (Boston: Houghton, Mifflin and Company, 1892); William P. Trent, *Southern Statesmen of the Old Regime: Washington, Jefferson, Randolph, Calhoun, Stephens, Toombs, and Jefferson Davis* (New York: Thomas Y. Crowell and Company, 1897); and Bruce Clayton, *The Savage Ideal: Intolerance and Intellectual Leadership in the South, 1890–1914* (Baltimore, MD: Johns Hopkins University Press, 1972), 69, 74.

14. William E. Dodd, "Some Difficulties of the History Teacher in the South," *South Atlantic Quarterly* 3 (April 1904): 119; and David W. Blight, *Race and Reunion: The Civil War in American Memory* (Cambridge, MA: Harvard University Press, 2001), 296.

15. William Faulkner, quoted in *Faulkner in the University: Class Conferences at the University of Virginia, 1957–1958*, ed. Frederick L. Gwynn and Joseph L. Blotner (Charlottesville: University Press of Virginia, 1995), 204, 116.

16. Ibid., 249.

17. Donald Davidson, *The Attack on Leviathan: Regionalism and Nationalism in the United States* (Chapel Hill: University of North Carolina Press, 1938), 322–23; Margaret Mitchell, quoted in Darden Asbury Pyron, *Southern Daughter: The Life of Margaret Mitchell* (New York: Harper and Row, 1992), 319; and Margaret Mitchell, *Gone with the Wind* (1936; repr., New York: Warner Books, 1993), 48–53, 600, 602.

18. Woodward to Rainey, 12 July 1936, folder 1, box 22, Rainey Papers; Woodward to Rainey, 29 April 1935, folder 1, box 22, Rainey Papers; J. Carlyle Sitterson, interview

by John Herbert Roper, 10 November 1978, folder 7, box 1, Roper Papers; Woodward to Rainey, October 1933, 4 December 1942, and 6 November 1937, folder 1; Woodward to Jack [last name unknown], 15 July 1937, folder 4, box 22, Rainey Papers; and 24 August [year unknown], folder 3, box 22, Rainey Papers.

19. Woodward to Antonina Jones Hansell, 11 April 1938, Antonina Hansell Looker Papers, Southern Historical Collection; and Woodward to Rainey, 6 November 1937, folder 1, box 22, Rainey Papers.

20. Littlefield, quoted in "Littlefield Fund for Southern History, Second Grant, Quotations from Major Littlefield's Will," folder "Correspondence, Classified, 1945–1952, and undated," box 2B104, Eugene C. Barker Papers, Center for American History, University of Texas at Austin; E. Merton Coulter, *The South during Reconstruction, 1867–1877* (Baton Rouge: Louisiana State University Press, 1947); and David H. Donald, "The Southern Memory," *New Leader*, July 31, 1948, 11, folder "E. Merton Coulter, 1955," box 7, Wendell Holmes Stephenson Papers, Perkins Library, Duke University.

21. Woodward to Rainey, 26 March 1939, folder 2, box 22, Rainey Papers; Rainey to Woodward, 14 November 1942, folder 2, box 22, Rainey Papers; Woodward to Rainey, 4 December 1942, folder 1, box 22, Rainey Papers; Beale to Woodward, 4 August 1939, folder 65, box 7, Woodward Papers; and Beale to Woodward, 3 December 1942, folder 1, box 26, Howard K. Beale Papers, Wisconsin State Historical Society, Madison.

22. Woodward, *Thinking Back*, 63; C. Vann Woodward, *Origins of the New South, 1877–1913* (Baton Rouge: Louisiana State University Press, 1951), 20; and C. Vann Woodward, "New South Fraud Is Papered by Old South Myth," *Washington Post*, July 9, 1961.

23. Sheldon Hackney, "Origins of the New South in Retrospect," *Journal of Southern History* 38 (May 1972): 216.

24. William Faulkner, *The Hamlet: A Novel of the Snopes Family* (1940; repr., New York: Vintage Books, 1964), 4–5 (emphasis removed).

25. Louis D. Rubin Jr., "W. J. Cash after Fifty Years," *Virginia Quarterly Review* 67 (Spring 1991): 214–28; and William G. Carleton, interview by John Herbert Roper, 21 July 1979, folder 12, box 1, Roper Papers.

26. William Faulkner, *Sartoris* (New York: Harcourt Brace and Company, 1929).

27. William Faulkner, *The Sound and the Fury* (1929; repr., New York: Vintage Books, 1954), 409, 286.

28. William Faulkner, *Absalom, Absalom!* (New York: Vintage Books, 1972), 220; Faulkner quoted in *Faulkner in the University*, 3; and William Faulkner, *The Sound and the Fury*, 408.

29. John Pendleton Kennedy, *Swallow Barn, or A Sojourn in the Old Dominion*, vol. 1 (Philadelphia: Carey and Lea, 1832); William Gilmore Simms, quoted in William R. Taylor, *Cavalier and Yankee: The Old South and American National Character* (New York: Oxford University Press, 1993), 286, 293.

30. H. L. Mencken, "The Calamity of Appomattox," *American Mercury* 21 (September 1930): 29–31; Thomas Wolfe, quoted in David Herbert Donald, "Look Homeward: Toward the South," *Southern Review* 23 (January 1987): 247; Robert Penn Warren, introduction to *Faulkner: A Collection of Critical Essays*, ed. Warren (Upper Saddle River, NJ: Prentice-Hall, 1967), 3; and William Faulkner, "An Introduction to *The Sound and the Fury*," ed. James B. Meriwether, *Mississippi Quarterly* 26 (Summer 1973): 411–12.

31. Woodward to Rainey, 12 July 1936, folder 1, box 22, Rainey Papers; Hackney, "Origins of the New South," 216; and Woodward, "New South Fraud."

32. C. Vann Woodward, *The Strange Career of Jim Crow* (New York: Oxford University Press, 1955); C. Vann Woodward, *Thinking Back*, 82–83.

33. Faulkner to Malcolm A. Franklin, 4 July 1943, in *Selected Letters of William Faulkner*, ed. Joseph Blotner (New York: Random House, 1977), 176; Faulkner to Franklin, 24 May 1943, quoted in Joseph Blotner, *Faulkner: A Biography* (New York: Random House, 1974), 1143–44; Warren, *Faulkner: A Collection of Critical Essays*, 9; and William Faulkner, *Intruder in the Dust* (1948; repr., New York: Vintage Books, 1972), 194, 203.

34. Richard Gray, *The Life of William Faulkner* (Cambridge, MA: Blackwell, 1994), 300; Edmund Wilson, "William Faulkner's Reply to the Civil Rights Program," *New Yorker* 23 (October 1948): 106, 110; and "A Way Out of the Swamp?" *Time* 52 (October 4, 1948): 111–12.

35. Louis D. Rubin Jr., "The Historical Image of Modern Southern Writing," *Journal of Southern History* 22 (May 1956): 159; Robert Penn Warren, *All the King's Men* (1946; repr., New York: Houghton Mifflin, 1996), 656; and C. Vann Woodward, *The Burden of Southern History* (Baton Rouge: Louisiana State University Press, 1993), 3–26, 187–212.

36. William Faulkner, *The Reivers* (New York: Random House, 1962).

37. Warren, *Faulkner: A Collection of Critical Essays*, 2; C. Vann Woodward, interview by John H. Roper, 18 July 1978, folder 10, box 1, Roper Papers; and C. Vann Woodward, *Burden of Southern History*, 280, 34, 39.

Contributors

W. Fitzhugh Brundage is William B. Umstead Professor of History at the University of North Carolina, Chapel Hill, where he joined the faculty in 2002. He is author of *Lynching in the New South: Georgia and Virginia, 1880–1930* (1993), *A Socialist Utopia in the New South: The Ruskin Colonies in Tennessee and Georgia, 1894–1901* (1996), and *The Southern Past: A Clash of Race and Memory* (2005), as well as several edited collections. In 2011–12 he was the recipient of a John Simon Guggenheim Fellowship.

Jordan Burke received his MAR in religion and literature at Yale Divinity School and is currently pursuing his PhD in English literature at the University of Virginia. His current work explores ways of coupling microhistorical treatments of Anglophone literature with transnational and systemic theories of literary exchange and circulation. While he has an abiding interest in Faulkner, he focuses primarily on the problem of the lyric in twentieth-century poetic theory, situating that conversation within a larger debate about the enduring shape of genres and cultural forms across temporal, national, and linguistic borders.

Rebecca Bennett Clark is a doctoral candidate in English at the University of California, Berkeley. She works on nineteenth- and twentieth-century American literature, with particular interests in visual culture and the literature of the US South.

James C. Cobb is B. Phinizy Spalding Distinguished Professor in the History of the American South at the University of Georgia, where he has taught since 1997. Among his many books are *The Most Southern Place on Earth: The Mississippi Delta and the Roots of Southern Identity* (1992), *Away Down South: A History of Southern Identity* (2005), and *The South and America since World War II* (2010). He served as president of the Southern Historical Association in 1999.

Anna Creadick is associate professor of English at Hobart and William Smith Colleges. Author of *Perfectly Average: The Pursuit of Normality in Postwar America* (2010), she has also published work in *Mosaic*,

Southern Literary Journal, and *Appalachian Journal*. Her new work investigates midcentury reading practices and social class.

Colin Dayan is Robert Penn Warren Professor in the Humanities, professor of English, and professor of law at Vanderbilt University, where she has taught since 2004. Her books include *Fables of Mind: An Inquiry into Poe's Fiction* (1987), *Haiti, History, and the Gods* (1998), *The Story of Cruel and Unusual* (2007), and *The Law Is a White Dog*, named a Choice Outstanding Academic Title for 2011. Her latest book, *With Dogs at the Edge of Life*, has just been published by Columbia University Press.

Wai Chee Dimock is William Lampson Professor of English and American Studies at Yale University, where she joined the faculty in 1997. She is author of *Empire for Liberty: Melville and the Poetics of Individualism* (1991), *Residues of Justice: Literature, Law, Philosophy* (1997), and *Through Other Continents: American Literature across Deep Time* (2008) and regularly teaches a class on Hemingway, Fitzgerald, and Faulkner as part of the Open Yale online education program.

Sarah E. Gardner is professor of history and director of Southern Studies at Mercer University. She is the author of *Blood and Irony: Southern White Women's Narratives of the Civil War, 1861–1937* (2004). Her manuscript, "Reviewing the South: Readers, Writers, Critics, and the Idea of an American Region," is at Cambridge University Press.

Hannah Godwin is a PhD candidate in English literature at the University of Oregon. She is at work on her dissertation, "American Modernism's Gothic Children."

Brooks E. Hefner is associate professor of English at James Madison University. His work on American literature and popular culture has appeared in *PMLA*, *MELUS*, *Modern Fiction Studies*, and the *Journal of Film and Video*.

Andrew B. Leiter is associate professor of English at Lycoming College in Williamsport, Pennsylvania. He is the author of *In the Shadow of the Black Beast: African American Masculinity in the Harlem and Southern Renaissances* (2010).

Sean McCann is professor of English at Wesleyan University. He is the author of *A Pinnacle of Feeling: American Literature and Presidential Government* (2008).

Conor Picken is assistant professor of English at Bellarmine University in Louisville, Kentucky. His teaching, research, and publications focus on southern literature, modernism, and social change.

Natalie J. Ring is associate professor of history at the University of Texas at Dallas, where she has taught since 2004. She is author of *The Problem South: Region, Empire, and the New Liberal State, 1880–1930* (2012) and coeditor of *The Folly of Jim Crow: Rethinking the Segregated South* (2012). She is currently at work on a history of the Louisiana State Penitentiary at Angola.

Calvin Schermerhorn is associate professor of history at Arizona State University. He coedited *Rambles of a Runaway from Southern Slavery by Henry Goings* (2012) and is author of *Money over Mastery, Family over Freedom: Slavery in the Antebellum Upper South* (2011), and *The Business of Slavery and the Rise of American Capitalism, 1815–1860* (2015).

Jay Watson is Howry Professor of Faulkner Studies at the University of Mississippi and the director of Faulkner and Yoknapatawpha. He is the author of *Forensic Fictions: The Lawyer Figure in Faulkner* and *Reading for the Body: The Recalcitrant Materiality of Southern Fiction, 1893–1985*, which received Honorable Mention for the 2013 C. Hugh Holman Award sponsored by the Society for the Study of Southern Literature. He is also the editor of *Faulkner and Whiteness*, *Conversations with Larry Brown*, and coeditor of three volumes of the Faulkner and Yoknapatawpha conference proceedings.

Index

Page numbers in *italics* refer to illustrations.

122–31; difference in female pro-
tagonist's name, 133n17
Wolfe, Thomas, 78, 169, 210–11, 212,
216, 222; *Look Homeward, Angel*,
217
Woodson, Carter, 68, 76, 78
Woodward, C. Vann, ix, xxi, 78,
210–25; *Burden of Southern
History, The*, 224; at Columbia
University, 212; at Georgia Tech,
212; *Origins of the New South,
1877–1913* (History of the South
Series), 78, 218, 219, 222; Rock-
efeller Foundation stipend, 213;
Rosenwald Fellowship, 212; *The
Strange Career of Jim Crow*, 223;
Tom Watson: Agrarian Rebel, 217;
at University of North Carolina at
Chapel Hill, 213, 216
Woollcott, Alexander, 150
World Republic of Letters, The (Casa-
nova), 4
World War I (Great War), xi, xviii,
110, 126, 128, 159, 210
World War II, xix, 6, 7, 10, 89, 92,
137, 149, 154
Wright, Richard, 78; *Invisible Man*,
78
Wrinkle, Margaret, xxvi

X, Malcolm, 21
Xingjian, Gao, 4

Yalden-Thompson, David, 160
Yale University, ix, 195, 206, 225
Yamaguchi University, 18
*Yellow Peril! An Archive of Anti-
Asian Fear* (Tchen and Yeats), 186
Yellow Peril narratives, xx, 185, 188
Yoknapatawpha County, xviii, xix, 32,
39, 47, 52, 53, 71, 77, 80, 95, 145,

148, 150, 153, 154, 155, 167, 177,
180, 189n3, 197, 198, 225; origins
of the word *Yoknapatawpha*, xiv,
12, 18

Zieger, Susan, 138

CPSIA information can be obtained
at www.ICGtesting.com
Printed in the USA
BVOW10*1917170217

476236BV00001B/2/P